SUPPLEMENTARY VOLUME LXXVI
2002

THE
ARISTOTELIAN
SOCIETY

THE SYMPOSIA READ AT THE
JOINT SESSION OF THE
ARISTOTELIAN SOCIETY
AND THE MIND ASSOCIATION
AT THE UNIVERSITY OF GLASGOW
JULY 2002

PUBLISHED BY

The Aristotelian Society

2002

First published 2002 by
The Aristotelian Society

© The Aristotelian Society 2002

ISBN 0 907111 47 5

ISSN 0309-7013

THE ARISTOTELIAN SOCIETY PUBLICATIONS

PROCEEDINGS: as a journal, three times a year, and as a bound volume annually in June.

SUPPLEMENTARY VOLUME: annually in June. This records the papers read at the annual Joint Session of the Aristotelian Society and the Mind Association.

BOOK SERIES: (in co-operation with Blackwell Publishers). The Society has editorial responsibility for these books, which are published by Blackwells. They are available at less than half price to members of the Society. Currently available:

Barry Taylor	*Modes of Occurrence: Verbs, Adverbs and Events* (1985)
Christopher Peacocke	*Thoughts: An Essay on Content* (1986)
David E. Cooper	*Metaphor* (1986)
Jonathan Westphal	*Colour: Some Philosophical Problems from Wittgenstein* (1987)
Anthony Savile	*Aesthetic Reconstructions: Lessing, Kant and Schiller* (1987)
Graeme Forbes	*Languages of Possibility* (1989)
Tim Maudlin	*Quantum Non-Locality and Relativity: Metaphysical Intimations of Modern Physics* (1994)
John Martin Fischer	*The Metaphysics of Free Will* (1994)
S. Lovibond & S. Williams (eds)	*Essays for David Wiggins: Identity, Truth and Value* (1996)
J. Corbi and J. Prades	*Minds, Causes and Mechanisms* (2000)
Tom Sorell	*Moral Theory and Anomaly* (2000)

ORDERS for past *Proceedings* and *Supplementary Volumes:* Single issues from the current and previous two volumes are available at the current single issue price from Blackwell Publishers Journals. Earlier issues may be obtained from Swets & Zeitlinger, Back Sets, Heereweg 347, PO Box 810, 2160 Lisse, The Netherlands. Email: backsets@swets.nl

All institutional enquiries should be addressed to the Distributors.

OTHER ENQUIRIES should be addressed to the Editor.

Printed in England by
J. W. Arrowsmith Ltd
Winterstoke Road
Bristol BS3 2NT

Journals Subscriptions Department
Marston Book Services
PO Box 87 Oxford OX2 0DT
Tel (01865) 791155
Fax (01865) 791927

Editor:
A. W. Price
Department of Philosophy
Birkbeck College
Malet Street
London WC1E 7HX

Please check in most recent volume for current addresses

CONTENTS

PROGRAMME

JOINT SESSION OF THE ARISTOTELIAN SOCIETY AND THE MIND ASSOCIATION
UNIVERSITY OF GLASGOW, JULY 5–7 2002

Friday 5.00 pm	The Inaugural Address Tom Baldwin Kantian Modality Chair: Bob Hale
Saturday 10.00 am	(i) Richard Glauser and Anthony Savile Aesthetics in Shaftesbury Chair: Gary Kemp
	(ii) Graeme Forbes and Jennifer Saul Intensionality Chair: Peter Sullivan
4.00 pm	Graduate Papers
8.00 pm	Philip Percival and Robert Stalnaker Epistemic Consequentialism Chair: Alan Miller
Sunday 10.00 am	(i) Garrett Cullity and Richard Holton Particularism and Moral Theory Chair: Michael Ridge
	(ii) Sebastian Gardner and Paul Franks From Kant to Post-Kantian Idealism Chair: Paul Gorner
4.00 pm	Submitted Papers
8.00 pm	Ronald de Sousa and Adam Morton Emotional Truth Chair: James Lenman

In Memory of
Gregory McCulloch
(1951–2001),
Professor of Philosophy,
University of Birmingham

The Inaugural Address

KANTIAN MODALITY

by Tom Baldwin

ABSTRACT Kant's claim that modality is a 'category' provides an approach to modality to be contrasted with Lewis's reductive analysis. Lewis's position is unsatisfactory, since it depends on an inherently modal conception of a world. This suggests that modality is 'primitive'; and the Kantian position is a *prima facie* plausible position of this kind, which is filled out by considering the relationship between modality and inference. This provides a context for comparing the Kantian position with Wright's non-cognitivist 'conventionalism'. Wright's position is vulnerable to the type of argument used against ethical non-cognitivism, and the Kantian position is further confirmed by Blackburn's acknowledgment that modality is 'antinaturalistic to its core'. The position is further elaborated to show that it can accommodate the famous Kripkean categories of the empirically necessary and the contingent *a priori*, and finally defended against the criticisms used by Quine against Carnap.

I

A word first about my title and the reference to Kant. The position I want to discuss was suggested to me by Kant's thesis that modality is a 'category'—an *a priori* concept of the pure understanding which matches one of the essential logical 'functions' of judgment. On looking more closely at Kant, however, it is apparent that much of the detail of his account of modality concerns the ways in which modal concepts are applied within judgments that concern experience. As a result he distinguishes the type of 'empirical' possibility with which he is primarily concerned (and concerning which he holds the determinist doctrine that whatever is possible is actual) from what he calls 'absolute possibility (which is valid in every respect)' which 'goes beyond all possible empirical use of the understanding'.[1] Since my discussion is not restricted to empirical possibility the Kantian allusion is therefore potentially misleading. Nonetheless, for reasons to be explained below, I think it is still suggestive. As I will also indicate later, the position I want to discuss can also

1. A232. Cf. his distinction between 'real' and 'merely logical' possibility—Bxxvi note a.

be associated with some of Wittgenstein's remarks concerning necessity, though I am not so rash as to attribute it to him.

II

I want to start, however, by discussing an aspect of a very different position—David Lewis's claim that his theory of possibility provides an *analysis* of modality.

It has not always been appreciated that Lewis's modal realism is intended to provide an analysis of modality, and Lewis's own description of his position as 'modal realism' is potentially misleading in this respect.[2] Nonetheless, from the start Lewis does in fact present his position as one which offers an 'analysis of modality',[3] though it is only in the course of his critical discussion of the 'ersatzism' he opposes that the matter becomes central. Lewis writes here 'I conclude that linguistic ersatzism must indeed take modality as primitive. If its entire point were to afford an analysis of modality, that would be a fatal objection.'[4] Lewis then allows that the ersatzer does not have to adopt the aim of providing an analysis of modality—such a person may argue that 'there is a choice between unwelcome ontology and unwelcome primitive modality' and that 'they prefer the latter' though Lewis does not share this preference. Thus it certainly matters to Lewis that his position provides an analysis which enables him to dispense with 'primitive modality'. If it were to turn out that this aspiration is not fulfilled, one of the main reasons he gives for preferring his position to that of the ersatzer would be undermined.

Lewis's analysis is, of course, that exemplified by the thesis that there might be blue swans iff there is a world w such that there are blue swans in w.[5] This thesis immediately provokes the objection that this is not an analysis which dispenses with 'primitive modality'. For is not a world a 'possible' world—a generalised possibility? So how can this approach present itself as a way of dispensing with primitive modality, as opposed to an account of

2. Lewis himself apologises for his use of the term (Lewis 1986 p. viii). There is, I think, much to be said for Plantinga's distinction between 'modal realism' and 'modal reductionism' (of which Lewis's theory is the prime example); see Plantinga (1987).

3. Lewis (1986), p. 15.

4. Lewis (1986), p. 156.

5. Ibid., p. 5

one group of modal concepts—operators such as 'Possibly'—in terms of a rather different modal concept—that of a possible world?

I think this objection is basically correct. But it needs to be handled with care, and we should first remind ourselves of Lewis's conception of a world as a mereological sum of spatio-temporally related objects.[6] Now there are at least two ways in which worlds so conceived may be regarded as 'possible'. One is just that it is permitted that such a world be non-actual. This, however, does not show that the very conception of a world itself is intrinsically modal. We tell Lewis's story about the kind of thing worlds are without employing modal concepts; if we then add that only one such world is actual we do not thereby bring modal concepts into the account.

Yet there is, I think, a second respect in which worlds are 'possible' which does have the implication that modality enters their conception. The point is best illustrated by considering a claim concerning something impossible: e.g. that it is impossible for anything to be a swan unless it came into existence by hatching out of an egg. Once this claim is construed Lewis-style it is treated as true iff there is no world w at which a swan came into existence without hatching out of an egg. For now the question arises as to what worlds there are, and in particular what attitude one is take to the hypothesis that there might be worlds other than those which there are. The issue is this: if one holds that this hypothesis can be dismissed, then one is regarding the mere possibility of the existence of a world as sufficient for its real existence—in which case the concept of possibility seems to enter constitutively into the conception of a world. Alternatively, if one rejects the hypothesis that for worlds possible existence implies real existence, then the account of the truth-conditions is intuitively unacceptable—since it implies that the existence of a swan which has not hatched from an egg is impossible even though one concedes that it is possible that there should be a world in which there is a swan which has not hatched from an egg.[7]

---

6. Ibid., pp. 69–71.

7. Plantinga argues that the second alternative here is mandatory, in that once one understands properly what Lewis's worlds are, one will see that the question of their existence is altogether independent of modal considerations (Plantinga 1987, p. 212). But I do not see why one should not take it that the first alternative is not equally available.

This last point is not altogether uncontentious since it draws on the S4 modal principle. Lewis's analysis can be expressed as follows:

Possibly A iff $(\exists w)(A(w))$

and the issue I have raised is this: is one to assume

$(\exists w)(A(w))$ iff Possibly $(\exists w)(A(w))$?

If not, one has to explain how, given the analysis, it can be that 'Possibly A' is false despite the fact that it is possible that $(\exists w)(A(w))$. Now one way to respond to this challenge would be to argue that it rests on the S4 principle

Possibly A iff Possibly (Possibly A)

since this immediately implies the assumption in question given Lewis's analysis. But since Lewis himself endorses S4 he cannot take this route; and this point is not, I think, just *ad hominem*, since if one adopts a Lewis-style analysis it is hard to see what good reason one could have for not endorsing S4 concerning unrestricted ('metaphysical') possibility. So this argument's dependence upon S4 is not, in this context, a serious weakness. Yet if one endorses the disputed principle and thereby accepts that the conception of a world is such that its possibility alone suffices for its existence, one invites the claim that possibility thereby enters into the conception of a world, and thus that the analysis of possibility is not reductive.

Lewis comes some way to acknowledging the point at issue here when discussing the 'principle of plenitude' that 'absolutely every way that a world could possibly be is a way that some world is'.[8] According to Lewis, however, the only way to make sense of the phrase 'a way in which a world could possibly be' is to interpret it as simply describing a world, so that the principle is just the triviality that every world is some world. But Lewis goes on to suggest that the substance of the principle of plenitude can be captured by a Humean 'principle of recombination'[9] to the effect that duplicates of any possible object coexist with duplicates of any other possible object, as

8. Lewis (1986), p. 86.
9. Ibid., p. 87.

long as the duplicate objects occupy distinct spatio-temporal regions, where each way of combining such duplicates is a world.[10] Yet we can ask again whether the possibility of a combination of duplicates suffices for its existence: if not, then we have no reason to think that that which is false in all such recombinations is impossible; but if the concept of a recombination is to be such that the mere possibility of a recombination suffices for its existence then again the impression that the resulting theory provides an analysis of modality is threatened. We are back with the same issue.

One might object that since worlds are intended to provide us with an analysis of modalities, it is just confused to ask whether there might be worlds other than those that there are. But this is incorrect. It is common practice, when one is confronted with a putative analysis, to consider whether the analysis might be true where the *analysandum* is not. After all, suppose someone were to propose that something is possible iff it obtains at some region of space-time; one would immediately object that something which fails to obtain in any region of space-time might nonetheless be possible. For example, it is possible for me to have blue hair even though space-time will never in fact include a state of this kind. But if one can shoot down my simple proposal in this way, then it is equally legitimate to raise the analogous question concerning Lewis's proposal.

This objection is to be distinguished from one which has been urged by Lycan,[11] to the effect that Lewis needs to exclude impossible worlds if he is to make his analysis plausible, and that he can only do so by tacitly conceiving of worlds as inherently possible from the start. For Lewis can respond to this that all that is required is that his conception of a world be such that worlds of the kind he envisages, namely those obtained by combining duplicates of objects in certain ways in a unified space-time, are intuitively possible.[12] He does not need to demonstrate that this is so in order to vindicate his analysis; rather, his analysis will be plausible insofar as this presumption is plausible—

10. Ibid., pp. 88–9.
11. Lycan (1988), p. 46.
12. Cf. Divers and Melia (2002), pp. 23–4.

which indeed perhaps it is.[13] But I am asking whether Lewis can legitimately regard his analysis as including all the relevant worlds, i.e. all those which are possible. And here intuition goes against Lewis: for, intuitively, it is just not true that mere possibility suffices for real existence in the case of space-times or concrete wholes of any kind. One of the lessons of the ontological argument, after all, is supposed to be that one should not be able to derive real existence from a mere concept, unless one is dealing with *possibilia* themselves. Thus the condition under which Lewis's analysis is plausible is that it is further maintained that, for worlds, mere possibility suffices for existence. But unless this proposition is derived from some more fundamental assumptions, it will have to be accepted that possibility enters constitutively into the conception of a world employed in what was supposed to be a reductive analysis of modality.

In thinking about this last point, the dialectical situation with respect to worlds should be compared with that which applies to talking donkeys. According to Lewis the possibility of a talking donkey implies its reality (though not, of course, its actuality). Does this then show that Lewis is committed to taking the concept of a talking donkey to be 'constitutively' modal? Intuitively, this seems wrong; hence there needs to be a way of distinguishing this case from that of Lewis's treatment of worlds. There is, however, a relevant difference: the argument from the possibility of a talking donkey to its real existence goes through the assumed reality of merely possible worlds in which there are talking donkeys. So, as long as this assumption is in place, nothing needs to be assumed about the concept of a talking donkey in order to reach the conclusion that possibility suffices for existence in this case. By contrast in order to sustain the acceptability of the analysis of possibility in terms of the existence of suitable worlds, the thesis that for worlds possibility suffices for existence has to

13. Lycan's objection depends on the assumption that because Lewis relies on sets of sentences to identify worlds he needs to be able to discriminate the consistent from the inconsistent ones. Lewis, however, explicitly rejects this assumption (see Lewis (1986), p. 7, fn. 1). A point on which Lewis clearly does feel himself somewhat vulnerable concerns the possibility of 'island universes'—the possibility of more than one isolated space-time region within a single world, contrary to his thesis that worlds are unified by space and time. On the one hand, such a possibility seems clearly conceivable and Lewis offers no argument against it; but he recognises that if he were to permit such worlds he would have to introduce a primitive 'world-mate' relation that would after all be a primitive modality (see Lewis (1986), pp. 71–3; Lewis (1992)).

be assumed right from the start. This is not a conclusion derived from other considerations; it is an *a priori* assumption which has to be taken as constitutive of the concept of a world.

III

The preceding argument has some similarities with Moore's famous 'naturalistic fallacy' argument. Hence the conclusion, that modality, like intrinsic value, is 'primitive' (or 'simple'), invites a metaphysics similar to Moore's account of intrinsic value, according to which possibility is a fundamental dimension of reality. Such a metaphysics would be a full-blooded modal realism, the type of position exemplified by that common misunderstanding of Lewis's position which is arrived at by omitting his commitment to the provision of an analysis of modality and assuming instead that his conception of a world is intended to identify the primitive modal structure of reality.

Thus misunderstood, Lewis's position falls into place as a modal analogue of ethical Platonism, as is well demonstrated by its susceptibility to familiar epistemological and ontological qualms concerning such allegedly 'queer' entities. But it is of course not the only way of attempting to do justice to the primitiveness of modality. As in ethics we can, I think, distinguish three further types of position: a broadly Aristotelian position that speaks of the essences of kinds of substance: a position that develops Kant's view that modal concepts are categories, *a priori* concepts of the understanding, whose warrant lies in the fact that they enter into the constitution of any possible conceptual scheme that provides for objective truth: and a Humean 'projectivist' view of necessity, as an expression of the irresistibility of certain judgments, or of the fact that we find their denial unimaginable.[14]

Before discussing directly the choice between these positions the issue of the *form* of the primitive modality should be briefly addressed. For it has been part of the analytical tradition in philosophy to hope to derive from formal considerations some leverage in promoting solutions to metaphysical disputes. Thus, since contemporary philosophical debate makes such extensive use of

14. Cf. Blackburn (1987/1993).

the expressive power of possible worlds, it may seem that formal considerations strongly favour the first modal realist position. One response to this has been the position of 'modalists' who maintain that one can in fact achieve all that is achieved by a possible world vocabulary with complex modal operators.[15] Whether this is correct is disputed, but it is not, I think, necessary to pursue the matter since in this area formal considerations are not crucial. For the alternatives to the modal realist position have resources from which alternative conceptions of possible worlds, or possibilities, can be constructed (worlds are of course just maximal possibilities and the familiar treatment of possibility and necessity can be readily adapted to allow for ordinary, non-maximal, possibilities).[16]

Thus on an Aristotelian position, one starts from a fundamental presumption that among an object's properties, some are essential to its identity and some are not and then constructs as abstract conception of a possibility by representing somehow (e.g. set-theoretically) a state of affairs in which an object of a certain kind has a property whose non-possession by it is not essential to it. More then needs to be said concerning the structure and representation of complex possibilities, but the details are not important here; what matters is that, starting from the distinction between essential and accidental properties, one can develop a workable conception of a possibility and thence of a possible world.

The Kantian position follows a similar strategy, except that because it locates modality within a discussion of the structure of concepts, it is committed to providing an account of possibility which deals in the first instance with features of conceptually articulated items, such as statements or sets of them. Most accounts then treat some of these items, e.g. consistent sets of them, as 'ersatz' possibilities themselves; but Armstrong's fictionalist variant, according to which possibilities are merely represented by these items, is equally available and is, I think, preferable.[17] Finally, since the Humean holds that judgements of

---

15. Cf. Forbes (1985), pp. 89–95.

16. Cf. Humberstone (1981).

17. Cf. Armstrong 1989, p. 49. It is worth stressing that this type of fictionalism is different from that advanced by Rosen, which relies on the use of a special 'fictional' operator in the possible world analysis, so that 'Possibly A' is said to be true iff *according to the theorist's fiction of a plurality of worlds*, there is a world w such that A in w (Rosen (1990)). I have discussed Rosen's position in Baldwin (1998).

possibility express a thinker's ability, or inability, to 'make any-thing of' a supposition, he is again dealing with thoughts or the statements which express them, and in this case Armstrong-style fictionalism concerning the possibilities represented by such statements will be a standard feature of the position.

IV

Of the alternatives to full-blooded realism, the Kantian position appears, to me at least, *prima facie* the most attractive. For it offers the prospect of an account which does not treat modality as a primitive feature of reality, in the way that an appeal to Aristotelian essences appears to, while equally avoiding the sub-jectivism of Humean projectivism. These judgements are, of course, facile; but I say more about both the Aristotelian and Humean positions below. Equally, in exploring a 'Kantian' pos-ition, let me repeat, I am not concerned to follow the details of Kant's actual discussion of modality as a category. Nonetheless I start from Kant's thesis that concepts are rules for the under-standing whose application to experience requires that they be also applicable by the imagination (A124–6). For this suggests that the ability to apply a concept correctly to observed actual situations requires the capacity to apply it in the course of delib-eration concerning possible situations as well, and thus that there is a intrinsically modal aspect to the possession and use of con-cepts. But all this needs more elucidation.

Concepts, on this account, are not simply capacities to respond accurately to types of observed phenomena by registering their presence. Their role in framing desires and intentions already shows an ability to apply them to what is thought of as non-actual. One mark of this enhanced role is given by Evans's 'Gen-erality Constraint', according to which someone who possesses concepts F and G should be able to understand what it would be for something to be both F and G.[18] For since nothing may have been observed to be both F and G, the understanding Evans requires involves the ability to appreciate hypotheses which are thought of as concerning a non-actual situation.

Yet although non-actuality is an ingredient of mere possibility, not everything non-actual is possible and more needs to be said

18. Evans (1982), p. 100.

to fill out the role of modality in characterising concept-possession. We get closer to this, I think, by considering what is characteristic of the ability to understand what it would be for something to be both F and G. For the obvious account is that it involves an ability to reason concerning the implications, both positive and negative, of the hypothesis that something is both F and G, where the ability to identify these implications does not require knowledge of whether or not they actually obtain. This suggestion connects concept-possession with a capacity for reasoning, and this is, I think, the fundamental aspect of the matter. The ability to employ concepts to frame objective thoughts about the world, thoughts which, as thinkers, we have to allow might be mistaken and so cannot regard as merely records of the passing scene, is inseparable from the ability to employ these concepts in reasonings in which a grasp of these concepts is deployed through a grasp of their implications.

So far modal concepts have not entered the discussion. But the relationship between reasoning and modal concepts in reasoning appears immediate: where A implies B it is impossible that A should be the case unless B is also the case. Hence, it seems to follow, the use of concepts requires a sense of their modal dimension, their necessary connections, since these determine the implications which are revealed in the course of the reasonings in which the concepts are employed. Logical concepts provide one easy example of this line of thought, but they are by no means the only one. For a central aspect of many concepts is that they belong within networks in which a range of connections and distinctions are discriminated. Kinship concepts, like *brother*, *sister*, *uncle*, *aunt*, *cousin* etc. are a good example here. Thus, the suggestion is, concepts belong within a field of internal relations, and the ability to reason from hypotheses constituted from such concepts is a matter of tracing out these internal relations, following out the modal dimensions inherent in the concepts involved.

Yet in two ways this may be felt to go too fast. First, it may be objected that reasoning and modality are not as closely related as is here assumed: for does not Tarski's conception of logical consequence as truth in all models suggest that there is a robust conception of the paradigm case of rational inference, logical implication, that is not dependent upon modal concepts? The response to this, I think, is that we take it that the models involved, typically set-theoretic structures, represent possible as well as actual situations. Tarski's conception is essentially one of formal validity and depends on the assumption that the symbols other than the logical constants are to be interpreted in ways which do not privilege the way things actually are, such as the size of the domain.[19]

Secondly, it may be felt that the argument above assumes too much in taking it that in using concepts in the course of reasoning we are guided by their inherent modal dimension. The most one can say, the objection goes, is that modal thoughts are a reflective endorsement of our inferential dispositions; and, as such, they are not constitutive of concept-possession in the way proposed in the conclusion of the argument above.

V

This objection requires a reassessment of the relationship between inference and modal thought. This issue was discussed by Crispin Wright in *Wittgenstein on the Foundations of Mathematics* which has been a starting-point for much subsequent discussion, especially concerning the significance of a character Wright introduces—the 'Cautious Man'.[20] Wright's Cautious Man is someone who regularly refuses to acknowledge the necessity of something whose necessity we normally regard as established by a proof. The Cautious Man follows a proof, step by step, accepts its conclusion on the basis of the proof, and yet refuses to allow that, where the proof is expressed as a conditional, this conditional expresses a necessary truth. Thus Wright's Cautious Man is a thinker who calls into question the warrant our normal practices of inference and proof provide for judgements of necessity.

Wright uses the apparent coherence of this limited form of modal scepticism as the basis for a defence of what he calls a 'conventionalist' account of necessity. This term harks back to the unsatisfactory positions characteristic of the logical positivists, but much of the content of Wright's use of the term arises

19. Cf. Etchemendy (1990), pp. 119–21.
20. Wright (1980), p. 453.

from a contrast with the position of the 'cognitivist' who is said
to hold that judgements of necessity are justified where a thinker
'recognises' the necessity inherent in the situation under consideration, such as a proof. So Wright's 'conventionalism' is a form
of non-cognitivism according to which our modal judgements
involve a 'decision' to accept the necessity of a proof, a decision
whose role is indicated precisely by the coherence of the Cautious
Man's attitude in refusing to accept this necessity despite his
grasp of the proof as a way of establishing the truth of its
conclusion.

I shall return to the Cautious Man and his significance for the
issue of cognitivism with respect to modal judgement. But I want
first to say a little on the issue of realism with respect to modality.
For Wright's description of the cognitivist conception of modal
judgement he rejects as one which depends on our capacity for
the 'recognition' of necessity suggests, through this use of a perceptual term, a conception of modality as a genuine property of
things, a property which we are, on occasion, able to identify
quasi-perceptually and thus 'recognise'. As debates in ethics
make familiar, cognitivism and realism do not always go
together; hence the realist issue requires some attention in its own
right, and I want to use it to qualify the conception of modality
proposed earlier, in particular the suggestion that in the course
of reasoning we are guided by our grasp of the internal relations
between the concepts involved. For on this view, concepts come,
like atoms, with an intrinsic modal 'valency' that enables them
to join up with other concepts in the molecular patterns that
our ordinary modal judgements capture. This would be a realist
account of the matter; and the objection to it is that it seems not
much less mysterious than the accounts of modality propounded
by those who rely on Aristotelian essences or merely possible
worlds. All that the conceptualist move has achieved is that the
grounds for unease have been shifted by locating primitive
modality at the level of sense (concepts) rather than at the level
of reference (properties, worlds); but this does not remove the
unease.

The alternative is to provide an anti-realist understanding of
the modal dimension of conceptual thought. The way to achieve
this, I think, is to regard modal judgements as the reflective
propositional expression of the norms inherent in reasoning, in

particular the norm of commitment. Thus, to take Wright's case of a conditional whose antecedent comprises the premisses P of a proof and whose consequent is the proof's conclusion C: someone who holds that it is a necessary truth that if P then C thereby acknowledges that they are committed to accepting C if they accept P. The modal judgement is an endorsement of the proof *as a proof* (which is precisely what the Cautious Man refuses to do). More generally, to hold that A is possible is to acknowledge no commitment to accepting not-A; and so on. Thus the basic idea is that modal judgements are a reflective expression of the norms inherent in the practice of reasoning. So whereas the realist conceives of inference as guided by recognition of the modal dimension inherent in our concepts, the anti-realist reverses these priorities and holds that modal judgement is the expression of norms inherent in the capacity that we have to reason from our thoughts which is essential to our capacity to have thoughts at all.

This is not a reductive analysis of modality of the kind offered by Lewis; for there is no attempt here to reduce modal facts to norms of reasoning. Nor is it, I think, appropriate to regard the account of modal judgement itself as reductive; for the claim just is that modal concepts express the norms of reasoning. But there is a different complaint that might well be urged, namely that the adoption of this anti-realist position amounts to giving up on the initial Kantian perspective and substituting instead a 'Humean' projectivist one. As before, I do not want to get bogged down with details about Kant and Hume; but one way to put the complaint is to urge that, in this context at least, anti-realism brings with it non-cognitivism, whereas anything that merits the title 'Kantian' needs to be cognitivist.

In order to address this complaint it is necessary to return to the Cautious Man, since it is from an understanding of his position that we are supposed to extract the reasons for adopting a non-cognitivist treatment of modal judgement. As I indicated earlier, the tale of the Cautious Man is supposed to demonstrate the coherence of a point of view that is altogether purged of modal thoughts—as Edward Craig puts it: 'The example of the Cautious Man strongly suggests that our species could survive the ditching of the concept of necessary truth.'[21] So the moral of

21. Craig (1985), p. 107.

the tale is to be that, because the Cautious Man is capable of agreeing with us concerning all the non-modal aspects of the world, he shows us that insofar as we go in for modal judgements, this is because we make 'the decision to adopt a certain policy towards a particular proposition',[22] namely a policy of refusing to countenance the truth or falsehood of those judgements whose falsehood or truth 'we find altogether unimaginable',[23] or of which 'we can make nothing'.[24]

If I am right, however, we should ourselves be cautious concerning this tale of the Cautious Man. For if this is to be the conception of a thinker whose thoughts make no use whatever of modal concepts, but who is in all other respects just like us, and, in particular is just like us in his capacity to reason, to make assumptions, to draw conclusions and to evaluate the reasonings of others, then the tale is intrinsically puzzling. Of course, if the Cautious Man is just an unreflective reasoner, there is no great problem; for on the Kantian view advanced above, modal judgements characteristically occur in the course of critical reflection on reasonings, as when one asks oneself whether there are possibilities not properly taken into account in the passage from premises to conclusion. So if the Cautious Man is like a child who reasons but has not yet learnt how to evaluate reasons, there is no incoherence in the conception; but equally no significant moral to be drawn from it. But if the Cautious Man is supposed to be someone who uses the normative vocabulary of 'commitment', 'proof', 'legitimacy' etc. in connection with the evaluation of arguments just as we do, but still refuses to make use of modal concepts, then we need to be told much more than we are as to how this is to be achieved.

Wright, whose conception of the coherence of the tale of the Cautious Man is in fact more equivocal than that of Craig and Blackburn,[25] suggests right at the end of his book a different way of making this very point, namely that, perhaps, 'No satisfactory

22. Ibid.
23. Ibid., p. 111.
24. Blackburn (1987/1993), p. 70.

25. Thus Wright remarks: 'It was not suggested that the original Cautious attitude could coherently be adopted absolutely universally, that somebody could coherently accept merely as practically certain everything which we regard as necessary, but only that it is available for a particular case' (Wright 1980, p. 461).

general account could be given of the range of circumstances in which the conventionalist's "policy" would apply.'[26] Wright does not endorse or repudiate this suggestion, but one can, I think, see here an analogue of the 'no-disentangling' argument commonly used in ethics against non-cognitivist positions. In order to be able to exhibit moral judgement as the expression of non-cognitive sentiments, it is said, we need to be able to suppose that a thinker can disentangle the cognitive side of 'thick' moral concepts such as rudeness from the evaluation of the phenomena thus picked out; and then the objection is that this disentangling cannot be achieved since what groups the phenomena together, e.g. as ways of being rude, is precisely the evaluation of them. Whether or not this argument is effective in ethics is not germane to the issue here; but in the context of modality, the comparable argument is that the tale of the Cautious Man is incoherent because it suggests that one can disentangle an understanding of concepts such as 'inference' and 'conclusion' from modal concepts. It is precisely this separation which my Kantian rejects and, I think, rightly. Hence, if modal non-cognitivism requires the possibility of thus disentangling modal concepts from non-modal ones, then my Kantian is not a non-cognitivist despite being an anti-realist.

This 'anti-disentangling' point is in a way manifest in the idioms used by the Humeans themselves, when they write of the Cautious Man as someone who agrees with us concerning whether one 'can make anything' of some supposition, or whether it is seriously 'imaginable'.[27] For if the Cautious Man does after all make judgements concerning what it is *possible* for him to imagine, then he is after all in the 'incautious' business of modal discrimination. A thinker wondering whether he can make anything of some supposition is focused not on the limits of his own mental powers, but on the content of the hypothesis; yet if modal thoughts concerning whether or not this content represents a possibility are supposed to be unavailable to the thinker, it is difficult to see how he can sensibly form a view about whether or not he himself can make anything of it.

26. Ibid., p. 466.
27. Craig (1985), p. 103. Blackburn likewise has the Cautious Man agreeing with us concerning 'the existence and centrality of imaginative blocks', but as someone who nonetheless 'refuses to modalize' (Blackburn (1987/1993), p. 66).

It is important at this point to separate the use of the tale of the Cautious Man to sustain the non-cognitivist position from its use simply to make a fallibilist point. When Wright urges that the Cautious Man's inability to 'make intelligible the idea that a particular step in a proof might turn out to be wrong' is to be separated from his acceptance of the necessity of the corresponding conditional, the point is fair enough. But it is not one which lends support to modal non-cognitivism; instead it represents the Cautious Man's acknowledgment of his own fallibility, and thus his hesitation in passing from appearances—his inability to imagine not-A—to judgement, the judgement that A is impossible. The role of the will in making this transition is not an indication of a Humean, non-cognitive, conception of modal judgement; instead it is reflects an aspect of judgement (or assent) that is indicative of a Cartesian, non-Humean, voluntarist account of judgement.

As the title of his paper ('Morals and Modals')[28] indicates, Blackburn uses ethical non-cognitivism as a template for his modal non-cognitivism. At the end of his paper, however, he acknowledges that there is a large asymmetry between the two cases: whereas, he maintains, it is possible to give a 'complete naturalistic' account of moral judgement (an account which does not use moral concepts at all), the same is not possible in the case of modal judgement. For a 'naturalistic' account of why we cannot make anything of, say, the supposition that $1 + 1 = 3$ would have to be an account which appeals only to non-modal facts to explain why there is this block on the imagination. But since we can 'make nothing' of this supposition, we cannot make anything of a naturalistic non-modal explanation of this inability which would suggest that there is, after all, a possibility that $1 + 1 = 3$ which are prevented from comprehending. Hence, Blackburn concludes, 'the phenomenon is anti-naturalistic at its core'.[29]

My Kantian agrees, of course, with this conclusion. But he infers that it shows that the non-cognitivist approach is misguided in this area. Blackburn's anti-naturalistic conclusion just confirms that modal concepts are *a priori* categories and that we

28. Blackburn (1987/1993).
29. Ibid., p. 72.

should not expect to be able to get a naturalistic 'sideways' view of our capacity to employ them. This is a point made very clearly by Wittgenstein in his 1930 *Philosophical Remarks* (p. 53):

> If I could describe the point of grammatical conventions by saying that they are made necessary by certain properties of the colours (say), then that would make the conventions superfluous, since in that case I would be able to say precisely that which the conventions exclude my saying. Conversely, if the conventions were necessary, i.e. if certain combinations of words had to be excluded as nonsensical, then for that very reason I cannot cite a property of colours which makes the conventions necessary, since it would then be conceivable that the colours should not have this property, and I could only express that by violating the conventions.

Indeed, although I have associated the position I have been developing with Kant, it can also be found in Wittgenstein's writings, as when he writes in his *Remarks on the Foundations of Mathematics* (VII 67)

> We say: 'If you really follow the rule in multiplying, you *must* all get the same result.' Now if this is only the somewhat hysterical way of putting things that you get in university talk, it need not interest us overmuch.
>
> It is however the expression of an attitude towards the technique of calculation, which comes out everywhere in our life. The emphasis of the *must* corresponds only to the inexorableness of this attitude both to the technique of calculating and to a host of related techniques.
>
> The mathematical Must is only another expression of the fact that mathematics forms concepts.
>
> And concepts help us to comprehend things. They correspond to a particular way of dealing with situations.
>
> Mathematics forms a network of norms.

VII

I now turn to confront an obvious objection: what about the *de re* empirical necessities made familiar and famous by Kripke, Putnam and others? If necessity and the rest are to be understood as expressions of norms of inference that are inherent in the use of concepts, it seems to follow that all necessity is *de dicto* and *a priori*. But it is not.

One response might be to distinguish between 'conceptual' and 'metaphysical' necessity. But that I take to be in effect an admission of partial defeat, since it will follow that the Kantian approach to modality I have been exploring does not apply to a central range of cases; instead, perhaps, an Aristotelian conception of essence will be invoked to handle these cases. So the Kantian must find a way of combining the emphasis on modality as fundamentally a conceptual phenomenon with a recognition of empirical *de re* necessities.

I start with the famous Barcan-Kripke thesis of the necessity of identity:

For all objects x, y, if x = y then, necessarily, (x = y).

This is standardly approached via such examples as the necessity that Hesperus be Phosphorus and the key stage in any argument for such a necessity is the claim that it is necessary *of* (*de re*) Hesperus that it *be Hesperus*. Since this necessity is *de re* there is no way of elucidating it by reference to the concept *Hesperus*; for it is not *qua* Hesperus that it is necessary *of* Hesperus that it be Hesperus. I suggest, however, that it is *qua* object that it is that it is necessary *of* Hesperus that it be whatever object it is— i.e. Hesperus. This looks as though it should work: for, on the one hand, the concepts *object* and *identity* are sufficiently accommodating to encompass all the ways of describing or referring to Hesperus; but, on the other hand, they still offer the prospect of an account of the necessity that is rooted in the employment of concepts and not just in the brute structure of reality.

The proposal, therefore, is that we should view the Barcan-Kripke principle as expressing commitments inherent in use of the concepts *identity* and *object*—commitments to holding fixed the actual identity of the objects under consideration in hypothetical suppositions. But why should we use concepts with these commitments? The basis for this, I think, lies in the fact that if hypothetical reasoning were not informed by this commitment, it would be futile; for each new thought, even if conceptualised with the same name, would be liable to concern new objects, and thus to be independent of preceding thoughts; so no structured reasoning could take place. Nonetheless, the resulting necessity can still be regarded as *de re*; because the concepts involved are so general they do not exclude any ways of referring to the object thus characterised. Hence once some specific, empirically determined, identity is introduced—e.g. that Hesperus is Phosphorus—the familiar empirical necessity, that Hesperus be Phosphorus, can be derived.

In considering how far one can extend this general approach to other putative essential properties, I do not wish to get drawn into an extended discussion of essentialist theses; nonetheless it appears to me reasonable to hold that if there are good reasons for maintaining a type of essentialist claim at all, then these reasons will turn out to revolve around one or two concepts whose application brings with them the essentialist claim in question.[30] Thus consider the 'necessity of origin' thesis: if there are good reasons to accept the conditional

> For all material objects x, y: if x originates from y then, necessarily, x originates from y,

then these reasons will concern the relationship between the concepts of a material object and its identity, on the one hand, and that of its origin, or occasion of coming into existence, on the other. Hence, if there is a necessity here, it is conceptual, although, because it concerns the objects in question simply *qua* material objects it will again give rise to a *de re* necessity which can be further specified by empirical details (e.g. concerning the parents of Elizabeth II). Similarly, if the typical Aristotelian form or sortal property is rightly regarded as an essential property of its instances, i.e. if one accepts

> For all objects x and sortals F: if Fx, then, necessarily Fx,

it will be because of the concepts involved—because the concept of a sortal property which provides criteria for the individuation and re-identification through time of an object is also conceived as giving rise to commitments concerning reference to the object in hypothetical reasoning. Thus, as before, although the argument is conceptual, it concerns the object however it be thought of or described so that the resulting necessity is *de re*. Finally, the Putnam-Kripke arguments concerning the necessity that water be H_2O revolve around the concept of a natural kind—the basic

---

30. Here I am in agreement with Forbes (1985), pp. 231 ff., Jackson (1998), Ch. 3, and (I think) Peacocke (1999), Ch. 4.

claim is that this concept picks out substances or kinds by reference to their 'nature', so that when we speculate hypothetically about such substances in very different environments (e.g. on Twin Earth) we are committed to importing the same underlying nature into that environment if we are to have the same substance or kind. It is of course an empirical matter what this nature turns out to be, but the basic necessity from which the relevant empirical necessity (e.g. Water = H_2O) can be derived is conceptual; e.g. it is because water is a natural kind that it has to have the nature it does have.[31]

The category of contingent *a priori* truth raises a similar issue, since these are truths which involve *de re* contingency. As with the *de re* necessities discussed just now, however, there is clearly a conceptual aspect to these contingent *a priori* truths: once one understands how one particular case works (e.g. 'The actual inventor of the zip invented the zip, if anyone did'), one sees how to generalise from it to other cases in which similar concepts are involved. So the problem should be soluble in a similar way, namely by clarifying the concepts involved in such a way that the commitments implied by their use are expressed by a *de re* modal judgement.

The general phenomenon of the contingent *a priori* is, I think, nicely represented in two-dimensional modal semantic theory.[32] Contingent *a priori* truths are represented in this theory by a pair of propositions (functions from worlds to truth-values): one, the 'horizontal' proposition, captures the fact that the truth of what is said in the actual world is not true in all possible worlds; the other, the 'diagonal' proposition, captures the fact that in any world considered as actual, what is said is true in that world— so that because one does not need to know which world is actual to know that the proposition is true, its truth is *a priori*. Hence to take the matter further, it needs to be shown how the concepts employed in these cases give rise to two types of commitment which can be represented by the two dimensions of a two-dimensional semantic matrix.

In discussing this I shall just concentrate on the example used above—'The actual inventor of the zip invented the zip, if anyone did.' It is clear that the key concept here is the indexical

---

31. I am in fact myself sceptical about this type of case; see Baldwin (2001b), pp. 133–6.
32. For an extended discussion, see Stalnaker (2001) and Baldwin (2001a).

'actual': so what needs to be explained is how its use gives rise to commitments of two different types. The duality concerns the commitments inherent in hypothetical reasoning involving the supposition that the actual inventor of the zip invented the zip, if anyone did, and it arises from two different ways in which hypotheses concerning what is non-actual can be introduced. One type of hypothesis concerns different contexts in which one is imagined to make this supposition; the other type concerns different situations in which the truth of the supposition, as actually made, is to be assessed. When the first type is under consideration, the use of the phrase 'the actual F' is such that it just describes the thing in the supposed context which is F, if there is one. Hence, one does not need to know anything about the context in which the sentence 'The actual inventor of the zip invented the zip' is to be considered as uttered to know that it is true; so it is *a priori*. Contingency, however, involves the second type of hypothetical reasoning: here we take the sentence as uttered in the actual world, and then ask what commitments accepting it as true give rise to when we assess whether it would be true in some hypothetical situation. In this case, the use of the indexical is taken to carry a commitment to preserving the identity of the object, if any, actually referred to as 'the actual inventor of the zip' when considering further suppositions about the actual inventor of the zip; but there is no similar commitment to supposing that this object has all the properties it actually has, so it has to be allowed that there are hypothetical situations in which what is thus supposed is false because the person in question, the actual inventor of the zip, did not invent the zip.

This is, of course, only one case, of the type 'The actual F is F, if anything is.' But I think it is reasonable to suppose that the two-dimensional structure of commitments explained here can be generalised to other cases which involve indexicals, and thus applied to the other cases of the contingent *a priori* which are represented in two-dimensional modal logic. Whether there are further cases of the contingent *a priori* not amenable to this treatment is, I think, a difficult matter which I shall not attempt to address here.

VIII

Finally, it is necessary to address briefly Quine's criticisms of the very idea of conceptual necessity. The central theme of Quine's critique has been that this idea requires a clear distinction between conceptual and empirical connections which is simply not to be found. Instead, even when we look to such paradigmatic areas as the concepts employed to characterise kinship and familial relations, we find that the supposed conceptual connections have tacit empirical assumptions which can be called into question. Thus for example, marriage used to be conceived as a relationship between men and women, such that it seemed a conceptually necessary truth that a married man is a husband. But once gay marriages are brought into the picture, it is not so clear that the partners to a gay marriage are *husbands*, though they are certainly married men. Others cases are readily extracted from the history of science—think of recent legal debates about whether the result of the cell nuclear replacement technique used to create Dolly the sheep was an embryo since no fertilisation took place. These cases show that conceptual networks stand in need of revision when beliefs and practices change and thus that concepts and their inferential relationships cannot be insulated from empirical beliefs. So is the idea of conceptual necessity a mistake?

That is Quine's conclusion; but is it warranted? The legitimation of gay marriages brings with it the need for changes in the concepts applied to married couples, such as the creation of the new, gender-neutral, concept 'partner'. Similarly, the development of the technique of cell nuclear replacement suggests a modification of the concept of an embryo. In both cases, therefore, the defender of conceptual necessity can hold that although empirical discoveries and social changes bring with them conceptual changes, there remain good reasons for 'hardening' the inferential norms inherent in concepts since it is only where some inferential connections are held firm that rational empirical enquiry can proceed.

Such a position is along the lines of Carnap's response to Quine—that the possibility of 'external' revision of concepts can be combined with an 'internal' distinction between the empirical and the conceptual. But this position comes at a price and it is important not to endorse the conclusions Carnap draws from it. The price to be paid is the acknowledgment that what have been taken to be conceptual connections sometimes turn out to have unrecognised, mistaken, empirical presuppositions, which, once recognised, require conceptual revision. This does not show that conceptual connections do not retain their distinctive function of making reasoning, and thus empirical inquiry, possible. But there is, nonetheless, an ineliminable role for 'decision' or 'convention' in this area, though it is not, as the Humean non-cognitivists would have it, a matter of a decision to go in for the 'incautious' business of modalising at all; instead the role of decision is just to select a new conceptual framework appropriate to the facts as currently, though fallibly, understood.

Carnap famously held that any such decision, prompted by an 'external' question, is essentially non-cognitive, and this led him into a radical relativism, whereby cognitive inquiries could only be 'internal', relative to an 'external' linguistic framework whose adoption is not subject to cognitive constraints.[33] Quine rightly protested against this result,[34] which he took to be, in effect, a *reductio ad absurdum* of the distinction between the conceptual and the empirical. But Carnap's position is far from mandatory. Conceptual revision is required where new discoveries or practices reveal or give rise to previously unanticipated similarities and distinctions, e.g. concerning the similarity between the result of cell nuclear transfer and ordinary fertilisation, and there is nothing non-cognitive about the recognition of such similarities. What does then call for the exercise of judgement is the decision as to which classification best characterises the different aspects of the situation as then understood. But these decisions are subject to cognitive appraisal in just the way in which the exercise of judgement in theoretical inquiries quite generally can be appraised. So Carnap's disastrous collapse of the conceptual/ empirical distinction into a non-cognitive/cognitive distinction can, and should, be avoided.

This result, I think, deflects much of the substance of Quine's criticisms of the very idea of conceptual necessity. Manifestly there is more to be said concerning his discussion of the status of logical and mathematical necessity; but his views on this subject have not attracted much support, and there is certainly no space for me to say anything worthwhile about them here.[35]

33. Cf. Carnap (1950).

34. See Quine (1951).

35. Many people have helped me develop my thoughts on this subject. I am particularly indebted to David Bostock, Marie McGinn, Tom Stoneham, Tim Williamson, and Crispin Wright.

REFERENCES

Armstrong, D. 1989. *A Combinatorial Theory of Possibility*, Cambridge: Cambridge University Press.

Baldwin, T. 1998. 'Modal Fictionalism and the Imagination', *Analysis* 58: 72–5.

Baldwin, T. 2001a. 'On Considering a Possible World as Actual', *Aristotelian Society Supplementary Volume* LXXV: 157–74.

Baldwin, T. 2001b. *Contemporary Philosophy*, Oxford: Oxford University Press.

Blackburn, S. 1987/1993. 'Morals and Modals' in his *Essays in Quasi-Realism*, Oxford: Oxford University Press, 52—74.

Carnap, R. 1950. 'Empiricism, Semantics and Ontology', *Revue Internationale de Philosophie* IV: 20—40.

Craig, E. 1985. 'Arithmetic and Fact' in I. Hacking (ed.) *Essays in Analysis*, Cambridge: Cambridge University Press, 89—112.

Divers, J. and Melia, J. 2002. 'The Analytic Limits of Genuine Modal Realism', *Mind* 111: 15–36.

Etchemendy, J. 1990. *The Concept of Logical Consequence*, Cambridge MA: Harvard University Press.

Evans, G. 1982. *The Varieties of Reference*, Oxford: Clarendon Press.

Forbes, G. 1985. *The Metaphysics of Modality*, Oxford: Clarendon Press.

Humberstone, L. 1981. 'From Worlds to Possibilities', *Journal of Philosophical Logic* 10: 313–39.

Jackson, F. 1998. *From Metaphysics to Ethics*, Oxford: Clarendon Press.

Lewis, D. 1986. *On the Plurality of Worlds*, Oxford: Blackwell.

Lewis, D. 1992. Review of Armstrong (1989), *Australasian Journal of Philosophy* 70, 211–224.

Lycan, W. 1988. Review of Lewis (1986), *Journal of Philosophy* 85: 42–7

Peacocke, C. 1999. *Being Known*, Oxford: Clarendon Press.

Plantinga, A. 1987. 'Two Concepts of Modality', in J. Tomberlin (ed.), *Philosophical Perspectives* 1, Atascadero, CA: Ridgeview, 189–231.

Quine, W. 1951. 'On Carnap's Views on Ontology', *Philosophical Studies* 2: 65–72.

Rosen, G. 1990. 'Modal Fictionalism', *Mind* 99: 327–54.

Stalnaker, R. 2001. 'On Considering a Possible World as Actual', *Aristotelian Society Supplementary Volume* LXXV: 141–56.

Wittgenstein, L. 1975. *Philosophical Remarks*, Oxford: Blackwell.

Wittgenstein, L. 1978. *Remarks on the Foundations of Mathematics*, 3rd ed., Oxford: Blackwell.

Wright, C. 1980. *Wittgenstein on the Foundations of Mathematics*, London: Duckworth.

AESTHETIC EXPERIENCE IN SHAFTESBURY

by Richard Glauser and Anthony Savile

I—Richard Glauser

ABSTRACT Shaftesbury's theory of aesthetic experience is based on his conception of a natural disposition to apprehend beauty, a real 'form' of things. I examine the implications of the disposition's naturalness. I argue that the disposition is not an extra faculty or a sixth sense, and attempt to situate Shaftesbury's position on this issue between those of Locke and Hutcheson. I argue that the natural disposition is to be perfected in many different ways in order to be exercised in the perception of the different degrees of beauty within Shaftesbury's hierarchy. This leads to the conclusion that the exercise of the disposition depends, from case to case, on many different cognitive and affective conditions, that are realised by the collaborative functionings of our ordinary faculties. Essential to Shaftesbury's conception of aesthetic experience is a disinterested, contemplative love, that causes (or contains) what we may call a 'disinterested pleasure', but also an interested pleasure. I argue that, within any given aesthetic experience, the role of the disinterested pleasure is secondary to that of the disinterested love. However, an important function of the disinterested pleasure is that, in combination with the interested pleasure, it leads one to aspire to pass from the aesthetic experience of lower degrees of beauty to the experience of higher ones in the hierarchy.

S haftesbury played a seminal role in the development of British aesthetics, and was to influence not only British, but also French and German writers during the 18th and 19th centuries. This view was established persuasively by Folkierski and Cassirer, among others, in the first half of the 20th century, and by Stolnitz in papers published in 1961.[1] Stolnitz has been criticised, sometimes justly, from different quarters on one count or

---

1. W. Folkierski, *Entre le Classicisme et le Romantisme: Etudes sur l'Esthétique et les Esthéticiens du XVIIIe Siècle* (Paris: Honoré Champion, 1925); E. Cassirer, *The Philosophy of the Enlightenment* (Princeton University Press, 1951); J. Stolnitz, 'On the Significance of Lord Shaftesbury in Modern Aesthetic Theory', *The Philosophical Quarterly* 11 (1961); 'On the Origins of 'Aesthetic Disinterestedness', *Journal of Aesthetics and Art Criticism* 20 (1961); 'Beauty: Some Stages in the History of an Idea', *Journal of the History of Ideas* 22 (1961).

another.[2] But this has not jeopardised the overall consensus as to the historical importance of Shaftesbury. Indeed, valuable work has subsequently been devoted to relating Shaftesbury's aesthetics to that of his predecessors, for instance some of the Cambridge Platonists, and to that of his contemporaries and successors, such as Addison, Hutcheson, Hume, Burke, Kant and Schopenhauer.[3] Yet Shaftesbury's theory of aesthetic *experience* seldom receives as much close scrutiny as is today commonly given the theories of several of the latter, partly because he is often taken to be less systematic than he is in fact.

So, what exactly is Shaftesbury's theory of aesthetic experience? (I use the expression 'aesthetic experience' in the non-technical and, I hope, innocent sense of an experience through which beauty is apprehended and appreciated.) Without an answer to this preliminary question it is hardly reasonable to pursue the matter of Shaftesbury's influence with any degree of precision, nor to describe precisely the relations between his theory and those of Hutcheson, Hume, Kant and so on. The question can be divided into two subordinate ones: (1) what is the nature of aesthetic experience according to Shaftesbury? (2) what are the objects of this experience in its fully developed form? The answer to the first question depends in part on the answer to the second. Sections I and II deal with the second question, sections III to V with the first.

I

Beauty, a Real and Natural Form. Shaftesbury's notion of beauty is classical; he equates beauty with a formal quality which he

---

2. For example: D. Townsend, 'Shaftesbury's Aesthetic Theory', *Journal of Aesthetics and Art Criticism* 41 (1982); G. Dickie, 'Stolnitz's Attitude: Taste and Perception', *Journal of Aesthetics and Art Criticism* 43 (1984); J. V. Arregui and P. Arnau, 'Shaftesbury: Father or Critic of Modern Aesthetics?', *British Journal of Aesthetics* 34 (1994); P. Mortensen, 'Shaftesbury and the Morality of Art Appreciation', *Journal of the History of Ideas* 55 (1994).

3. For example: P. Kivy, *The Seventh Sense* (New York: Burt Franklin 1976); J-P. Larthomas, *De Shaftesbury à Kant* (Paris: Didier Erudition, 1985); D. Townsend, 'From Shaftesbury to Kant: the Development of the Concept of Aesthetic Experience', *Journal of the History of Ideas* 48 (1987); D. Lories, 'Du Désintéressement et du Sens Commun: Réflexions sur Shaftesbury et Kant', *Etudes Phénoménologiques* 9–10 (1989); D. Townsend, *Hume's Aesthetic Theory* (London: Routledge, 2001), chap. 1.

calls variously 'harmony', 'order', 'symmetry', 'design', 'proportion' or 'numbers'. It is thus a complex property, for harmony and proportion imply relations of different parts or elements to each other. Even in relatively simple qualities such as shapes, motions and colours, beauty lies in the proportion and arrangement of their respective parts: 'The shapes, motions, colours and proportions of these latter being presented to our eye, there necessarily results a beauty or deformity, according to the different measure, arrangement and disposition of their several parts.'[4] Even in the 'simplest of figures' it is the proportions of their parts that strike one with their beauty.[5] If we move from relatively simple, but abstract qualities, to complex natural beings on the one hand, and to works of art on the other, their beauty is not only a complex quality, but also a quality that betokens design and finality: 'Whatever things have order, the same have unity of design and concur in one, are parts constituent of one whole or are, in themselves, entire systems.'[6]

Contrary to Hutcheson and Hume, however, Shaftesbury generally holds a realist conception of beauty. Hutcheson distinguishes between beauty on the one hand, and, on the other, the objective foundation or cause, in things themselves, of our appreciation of their appearing beautiful. For Hutcheson beauty is a mere idea, relative—but common—to the minds of all mankind. For Hutcheson, as for Crousaz,[7] the cause in things themselves of our idea of beauty is a formal quality called 'uniformity amidst variety'. Hutcheson holds that this quality belongs both to sensible and to purely intelligible things, such as theorems. Shaftesbury holds the same for harmony or proportion. However, unlike Hutcheson, Shaftesbury equates beauty with harmony or proportion, and thus for him beauty is generally a real form of things. It is unclear, though, whether he believes that beauty is composed of other qualities (physical or mental), or whether it depends on them as does an emergent or supervenient quality.

4. *Characteristics of Men, Manners, Opinions, Times*, ed. L. E. Klein (Cambridge University Press, 1999), p. 172. All subsequent references are to this edition.

5. *Characteristics*, p. 326.

6. *Characteristics*, p. 274.

7. J-P. de Crousaz, *Traité du Beau* (1715. Paris: Fayard, 1985), p. 29.

What does Shaftesbury mean by calling beauty 'real'? He expresses himself in terms of the opposition between realism and nominalism. Beauty is a real form of things in a quasi-Aristotelian sense of 'form': it is a natural feature depending neither on social convention nor on individual taste. For Shaftesbury, to say that beauty is a real, natural feature is to say both: (1) that it is not non-natural, for it is nothing over and above harmony, order or proportion; and (2) that it is a quality that things possess either by virtue of their natural, internal constitution, or by some natural growth and development. This can be borne out by a number of passages, which concern all sorts of beauty, such as artistic beauty, moral beauty (the beauty of virtue) and the beauty of natural objects. (Although Shaftesbury never attempts to reduce ethics to aesthetics, both fields of investigation being distinct as to method and to aim, he considers moral value a sort of aesthetic value.) For instance, in the *Soliloquy* he claims that

> Harmony is harmony by nature, let men judge ever so ridiculously of music. So is symmetry and proportion founded still in nature, let men's fancy prove ever so barbarous or their fashions ever so Gothic in their architecture, sculpture or whatever other designing art. It is the same where life and manners are concerned. Virtue has the same fixed standard. The same numbers, harmony and proportion will have place in morals and are discoverable in the characters and affections of mankind, in which are laid the just foundations of an art and science superior to every other of human practice and invention.[8]

In the *Moralists*, he distinguishes between 'realists in respect of virtue' and 'nominal moralists' who make 'virtue nothing in itself, a creature of will only or a mere name of fashion'.[9] He then goes on to defend moral realism (realism in respect of virtue) and 'endeavours to show that it [virtue] is really something in itself and in the nature of things, not arbitrary or factitious (if I may so speak), not constituted from without or dependent on custom, fancy or will, not even on the supreme will itself, which can no way govern it but, being necessarily good, is governed by

---

8. *Characteristics*, pp. 157–158. This is why 'In the very nature of things there must of necessity be the foundation of a right and wrong taste, as well in respect of inward characters and features as of outward person, behaviour and action' (p. 150).

9. *Characteristics*, p. 262.

it and ever uniform with it'.[10] Shaftesbury does not say that if beauty is a real, natural form of things, it is a quality that things possess independently of our aesthetic experiences. But this view can reasonably be attributed to him as well.

II

The Hierarchy of the Degrees of Beauty. The number of kinds of beautiful things in Shaftesbury's universe is indefinitely great. This is only to be expected since whatever has some harmony, order and proportion has beauty to some extent. Yet Shaftesbury does sketch out a general hierarchy of the degrees of beauty. Let us try to work from the bottom up, since, in Platonic fashion, such is the order of discovery.

In the *Moralists*, Theocles, a rational enthusiast, wishes to show Philocles, a reasonable sceptic, that spiritual beauty is greater than that of material objects, natural or artistic. He brings Philocles to acknowledge that in a work of art, for example, it is not the physical support ('the metal or matter') that is really beautiful, but the art 'which beautifies' the support. Notice, however, that to say that art beautifies 'the metal or matter' is clearly to imply that the beautified physical support does have beauty, albeit a beauty which has its source in the beautifying art. Hence, Shaftesbury cannot be taken to mean that the physical support entirely lacks beauty, otherwise art would not be beautifying. All that can be construed is that art, because it is beautifying, has greater reality than whatever physical support is beautified by it: 'The beautifying, not the beautified, is the really beautiful.'[11] Theocles's point is that a physical support can contingently receive or lose beauty, and because its beauty is transient or fleeting, whatever received beauty it does have is not as real or as great as the beauty of art itself, which is beautifying. The same goes for living bodies: whatever beauty they have depends on their organisation, but the organisation itself depends on an animating soul. Such an organisation, or beauty, comes and goes according to whether the body is animated by a soul

10. *Characteristics*, pp. 266–267.
11. *Characteristics*, p. 322. Subsequent quotations, until further mention, are from pp. 322–323.

or not. Art is more beautiful than a physical support because it is a beautifying principle; a soul is more beautiful than a living body for the same reason. Yet, precisely because a physical support and a living body are temporarily beautified by their respective principles, they do have beauty, although in some lesser measure. This must be kept in mind when reading that 'The beautiful, the fair, the comely, were never in the matter but in the art and design, never in body itself but in the form or forming power.' Shaftesbury is sometimes carried away by his own rhetoric, since all that he has previously said shows, not that beauty is never in matter and body, but only that if it is, it is temporarily so. Theocles gets things right a few lines further, asking: 'What is it you admire but mind or the effect of mind?'

He then sketches a hierarchy of degrees of beauty. Living bodies and physical supports of art, taken in abstraction from their respective beautifying principles, are 'dead forms', since, although they are beautified, they are not beautifying principles. They are 'formed, whether by man or nature, but have no forming power, no action or intelligence'. Yet, below the beautified 'dead forms' are unbeautified 'dead forms', because 'All which is void of mind is horrid, and matter formless is deformity itself.' This is a zero degree of beauty. Furthermore, a distinction must be made among the beautified dead forms, between natural beings and works of art. Shaftesbury clearly ranks the former above the latter: 'I ... gladly give the advantage to the human form, above those other beauties of man's formation. The palaces, equipages and estates shall never in my account be brought in competition with the original living forms of flesh and blood.' Above the beautified 'dead forms' are the 'forming forms'. These are the forms that 'have a power of making other forms themselves'; they have 'intelligence, action and operation'. Forming forms, then, are finite minds. A problem arises which Shaftesbury does not deal with. For in his own scheme art is not a forming form, since it does not literally have 'intelligence, action and operation', nor is it a dead form, since it is a beautifying principle. So, although Shaftesbury does not say so, art seems to have a status intermediate between beautified dead forms and the forming forms which are finite minds. Finally, a few pages later we learn that the most perfect beauty belongs to God, the only forming form capable of producing other (finite) forming forms.

In the *Moralists* Shaftesbury mentions explicitly only three general degrees of beauty: dead forms, finite forming forms and the infinite forming form. In fact his hierarchy comprises at least seven degrees: (1) unbeautified dead forms (zero degree of beauty); (2) beautiful dead forms that are relatively simple qualities; (3) beautified dead forms that are works of art; (4) beautified dead forms that are natural beings; (5) art itself, which is a beautifying principle, hence not a dead form, but not a forming form either, since it is not a mind, but a product of finite mind; (6) forming forms which are finite minds (these are at least triply beautifying in that they animate bodies, produce works of art, and are capable of self-improvement towards moral goodness and virtue);[12] and finally God, the infinite forming form of finite forming forms, from whom, as we shall see, all beauty flows directly or indirectly.[13] The higher one moves in the hierarchy, the greater the reality of beauty.

Yet this sevenfold hierarchy is far from representing all that Shaftesbury wished to arrive at, for he elsewhere attempts to fill out much of what is comprised under the distinction between dead and forming forms by a distinction between the respective beauties of inanimate, animate and mixed beings. Inanimate beauty: 'beginning from those figures with which we are delighted, to the proportions of architecture. The same in sounds'. 'In things inanimate, nature before the arts, and thus from stones, diamonds, rock, minerals; to vegetables, woods, aggregate parts of the world, as sea, rivers, hills, vales. The globe, celestial bodies and their order; the great architecture of Nature—Nature itself.' Animate beauty: 'from animals (and their several natures) to men, and from single persons of men—their humours, dispositions, tempers, characters, manners—to communities, societies, commonwealths.' 'In things animate, from flocks, herds, to men and other orders of intelligences, to the supreme intelligence—God'. Next, he classifies as 'mixed' of inanimate and animate beauty the highly complex organisations to be found 'in communities; a territory, land, culture, structures

12. Cf. *Characteristics*, pp. 331–332.
13. Notice, however, that even this classification is problematic since works of art, according to Shaftesbury, are less beautiful than natural bodies, yet are capable of representing moral beauty, whereas many natural bodies are not.

and the ornaments of a city, mixed and making up (in conjunction) that idea of a native country'.[14] This hierarchy must be related to Shaftesbury's conception—expounded in the *Inquiry*—of the universe as a completely harmonious system of an indefinitely great number of stratified, teleologically structured, and relatively harmonious subsystems, all the way down to individual plants and rocks, which are themselves complex subsystems. The strata are designated as physical, geological, biological, artistic, moral, social and political, astronomical, cosmological, and theological.[15]

The entire scheme serves as the background to Shaftesbury's conception of moral beauty. Within this scheme the moral beauty of finite minds has at least three degrees. First of all, just as the beauty of living bodies depends on their health, any normal finite soul (animal or human) has a minimal inner proportion or harmony which is realised by its mental balance, the psychic equilibrium formed by its numerous and complex affections, dispositions, character traits and so on.[16] Secondly, a higher degree of harmony, both internal and external, is realised inasmuch as the being is good. Goodness is realised in an animal or a human being by a higher degree of the internal harmony of their affections, and correspondingly, by a resulting external harmony between their behaviour and the optimal state of whatever higher proximate (sub)systems to which they respectively belong (families, flocks, packs, herds, etc., tribes, societies and species).[17] Thirdly, a still higher degree of beauty is to be found in rational and self-conscious minds alone, and depends on their moral virtue. Virtue consists of a perfect harmony among three kinds of affections: natural social affections that further the public good; private natural affections that further one's own interest; and unnatural affections, which are capable of subverting the former two. The perfect balance consists in having neither of the first

---

14. *The Life, Unpublished Letters, and Philosophical Regimen of Anthony, Earl of Shaftesbury*, ed. B. Rand (Bristol: Thoemmes Press, 1999), p. 244. Cf. *Characteristics*, p. 416 footnote.

15. *Characteristics*, pp. 168 ff.

16. Cf. *Characteristics*, pp. 215, 282, 302–304 and 384.

17. 'When in general all the affections or passions are suited to the public good or good of the species ...', then is the natural temper entirely good' (*Characteristics*, p. 172).

two be too strong nor too weak, and in having none of the third. As with goodness, virtue is both an internal and external harmony. It is internal insofar as it is a harmony to be found specifically between the agent's natural social and private affections, and in the absence of non-natural affections. This internal harmony of virtue is greater than in mere goodness because the internal harmony exists not only between such natural affections themselves, but also between these first-order affections and the rational agent's awareness and critical appreciation of them, his second-order affections. Thus, a conscious virtuous agent is less prone than a vicious person to the inner dissension brought about by regret, self-accusation and remorse; internal dialogue replaces dispute with oneself. Virtue's harmony is external, too, inasmuch as the internal harmony produces a harmony in the rational agent's behaviour, between the furthering of his own good and the furthering of the optimal state of the public good. Yet this external harmony is greater than in the case of mere goodness, because it is conscious and critically appreciated by the agent himself. Of course, virtue, as goodness, varies in degrees; one can be more or less good, more or less virtuous. Nevertheless, as in Stoicism, a perfectly virtuous person not only accomplishes the role in the world-order that is teleologically natural for him to fulfil, but he is also approvingly conscious of doing so. In fully playing his role within the human subsystem, and knowing that he does so, he develops his human nature.

Thus, the hierarchy of degrees of beauty depends on God, either directly as in the beauty of natural beings and their goodness, or only indirectly as in artistic beauty and the beauty of virtue: 'That which fashions even minds themselves contains in itself all the beauties fashioned by those minds and is consequently the principle, source and fountain of all beauty.'[18] However, the beauty of the universe itself is not entirely exterior to God's own beauty. For in one of the versions of the cosmological argument used to prove God's existence, the conclusion shows that God animates the universe continually. He functions as a principle of unity and of identity of the world, in a way analogous to that in which a finite soul animates a body.[19] Moreover,

18. *Characteristics*, p. 324.
19. Cf. *Characteristics*, pp. 303–304.

it is not merely that all beauty within the world depends directly or indirectly on God as its creator; it also depends more specifically on God's beauty itself. For 'Whatever beauty appears in our second order of forms or whatever is derived or produced from thence, all this is *eminently, principally and originally* in this last order of supreme and sovereign beauty;' 'Whatever in nature is beautiful or charming is only the *faint shadow* of that first beauty.'[20] This suggests that—in a way distantly reminiscent of Plato—all worldly beauty participates of divine beauty, which seems to function as an exemplary cause. This is surely the reason for which Shaftesbury approvingly quotes Maximus Tyrius: 'The river's beauty, the sea's, the heaven's and heavenly constellations' all flow from hence [i. e. from 'divinity itself ... of all beauties the brightest'] as from a source eternal and incorruptible. As beings partake of this, they are fair and flourishing and happy; as they are lost to this, they are deformed, perished and lost.'[21]

In two senses, then, beauty is mind-dependent. First, all beauty ontologically depends on God's beauty, which is the beauty of an infinitely wise, virtuous and providential mind. Secondly, artistic and moral beauty depend directly on finite minds since they are produced by them. But this is compatible with the realist tenet, rejected by Hutcheson, that beauty is independent of finite minds' aesthetic experiences.[22]

Here, four points should be suggested. First, given that beauty is not only a real, natural quality, but a highly pervasive one, permeating nearly everything in the universe from relatively simple qualities to the structure of the universe and to God himself, there is bound to be in human minds a natural disposition to perceive beauty. Secondly, it is impossible for this disposition to be exercised with regard to the beauty of a great many things in the absence of considerable scientific, psychological, moral and theological knowledge. Even given the last three, a person wishing to discover the beauties of the material world would need a

---

20. *Characteristics*, pp. 324 and 318, my italics.

21. *Characteristics*, p. 277.

22. There are two passages (p. 172 and p. 326) where it is said that beauty 'results from' our perceiving the objects that have proportion and harmony. But if one takes the expression 'results from' in a literal sense, which would make beauty dependent on our experiences, such a construal is contrary to the realist line of Shaftesbury's thought expressed in the contexts of the passages themselves.

great deal of knowledge in physics, geology, biology, astronomy and cosmology. Although Shaftesbury does not explicitly stress this point, it is fair to say that whatever his conception of aesthetic experience is, it is bound to rely heavily in many cases on the accumulation of a great deal of rational knowledge. This is important to stress in the face of romantic interpretations of Shaftesbury. Rather, his whole approach to beauty leans on the hopeful promise of important progress in scientific, psychological and moral knowledge. This is why he is a figure of the Enlightenment. Thirdly, because the kind of knowledge required in order to perceive the beauty of whatever is contemplated must be different from case to case, one cannot hope to come up with a uniform account of aesthetic experience applicable to all cases. The aesthetic experience of the beauty of relatively simple qualities, of crystals, of horses, of the solar system, of the complex mental balance of human minds, of virtue, of social systems, etc., will require, from case to case, vastly different cognitive conditions. Further, it is not just that the prerequisite kinds of knowledge will have to be different, but also that the mental faculties and operations needed to perceive the different kinds of beauty will have to differ from case to case. Fourthly, since there is a hierarchy of degrees of beauty, and since we are supposed to move up—in Platonic fashion—from the aesthetic experience of the lower degrees to that of the higher degrees, what is the driving force that moves us from one degree to the next? Why does Shaftesbury believe that a mind will be motivated to progress from a child's aesthetic contemplation of the figures of his ball and die all the way up to a perception of the higher orders of beauty, perhaps even to the beauty of God?[23] I discuss this in the last section.

III

A Natural Disposition to Experience Beauty. According to Shaftesbury we have a natural disposition to experience beauty. The

23. That Shaftesbury believes it possible to contemplate in some limited measure the beauty of the universe, although it is only partly known, and also of God, cf. *Characteristics*, pp. 191, 257 and 277; *The Life, Unpublished Letters, and Philosophical Regimen of Anthony Earl of Shaftesbury*, p. 252; F. H. Heinemann, 'The Philosopher of Enthusiasm, With Material Hitherto Unpublished', *Revue Internationale de Philosophie* 6 (1952), p. 316; and S. Grean, *Shaftesbury's Philosophy of Religion and Ethics* (Ohio University Press, 1967), p. 249.

meaning of 'natural' varies in Shaftesbury according to the entity qualified and to the context of its use. So the first thing to do is to explain the sense and implications it has here. The issue is related to Locke's rejection of innate ideas and to Shaftesbury's dissatisfaction with this rejection. He believes that Locke misused the word 'innate'. But he prefers to steer clear of the controversy raging over the question of innateness in his day, and to use instead the terms 'natural', 'connatural' and 'instinct'.[24] Were it not for the dispute concerning innateness, Shaftesbury would be happy to call 'innate' or 'instinct' both the disposition to experience beauty and the idea of beauty.[25] Even so, he does not want to imply that the disposition and the idea are not acquired some time after birth. In fact he scorns as idle speculation attempts to determine whether they are implanted in the mind before birth, at birth, or after birth, and if the last, how long after birth. What he sees as the substantial question is whether, if they are acquired after birth, they are acquired naturally, that is by natural means as opposed to artificial means such as 'art, culture or discipline'. If such is the issue a disposition will be natural whether it is part of man's constitution at birth or whether it is acquired at some later stage by a process 'exclusive of art, culture or discipline'. The model along the lines of which Shaftesbury is thinking is that of a biological organism. A rose plant has many qualities that are natural to it in that they are actual as soon as the plant exists; other qualities are also natural to it, such as having flowers, but they will only appear later. In any case, if the disposition to experience beauty is acquired, it is so at a very early stage, for small children enjoy it, as when they take pleasure in discerning the regular forms of a ball or a die.[26] Also, it is acquired naturally, by means 'exclusive of art, culture or discipline', for it is the 'first view' of the proportions of a ball or die that pleases an infant. In general 'There is in certain figures a natural beauty, which the eye finds as soon as the object is presented to it.' In

24. Cf. letter to Ainsworth, in *The Life, Unpublished Letters, and Philosophical Regimen of Anthony, Earl of Shaftesbury*, p. 403.

25. Cf. *Characteristics*, p. 325.

26. 'It is enough if we consider the simplest of figures, as either a round ball, a cube or die. Why is even an infant pleased with the first view of these proportions?' (p. 326). Cf. also p. 416 footnote: 'beginning from those regular figures and symmetries, with which children are delighted'.

such cases 'No sooner the eye opens upon figures, the ear to sounds, than straight the beautiful results and grace and harmony are known and acknowledged.'[27] For this reason, and because the disposition to perceive beauty is natural, the idea of beauty is too: 'Nothing surely is more strongly imprinted on our minds or more closely interwoven with our souls than the idea or sense of order and proportion.'[28] Another important analogy with a living organism is that the natural disposition, like a rose plant, has a development which can be natural or not. This should seem obvious, since the disposition to perceive beauty that a child exercises will have to be developed, sometimes highly, and also in different directions, before it can be properly exercised in the perception of the beauty of an oratorio, a social system, or an astronomical system, not to mention the beauty of virtue and of God himself.

The disposition is natural in the further sense that it is universal, common to all persons.[29] But here, too, one must keep in mind the analogy with a living organism. It is natural for all rose plants to bear flowers sooner or later, but insufficient conditions and natural accidents either prevent flowering altogether or mutilate whatever flowers there are. Similarly with human beings and their disposition to experience beauty. Because of insufficient affective and cognitive conditions, or because of natural accidents, the disposition may be mutilated or insufficiently developed in some persons, and just about absent in others. Hence, one could not refute Shaftesbury merely by pointing to cases of persons incapable of appreciating the complex beauty of a Titian or of some physical subsystem.

IV

Is the Disposition to Perceive Beauty a Sixth Sense? In the quotation given in the last footnote, Shaftesbury calls the disposition to experience beauty a 'natural sense of a sublime and beautiful in things'. Is he saying that the disposition is literally a sixth

27. *Characteristics*, p. 326.

28. *Characteristics*, p. 273.

29. 'So that to deny the *common and natural sense* of a sublime and beautiful in things will appear an affectation merely to anyone who considers duly of this affair' (*Characteristics*, p. 173, my italics).

sense? What might seem to favour an affirmative reply is, first, that the disposition is called a 'natural sense', and secondly, that Hutcheson, advocate of a special, 'inner' sense for the perception of beauty, claims to have been influenced by Shaftesbury.[30] However, Hutcheson does not say that this influence has anything to do specifically with the perception of beauty. Also, we commonly use 'sense' casually, as in speaking of a sense of duty or a sense of rhythm. In Shaftesbury and Hutcheson's time it was not uncommon to use the expression 'sixth sense' casually in the context of aesthetic experience. For instance, the Abbé Du Bos in his *Réflexions Critiques sur la Poésie et sur la Peinture* (1719), speaks of a 'sixth sense which is in us without our seeing its organs'. But this is merely a general sensitivity (*le sentiment*) that he calls 'the heart'.[31] So, if we lacked any prior knowledge of Hutcheson, would we be inclined to read more than a casual use of 'sense' into Shaftesbury, and attribute to him a proper sixth sense theory? I believe not. Shaftesbury's position is closer to Burke's, who claims that taste can be accounted for by the joint, collaborative functioning of our ordinary faculties, without invoking an extra sense.[32] Nevertheless, Hutcheson did not develop his theory out of thin air. What must be shown, I believe, is an important and somewhat complex connection between Shaftesbury and Hutcheson, a connection that justifies the latter's claim to be influenced by the former, but which does not justify our treating Shaftesbury's natural disposition as a special sense in addition to the ordinary ones. So, let us attempt to show that Shaftesbury takes at least two significant steps down a road which, as things will turn out, can be seen as leading towards Hutcheson.

Two well known passages of the *Characteristics* seem to lend themselves to a Hutchesonian reading. The first is from the *Inquiry*. The second and third paragraphs quoted below are the first two of a sequence of four which did not appear in the first

30. Cf. F. Hutcheson, *An Inquiry Concerning Beauty, Order, Harmony, Design*, ed. P. Kivy (The Hague: Nijhoff, 1973), pp. 3, 25 and 27.

31. Abbé Du Bos, *Réflexions Critiques sur la Poésie et sur la Peinture* (Paris: ENSBA, 1993), p. 277.

32. Cf. E. Burke, *A Philosophical Enquiry into the Origin of our Ideas of the Sublime and Beautiful*, ed. J. T. Boulton (Oxford: Blackwell, 1987), p. 26.

edition (1699), but were added in the later, revised edition of 1711.

> In a creature capable of forming general notions of things, not only the outward beings which offer themselves to the sense are the objects of the affection, but the very actions themselves and the affections of pity, kindness, gratitude and their contraries, being brought into the mind by *reflection*, become objects. So that, by means of this *reflected sense*, there arises another kind of affection towards those very affections themselves, which have been already felt and have now become the subject of a new liking or dislike.
>
> The case is the same in the mental or moral subjects as in the ordinary bodies or common subjects of sense. The shapes, motions, colours and proportions of these latter being presented to our eye, there necessarily results a beauty or deformity, according to the different measure, arrangement and disposition of their several parts. So in behaviour and actions, when presented to our understanding, there must be found, of necessity, an apparent difference, according to the regularity or irregularity of the subjects.
>
> The mind, which is spectator or auditor of other minds, cannot be without *its eye and ear so as to discern proportion, distinguish sound and scan each sentiment or thought which comes before it.* It can let nothing escape its censure. It feels the soft and harsh, the agreeable and disagreeable in the affections, and finds a foul and fair, a harmonious and a dissonant, as really and truly here as in any musical numbers or in the outward forms or representations of sensible things. Nor can it withhold its admiration and ecstasy, its aversion and scorn, any more in what relates to one than to the other of these subjects. So that to deny the *common and natural sense of a sublime and beautiful* in things will appear an affectation merely to anyone who considers duly of this affair.[33]

The second passage is from *The Moralists* (first edition, 1709):

> 'Let us view the charm in what is simplest of all, mere figure. Nor need we go so high as sculpture, architecture or the designs of those who from this study of beauty have raised such delightful arts. It is enough if we consider the simplest of figures, as either a round ball, a cube or die. Why is an infant pleased with the first view of these proportions? Why is the sphere or globe, the cylinder and obelisk, preferred and the irregular figures, in respect of these, rejected and despised?'

---

33. *Characteristics*, pp. 172–173.

'Is there then', said he, 'a natural beauty of figures and is there not as natural a one of actions? No sooner the eye opens upon figures, the ear to sounds, than straight the beautiful results and grace and harmony are known and acknowledged. No sooner are actions viewed, no sooner the human affections and passions discerned (and they are most of them as soon discerned as felt) than straight an inward eye distinguishes and sees the fair and shapely, the amiable and admirable, apart from the deformed, the foul, the odious or the despicable. How is it possible therefore not to own that as these distinctions have their foundation in nature, the discernment itself is natural and from nature alone?'[34]

The overall aim of both passages is to introduce the idea of a disposition to perceive and appreciate the moral worth of affections and actions, whether they be one's own or someone else's. Shaftesbury's strategy—which will be duplicated by Hutcheson[35]—is to use the natural disposition to perceive beauty as a stepping-stone towards introducing a natural disposition to perceive moral worth, in the belief that the former will be more readily accepted than the latter. The first passage has the further purpose of presenting in part the important distinction Shaftesbury makes between mere goodness and moral virtue. Virtue requires two intellectual functions: (1) the capacity to form concepts, 'general notions of things', and (2) inward consciousness of one's actions and affections.

Shaftesbury uses Locke's term 'reflection' to name consciousness: 'The very actions themselves and the affections of pity, kindness, gratitude and their contraries, being brought into the mind by reflection, become objects.' It is important to note that Locke called consciousness or reflection an 'internal sense'.[36] Conflating two of Locke's expressions, Shaftesbury coins a new name for the same old Lockean faculty: 'reflected sense'. However, he adds three features that, as far as I know, do not feature—certainly not prominently—in Locke's account of

---

34. *Characteristics*, pp. 326–327.

35. Cf. Hutcheson, *op. cit.*, p. 26.

36. 'This source of ideas, every man has wholly in himself: and though it be not sense, as having nothing to do with external objects; yet it is very like it, and might properly enough be called internal sense. But as I call the other *Sensation*, so I call this reflection, the ideas it affords being such only, as the mind gets by reflecting on its own operations within itself' (J. Locke, *An Essay Concerning Human Understanding*, ed. P. Nidditch (Oxford University Press, 1975): II, 1, §4, p. 105).

consciousness. They come to the foreground here, and make Shaftesbury's 'reflected sense' something more than mere introspective awareness. First, Shaftesbury's 'reflected sense' depends on the intellect, since, according to the first passage quoted above, it depends on the mind's 'forming general notions of things'. Secondly, it is nevertheless an emotive capacity. For '[the mind cannot] withhold its admiration and ecstasy, its aversion and scorn'; it produces 'another kind of affection towards those very affections themselves, which have been already felt and have now become the subject of a new liking or dislike'. The awareness of some actions and (first-order) affections produces an emotional response which is a second-order affection. Thirdly, whereas Locke's 'reflection' is basically a source of *ideas*, Shaftesbury's 'reflected sense' is an active source of *evaluative judgements*, for 'the heart cannot possibly remain neutral but constantly takes part one way or other'.[37] Inasmuch as the second-order affection is a liking or a disliking (of an action or of a first-order affection), it comprises or depends on a moral approval or disapproval, an evaluative judgement. In these respects, then, Shaftesbury's 'reflected sense' is not mere consciousness or awareness, which is why he calls it a 'natural moral sense'.[38] Because of these features one should grant that Shaftesbury's 'reflected sense' is situated, as it were, between Locke's mere consciousness or 'internal sense' and Hutcheson's inner sense.

Shaftesbury's point is that, precisely because of the two last features mentioned—emotive and evaluative—the disposition to perceive and appreciate the moral value of actions and affections is similar to the disposition to perceive beauty in external, physical objects. Also, moral value is itself a kind of beauty. So much for the similarity of (what up to here we have been invited to take as) the 'two' natural dispositions. What of their differences? One should notice, first of all, that the examples given of beautiful things in both passages are not of complex objects such as natural beings, works of art, and so on, but only of relatively simple qualities: 'shapes, motions, colours and proportions' in the *Inquiry*; 'the simplest of figures, as either a round ball, a cube

37. *Characteristics*, p. 173.
38. *Characteristics*, p. 180.

or die' in the *Moralists*. Bearing this in mind, note that in both passages the capacity of perceiving the beauty of such qualities is that of the external senses (the eye, the ear). Nothing whatever is hinted at concerning the need for an 'inner sense' for apprehending the beauty of these qualities. Pursuing the contrast between the moral objects of 'reflected sense' and the beautiful, external objects of the senses, Shaftesbury generalises what he has said about relatively simple sensible qualities to include the whole domain of complex sensible objects. For he clearly implies that the external senses, not 'reflected sense', perceive the beauty to be found in natural beings and in works of art: 'in any musical numbers or in the outward forms or representations of sensible things'. No 'reflected sense' or 'inner sense' is invoked to explain our perception of the beauty of external things, whether they be simple qualities or complex objects, natural or artefactual.

Of course, the external senses will not *suffice* for the perception of the beauty of just any external entity, for two reasons at least. The first is that, as we have seen, many external objects are not sensible. The second is that even when they are sensible, as soon as we move from simple qualities to complex sensible objects, it is no longer true that the perception of beauty is immediate. That is to say, Shaftesbury does not hold for complex sensible objects, whether natural or artefactual, what he holds for simple qualities ('No sooner the eye opens upon figures, the ear to sounds, than straight the beautiful results and grace and harmony are known and acknowledged'). On the contrary, he holds in general that 'Never can the form be of real force where it is uncontemplated, unjudged of, unexamined.'[39] The context of this statement is a passage in which Shaftesbury—in Platonic fashion—distinguishes intellect from sense. Hence, we should gather that the contemplation, judgement and examination required for the beauteous form to 'be of real force' depend much more on the intellect than on the external senses. So it seems, indeed, that cases where the perception of beauty is accomplished merely by the external senses are so scarce as to be confined merely to very simple qualities. Further, even if in the vast majority of cases the experience of beauty requires the intellect in addition to the external senses, we still have no requirement for a special, sixth, 'inner'

39. *Characteristics*, p. 331.

sense. All that we have up to this point is a natural disposition that depends on the collaborative functioning of ordinary faculties and operations. Inner, 'reflected sense' is invoked solely in connection with the perception of the moral beauty of 'inner' objects: actions and affections.[40]

Hutcheson believes that a special inner sense, one and the same, is required for each and every experience of beauty; there is no experience of beauty that does not require a sixth sense. Shaftesbury claims nothing of the sort. Not only is his internal 'reflected sense' restricted to the perception of moral beauty, it is also not an additional faculty, but merely an admittedly amplified and elaborate version of Locke's consciousness. Thus, when compared to Shaftesbury, Hutcheson makes two crucial moves: (1) he believes that the evaluative and affective functions that Shaftesbury added on to Locke's power of consciousness can only be performed by another, additional sense, distinct from the five external senses and from mere consciousness; and (2) he claims that each and every experience of beauty, whatever the beautiful object, requires this additional sense.

Even so, there is no question of removing Shaftesbury's 'reflected sense' from the natural disposition to perceive beauty. For what 'reflected sense' perceives and appreciates is a special kind of beauty, moral beauty. So there is a kind of beauty for the perception and appreciation of which an 'inner sense', a 'natural moral sense', is indispensable. Yet this is not an additional faculty, but rather an augmented version of Locke's consciousness working with the intellect.

The claim that moral goodness and virtue are species of beauty has implications which must be seen from two different perspectives. On the one hand, there are consequences that should be studied from the point of view of moral philosophy. I cannot go into those here.[41] On the other hand, there are equally important

40. In the *Soliloquy* Shaftesbury speaks of an 'eye or ear for these interior numbers' (p. 150). But this has to do only with the 'moral truth, the beauty of sentiments, the sublime of characters', not with the beauty of sensible objects. In *The Moralists* he says that 'This difference [between beauty and the lack of it] is immediately perceived by *a plain internal sensation*' (p. 274). I suggest that our response is called a 'sensation' because it is an emotional, evaluative response, and 'internal' because, trivially, all responses are internal.

41. On this issue, cf. S. Darwall, *The British Moralists and the Internal 'Ought'* (Cambridge University Press, 1995).

consequences for aesthetics. Here, the first implication is that, although Shaftesbury introduces his natural moral sense, in the passages quoted above, by comparing it with our ability to perceive the beauty of external objects, they are not in fact two faculties, nor two dispositions situated at the same level. 'Reflected sense', we have seen, is indeed a proper faculty, operating in conjunction with the intellect when our natural disposition to perceive beauty is exercised on moral beauty. The natural disposition can also be exercised towards the beauty of non-moral objects without the operation of 'reflected sense', but with other faculties. The exercise of the natural disposition depends on whatever ordinary cognitive, evaluative and affective faculties and operations are necessary to attain the perception of whatever kind of beauty is at hand. According to the kind of beauty, the exercise of the self-same disposition will require different collaborative functionings of ordinary cognitive and affective faculties. Sometimes 'reflected sense' will be called for, sometimes not; it depends on the kind of beauty to be discovered and appreciated. This reading suggests that Shaftesbury's natural disposition to perceive beauty is to a large degree a higher-order, essentially dependent disposition.

Many of its different exercises, according to the diverse kinds of beauty to be perceived, require the development and perfecting of the disposition. And perfecting it depends on previously acquiring whatever cognitive, evaluative and affective abilities are necessary to the exercise of the disposition towards this or that kind of beauty. Inasmuch as it depends on 'art, culture or discipline', the development is not natural. Consider, for example, artistic beauty. Shaftesbury says that a 'refined taste' depends on 'use, practice and culture'. Although the disposition to perceive beauty is natural, a sure taste in the fine arts is not natural in the sense of 'innate': 'A legitimate and just taste can neither be begotten, made, conceived or produced without the antecedent labours and pains of criticism.' For this reason he declares 'open war' against those who 'reject the criticizing art, by which alone they are able to discover the true beauty and worth of every object',[42] and assigns to criticism the role of educating the natural disposition and transforming it into refined

42. *Characteristics*, p. 408. Cf. also pp. 320–321.

taste. Criticism includes many different elements, such as learning from the test of time, rational discussion, enlightened raillery and, given Shaftesbury's distrust of introspection,[43] self-criticism in soliloquy. Refined artistic taste, however, is merely a cultivated development and perfection of the natural disposition. And it is a perfection in one direction only, that of artistic beauty, which furthermore stands at a comparatively low position in the scale of forms of beauty. Nevertheless, the implication is clear: by analogy, similar education is necessary for the same disposition to be ably exercised towards the perception of all the higher degrees of beauty within the hierarchy: 'Is it a wonder we should be dull then, as we are, confounded and at a loss in these affairs, blind as to this higher scene, these nobler representations? ... Is study, science or learning necessary to understand all beauties else? And, for the sovereign beauty, is there no skill or science required?'[44] Not only is the natural disposition supposed to be extensively developed through rational knowledge, culture and critical appreciation, but there are also many different directions of development required, each direction depending on different cognitive, evaluative and affective abilities. Hence, there is no self-same psychic model or mental structure according to which the disposition to aesthetic contemplation and appreciation is exercised in all cases. In some cases few faculties, operations and abilities will be required; in other cases, many more will be needed. This is why it is wrong to claim, as is often done, that aesthetic experience is *always* an immediate response in Shaftesbury. It is naturally so only in cases of relatively simple, abstract qualities; for the rest it can only become immediate once the disposition has been painstakingly perfected. However, each and every acquired perfection of the disposition contributes to making its owner a better person: 'The admiration and love of order, harmony and proportion, in whatever kind, is naturally improving to the temper, advantageous to social affection, and highly assistant to virtue, which is itself no other than the love of order and harmony in society.'[45] Developing the natural disposition is a moral matter, essential to the full realisation of a person's nature.

43. *Characteristics*, pp. 77–78.
44. *Characteristics*, p. 321.
45. *Characteristics*, p. 191.

V

A Pleasurable Ascension. To deny a self-same mental structure
for all cases of aesthetic contemplation and appreciation is not
to deny some common features. One common feature is what
has been called 'disinterested pleasure'; another is disinterested
love. The notion of disinterested pleasure was to have a celebrated and controversial historical fortune in the hands of Hutcheson, Kant and many others in more recent times. But it is
important not to lay too much weight on this notion in Shaftesbury. I would like to show that what we may rightly call 'disinterested pleasure' in Shaftesbury, although prominent in his
theory of aesthetic experience, is less important than disinterested
love, and entirely depends on it.

Stolnitz has shown how Shaftesbury uses the terms 'interest',
'interested' and 'disinterested'.[46] 'Interest' has both an axiological
and a conative sense. In the axiological sense it denotes a being's
real good, whether it be known by the being to be its real good
or not, and whether it be desired or not. In this sense Shaftesbury
holds that 'by improving, we may be sure to advance our worth
and real self-interest'.[47] In the conative sense, 'interest' refers to
whatever is taken, either rightly or wrongly, by an individual to
be his good, and is desired by him. 'Interested' is used by Shaftesbury in connection with the conative sense of 'interest': an interested action, desire, or character trait is one that tends to further
whatever it is that the individual takes, rightly or wrongly, to be
his good. A synonym for 'interested' in this sense would be
'selfish', as long as we keep in mind that a selfish affection or
desire, if moderate, can either be, or not, 'consistent with public
good' and 'in some measure contributing to it', and thus either
morally good or not.[48] If 'disinterested' is taken as the contrary
of 'interested', then it is close to 'unselfish', 'altruistic', 'benevol-
ent' or 'aiming at the public good'. This sense of 'disinterested',
however, is irrelevant to aesthetics. But the use that Shaftesbury
makes of 'disinterested' that is relevant to aesthetics is the contradictory, privative sense of 'interested', i.e. 'non-selfish', which,

46. 'On the Significance of Lord Shaftesbury in Modern Aesthetic Theory', pp. 105
ff.
47. *Characteristics*, p. 320.
48. *Characteristics*, p. 170.

according to the context of its use, means 'impartial', 'unbiased' or 'impersonal'. An instance of this is the disinterested love of God or virtue; it is 'the love of God or virtue for God or virtue's sake', which 'has no other object than merely the excellency of that being itself'.[49] This is opposed to 'loving' God interestedly, as in the hope of reward or out of fear of punishment.

Let us part with Stolnitz and say a bit more about disinterested love. What does it mean to say that something is loved for itself? According to Shaftesbury, 'every real love' is 'only the contemplation of beauty'.[50] Thus, to say that something is loved for itself can mean two things. If the thing simply *is* a form of beauty and harmony, such as virtue, it is contemplatively loved for itself, and that is it. If, on the contrary, the being *has* some form of beauty or virtue, then to say that it is loved for itself is to say that it is contemplatively loved merely for its beauty, moral or otherwise. This is the case, first of all, with God. If he is loved disinterestedly, explains Shaftesbury, the love 'has no other object than merely the excellency of that being itself', which is to say that he is loved for his mere value, his supreme beauty. By analogy the same applies to the disinterested love of lower sorts of beings that have some degree of beauty, moral or otherwise, transient or not: if virtuous persons and their character traits, affections and actions are loved disinterestedly, or if natural beings, works of art, and even relatively simple sensible qualities are loved disinterestedly, they are loved for whatever kind of 'excellency' or beauty they have. And if a being that has different sorts of beauty—such as a person, who may be both physically and morally beautiful—is loved disinterestedly, it is loved for its highest form of beauty, for this is the kind of 'excellency' with which the person is then associated.

As suggested above, disinterested love does not apply only to God, but, in a fully accomplished person, to whatever in the hierarchy either is beautiful or has some degree of beauty. Shaftesbury makes this clear by calling disinterested love 'enthusiasm' in a positive sense, and arguing that positive enthusiasm in an accomplished person ranges over the whole scale of beautiful things from the bottom up.[51]

49. *Characteristics*, p. 268.
50. *Characteristics*, p. 318.
51. For instance, *Characteristics*, p. 320

All sound love and admiration is enthusiasm. The transports of poets, the sublime of orators, the rapture of musicians ... all mere enthusiasm! ... [I] am content you should call this love of ours 'enthusiasm' ... For is there a fair and plausible enthusiasm, a reasonable ecstasy and transport allowed to other subjects, such as architecture, painting, music, and shall it be exploded here? Are there senses by which all those other graces and perfections are perceived, and none by which this higher perfection and grace is comprehended? Is it so preposterous to bring that enthusiasm hither and transfer it from those secondary and scanty objects to this original and comprehensive one [God]?[52]

Thus, disinterested love or positive enthusiasm is a feature common to all aesthetic experiences, ranging over the entire scale of beautiful things. It is to be identified with what we encountered in the previous section in the guise of 'a new liking', the affective, evaluative approval immanent in aesthetic experience.

As for 'disinterested pleasure', Shaftesbury does not use this expression, nor does he use 'disinterested perception' and 'disinterested attitude'. But he points emphatically to a pleasure immanent in the aesthetic experience of beautiful objects, and which is different from the pleasures that result from an interested perspective on the same objects. The *locus classicus* is a passage in the *Moralists*,[53] where the context is a discussion of 'real love', disinterested love. Theocles begins by explaining that 'every real love' is 'only the contemplation of beauty'. This love produces a certain pleasure, and Theocles distinguishes this pleasure from those arising from an interested perspective on the same object. The interested perspectives to which disinterested love is contrasted are the intentions of commanding, of possessing and of consuming. If one loves 'the beauty of the ocean', for example, the resulting pleasure is distinct from that which would ensue (*per impossibile*) from commanding or possessing it. The pleasure found in contemplating 'such a tract of country as this delicious vale' is different from that which would follow from owning it. The pleasure of 'the beauty of those trees under whose shade we

---

52. *Characteristics*, p. 320. See also, pp. 27–28 and pp. 351 ff., especially 353. Cf. my 'Shaftesbury: Enthousiasme et Expérience Religieuse', forthcoming in Revue de Théologie et de Philosophie (2002).
53. *Characteristics*, pp. 318–319.

rest' is distinct from that which would arise from eating their fruit.

The point Shaftesbury wants to make is not that it is psychologically impossible for *some* of the pleasures resulting from the satisfaction of interested perspectives, such as commanding, possessing, consuming, to coexist with the pleasure resulting from the disinterested love of the beauty of the same object. Surely one can simultaneously be pleased to own a Veronese and be pleased by its beauty. In other cases, however, the two kinds of pleasures do seem to be psychologically incompatible: if a person takes pleasure in commanding another, this pleasure can hardly coexist with that resulting from a disinterested love of the person's moral beauty.

Nor does Shaftesbury deny that the disinterested pleasure taken in the aesthetic experience of an objet can raise an interested perspective towards the object, such as a desire to possess it. Rather, he means that even if an interested perspective towards the object is caused by a disinterested pleasure, cause and effect necessarily remain distinct. In order to have such an effect, the disinterested pleasure must first be an accomplished experience. As such it is independent of the effect—the desire— that it may or may not elicit. A disinterested pleasure remains disinterested whether or not it causes an interested perspective on the object; and if it does cause one, it remains disinterested whether or not the interested perspective is satisfied.

The positive points that Shaftesbury wishes to make are that: (1) an aesthetic experience is basically a form of contemplative disinterested love of an object's beauty; (2) the pleasure that arises from disinterested love is of a different kind from, but not necessarily psychologically incompatible with, some other pleasures regarding the same object; (3) the pleasure that arises from a disinterested love of an object's beauty is the only one that is appropriate to the object's beauty. There is nothing wrong in calling this aesthetic pleasure 'disinterested', just as long as we keep in mind two things. (1) Such a pleasure as Shaftesbury wants to draw our attention to in aesthetic experience depends on—and can only be explained in terms of—disinterested contemplative love. The notion of 'disinterested pleasure' present in his aesthetics bears the marks, as it were, of its religious origins and context, and the historian of philosophy should avoid the temptation to construe Shaftesbury's notion of what we call 'disinterested pleasure' in such a way as to divorce it from them. (2) According to what we, today, put under the headings 'disinterested' and 'interested', there may or may not be in Shaftesbury some disinterested pleasures which do not stem from disinterested love, and which are non-aesthetic.[54]

Disinterested love is a feature more basic to aesthetic experience in Shaftesbury than the kind of pleasure resulting from it. Furthermore, disinterested pleasure as such is not a reliable criterion of the *degree* of beauty, in the case of beauties that require a cultivated taste in order to be apprehended. An insufficiently educated person may have great pleasure in contemplating lower forms of beauty, and little or no pleasure with regard to higher forms. What counts is a degree of pleasure appropriate to the degree of the beauty of the contemplated object. For the question is, explains Shaftesbury, 'Whether we are *rightly* pleased and choose as we *should* do?' One must 'learn to fancy, to admire, to please, as the subjects themselves are *deserving*'. One should always ask: 'But is this pleasure *right*?'[55]

Townsend is correct in saying that disinterestedness of pleasure 'is not really proposed as any kind of test, nor does it characterize a special class of perceptions or judgements. It is much more important to Shaftesbury to determine what our true interests are'[56]. Were Shaftesbury to distinguish the aesthetic experience from other experiences, he would do so, contrary to Kant, in terms of disinterested love rather than disinterested pleasure. And he would not explain beauty in terms of disinterested pleasure, as Kant sometimes does,[57] but would explain the disinterested pleasure stemming from disinterested love as the kind of pleasure appropriate to beauty. Furthermore, he would not seek to distinguish sharply between aesthetic, moral and religious

54. It should be noted that, according to Hutcheson, one of the reasons why it is necessary to postulate an internal, sixth sense for aesthetic contemplation is precisely that aesthetic perception shares with the (non-aesthetic) perceptions of the five other senses the common feature of producing disinterested pleasures (cf. *An Inquiry Concerning Beauty, Order, Harmony, Design*, Section I, §6, pp. 31–32, and one aspect of the complex argument running through §12–14, pp. 35–38). According to him there are non-aesthetic disinterested pleasures.

55. *Characteristics*, pp. 250 and 151, my italics.

56. 55 D. Townsend, 'Shaftesbury's Aesthetic Theory', p. 211.

57. *Critique of Judgment*, ed. W. S. Pluhar (Indianapolis: Hackett, 1987), p. 53.

experiences, since both of the latter are kinds of aesthetic experiences; they are, respectively, the experience of the moral beauty of finite minds and the experience of the (moral) beauty of God, either in himself or as is manifested in the universe.

If an aesthetic experience is basically a form of pleasurable disinterested love, it is both a contemplative and a practical experience. We have seen that the contemplative aspect of the experience is bound to vary enormously in cognitive preconditions from case to case according to the kind of beauty contemplated within the hierarchy. The appropriate practical loving reactions are bound to vary just as much from case to case: one does not act appropriately towards a person whom one loves disinterestedly in the same way that one acts appropriately towards God if one loves him disinterestedly. Nor in the same way that a child can react lovingly when he perceives the beauty of the figures of his ball or die.

We must now return to an unanswered question. In an accomplished person, the natural disposition to experience beauty is to be extensively developed in two ways: vertically, inasmuch as we are supposed to perfect the disposition so as to be able to contemplatively love higher and higher forms of beauty; horizontally, inasmuch as we are supposed to perfect the disposition in order to be able to contemplatively love all the forms of beauty present at any given level of the hierarchy. The least that can be said is that both developments, vertical and horizontal, require considerable 'labours and pains'. What, then, is the motivating, driving force that is to lead us to aspire, in optimal cases, to perfect our natural disposition in both directions?

'The mathematician who labours at his problem, the bookish man who toils, the artist who endures voluntarily the greatest hardships and fatigues—none of these are said 'to follow pleasure',' as the expression is ordinarily taken.[58] Yet, Shaftesbury claims, follow pleasure they do. In the *Inquiry*, Shaftesbury gives another example of the kind of pleasure proper to disinterested love, a love pertaining in this case to the beauty of mathematics:

> When we have thoroughly searched into the nature of this contemplative delight [in mathematics], we shall find it of a kind which

58. *Characteristics*, p. 252.

relates not in the least to the private interest of the creature, nor
has for its object any self-good or advantage of the private system.
The admiration, joy or love turns wholly upon what is exterior
and foreign to ourselves. And although the reflected joy or pleasure which arises from the notice of this pleasure once perceived
may be interpreted as self-passion or interested regard, yet the
original satisfaction can be no other than what results from the
love of truth, proportion, symmetry in the things without.[59]

Shaftesbury distinguishes two pleasures. The first is the disinterested pleasure caused by, or contained in, a disinterested contemplative love of beauty. The second pleasure is a 'reflected joy'
because it depends on the 'the notice' of the first pleasure. (Due
to 'reflected sense' we have first and second-order natural affections in the perception and evaluative appreciation of *moral*
beauty; but we also have first and second-order pleasures in the
perception and evaluative appreciation of *all* beauties, such as
those of mathematics. The two distinctions—between, on one
hand, orders of natural affection and, on the other, orders of
pleasure—are different.) What is the second pleasure? Since it
depends on the awareness of the first-order pleasure, it has that
pleasure as its object: one is pleased to be pleased. And since the
first-order pleasure is known to be one's own, the second-order
pleasure is a 'self-passion'. But why is the latter an 'interested
regard'? I suggest the following reading as best fitting what we
have previously seen. The 'reflected joy' is not only a pleasure in
being pleased; it is also a pleasure in being *disinterestedly* pleased,
due to an implicit awareness that *having* disinterested pleasure is
somehow conducive to our real self-interest. Whether we know
it or not, the reason why disinterested pleasure is conducive to
our real self-interest is that it directly results from disinterested
love. Of course, the first pleasure does not have one's (real) self-
interest as its object; it has 'no object within the compass of the
private system'.[60] Its object is merely the beauty that is 'exterior
and foreign to ourselves'. But the ensuing 'reflected joy' comes
not only from the consciousness of the first pleasure, but also
from some awareness, faint or lively, that experiencing the first
pleasure somehow contributes to our true self-interest. If this

59. *Characteristics*, pp. 202–203.
60. *Characteristics*, p. 203.

reading is correct, Shaftesbury means that the mathematician, the 'bookish man', the artist, indeed all persons ('we all of us know something of this principle'),[61] have an awareness, dim or acute, that they become better persons by exercising their natural disposition to experience beauty, by loving it disinterestedly and taking pleasure in it.

Pleasures often foster a desire to renew the same pleasure or to have greater ones of the same kind. Presumably, then, Shaftesbury believes that the two pleasures—the first-order, disinterested one and the second-order, interested one—produce a desire to renew the same disinterested pleasure or to have greater ones. Yet an aesthetic pleasure is necessarily caused directly by (or contained in) disinterested love ('the original satisfaction can be no other than what results from the love of truth, proportion, symmetry in the things without'). So, if the desire to have a renewed or greater disinterested pleasure is satisfied, the pleasure will be the direct effect of a renewed or greater disinterested love, itself an effect—although only an indirect one—of the desire. But the fact that the new aesthetic pleasure is an (indirect) effect of the desire that it satisfies does not jeopardise the pleasure's disinterestedness. For it can surely remain true that the new, desired aesthetic pleasure 'relates not in the least to the private interest of the creature' *in the sense* that it does not have 'for its *object* any self-good or advantage of the private system', and that it is directly caused by a disinterested love of 'what is exterior and foreign to ourselves'. This is so even if *having* a disinterested pleasure does relate, causally, to the 'private interest of the creature' in contributing to making it a better person. But again, this sort of 'private interest' is not only compatible with, but conducive to morality and 'the public good'.

In endeavouring to satisfy the desire for renewed or greater disinterested pleasures, one will be motivated to seek pleasures appropriate to beauties situated higher in the hierarchy, and in perhaps exceptional cases, appropriate to the beauty of God, either in himself or at least as manifested in the universe. Hence, although within any given aesthetic experience the role of the disinterested pleasure is secondary to that of the disinterested

61. *Characteristics*, p. 351.

love, an important function of the disinterested pleasure, I suggest, is that, in combination with the interested pleasure, it leads one to aspire to pass from the aesthetic experience of lower degrees of beauty to the experience of higher ones. If this reading is on the right track, the importance of 'disinterested pleasure' is to be found at least as much in the ascending *transition* from one aesthetic experience to another, as *within* aesthetic experiences themselves.[62]

62. I wish to thank Laurent Jaffro and David Spurr for their helpful comments.

AESTHETIC EXPERIENCE IN SHAFTESBURY

by Richard Glauser and Anthony Savile

II—Anthony Savile

ABSTRACT (1) If Shaftesbury is to be seen as the doyen of modern aesthetics, his most valuable legacy to us may not so much be his viewing aesthetic response as a *sui generis* disinterested delight as his insistence on its turning 'wholly on [experience of] what is exterior and foreign to ourselves'. Not that we cannot experience ourselves, or what is our own, as a source of such admiration. Rather our responses, favourable or no, are improperly grounded in any essentially reflexive, or first-personal, ways of taking what engages us. The suggestion is tested against the case of Narcissus. (2) Glauser interestingly emphasizes Shaftesbury's neo-Platonic conception of a hierarchy of aesthetic experience that culminates in the joyful contemplation of God. That hierarchy must be something that is less unitary and systematic than Shaftesbury himself had supposed, even when his emphasis on the tie between aesthetic pleasure and contemplative experience is allowed to extend beyond perception and to encompass episodes of thought itself.

I

'The most ingenious way of becoming foolish is by a system' said Shaftesbury, encouraging us to view him as a fundamentally unsystematic thinker. In his paper Professor Glauser has done much to dispel that perception, and shown with clarity the system that there is in the *Characteristics*. I have learnt much from his lucid exposition and am grateful to him for it. In my own contribution to our symposium I shall not attempt to rewrite the history we have been told, nor to enlarge upon it in the hope of throwing light into corners not already illuminated. Instead, I shall spend time expanding some of the detail of Shaftesbury's thought and ask whether, in the light of that, there are not respects in which it recommends itself to us today more readily than we might expect. The topic on which I shall initially focus is one which has been central to our understanding of the aesthetic since the early eighteenth century, and which is generally seen as Shaftesbury's single most important gift to the subject. I allude of course to his doctrine that truly aesthetic satisfactions are of their nature disinterested ones.

To orient discussion I shall examine the passage to which Glauser draws attention at the very end of his paper, to wit those lines from the *Inquiry* that treat of the contemplative delight we take in mathematics. There Shaftesbury writes:

> When we have thoroughly searched into the nature of this contemplative delight, we shall find it of a kind which relates not in the least to any private interest of the creature, nor has it for its object any self-good or advantage of the private system. The admiration, joy or love turns wholly on what is exterior and foreign to ourselves. And though the reflected joy or pleasure which arises from the notice of this pleasure once perceived may be interpreted as self-passion or interested regard, yet the original satisfaction can be no other than what results from love of truth, proportion, order and symmetry in the things without.[1]

Here we are introduced to the idea of pleasures that are interested, and hence non-aesthetic, in two distinct ways. The first of them does so by reference to a pleasure's internal object. I notice myself taking a delight in certain mathematical proofs and, says Shaftesbury, that can give rise to a further pleasure, one which is interested just because it has a state of myself as its object. This second-order pleasure is implicitly contrasted with the first-order pleasure—the aesthetic one—whose object is the mathematical proof itself.

With his example Shaftesbury is considering two sorts of what we may call 'unmotivated' pleasure. By this I mean no more than that in neither case does the pleasure essentially result from the satisfaction of a desire that has occasioned some successfully accomplished action. Now it is certainly not the case that we today would call the second-order unmotivated pleasure that Shaftesbury has in mind 'interested', since talk of interest immediately brings with it consideration of motive. More to the point though—there is after all no particular reason to expect Shaftesbury's usage to accord entirely with our own—the natural contrast that he implies (though without explicitly stating it), and which we might at a pinch think of as both unmotivated and 'disinterested', would be a pleasure that I take involving the pleasure of someone other than myself. So, for example, I can take a second-order pleasure in your first-order liking for the Cologne

---

1. Klein (ed.), 202–3.

I recommended to you last week, or I may simply be delighted that you are reasonably stable again now after recovering from a period of crippling depression. Here we have second-order pleasures whose internal objects are the pleasures of someone other than ourselves, and hence not interested ones as Shaftesbury is apparently using the term. In neither case though is my second-order and as it were 'disinterested' pleasure an aesthetic one.

Not all unmotivated pleasures are second-order ones, of course, and salient among those that are not are our aesthetic delights. But again there are among our first-order unmotivated pleasures plenty that do not have ourselves as their object (and hence by Shaftesbury's reckoning are not interested) without being of an aesthetic order for all that. I am glad that the kitchen knives are no longer blunt; I rejoice that the government has finally fallen; I am relieved that you have at last got round to making an appointment with the dentist, and so on. Our aesthetic pleasures are for the most part like these in that they do indeed generally concern things other than ourselves, but that aspect of them neither captures what we have in mind when we call them 'disinterested', nor, in any undeveloped form, does it take us anywhere near the heart of the matter. After all we can perfectly well consider ourselves from the aesthetic point of view; were that not so, it would be hard to explain why most of us here wouldn't much care to be seen in public wearing a baseball cap or for that matter a full-bottomed wig. (In Section IV I shall ask whether Shaftesbury's apparently uninviting idea admits of fruitful expansion.)

II

The other route Shaftesbury takes towards the introduction of disinterested delight is precisely concerned with motivation. He puts it by saying that 'We shall find [the nature of this contemplative delight] of a kind which relates not in the least to any private interest of the creature, nor has it for its object any self-good or advantage of the private system.' Undoubtedly there is ellipsis here, for it cannot properly be said that any pleasure has (or fails to have) an advantage as its object, in the sense of its *goal*. What I take him to mean is that the pleasure he is concerned with is not a response to the awareness that some activity or behaviour of ours has achieved any self-benefiting aim we have set ourselves. Were it of such a kind, it would be an interested pleasure, and clearly our aesthetic pleasures are not of that sort. Hence we are inclined to call them 'disinterested' to set them apart, though, as Glauser observes, the phrase 'disinterested pleasure' is not one that Shaftesbury uses, and, to be sure, in the passage I am talking about the word 'disinterested' doesn't appear at all.

If I have understood Shaftesbury correctly, two things are going on which we ought to applaud. The first is that the idea of disinterestedness is being accounted for in terms of what it contrasts with, the trouser-wearing notion of *interest*. Secondly, pleasures are being called disinterested or interested as they arise in response to behaviour that is interested or not. That is, a *pleasure* is interested or disinterested only derivatively, not originally. However, at the same time we do well to notice how misleading it would be to assimilate Shaftesbury's idea to anything we ourselves might naturally express in terms of interest or disinterest.

Suppose I gash my hand at home on a piece of glass and hurry off to A&E to get the flow of blood stanched. How pleased I am to have got there without too great a loss of the precious liquid. For Shaftesbury, my pleasure is then an interested one since it turns on an action that seeks benefit to 'the private system'; yet as far as we today are concerned, such behaviour is neither interested nor disinterested, and it would be misleading to suggest otherwise, except in the irrelevant sense that it is in my interest to get to the hospital quickly. For us moderns both terms do indeed find their prime application to motivated behaviour, but the situation is far more complicated than anything that Shaftesbury had in mind. Many self-regarding actions, like that of my example, do not display interest, while not being disinterested either. What makes an action an interested one is that it is criticisably undertaken for the agent's own advantage (or that of his close associates, family or friends), and usually at the expense or the detriment of someone else. There was nothing remotely criticisable about my rushing to the hospital with my bleeding hand, and my doing that certainly didn't in any way involve the abuse of any one else's trust or my doing someone else down.

As for disinterested behaviour, that isn't just behaviour that fails to be interested in the modern sense. Flossing my teeth at night is that all right, but it would just be silly to say that I am a disinterested nocturnal tooth-flosser. Rather, the word finds its place because typically someone who behaves in an interested way recognises that he is criticisable in doing so, and will tend defensively to represent himself as acting impartially or altruistically or in some other quite inoffensive manner. Behaviour that we call disinterested is simply behaviour that is not of a kind calculated to get people to believe that it is other than interested. I may interestedly give you a good stock-market tip, doing so with the ulterior and unavowed motive of winning your support in my attempts to join the board (a case where no one is done down, but I am still criticisable for lack of frankness). If I say to you on the other hand, that I gave you the tip quite disinterestedly, and say so truly, then I am drawing your attention to the fact that I was not acting out of some ulterior and criticisable motive.[2]

To get this absolutely right would take work, and that is not what I am concerned with. In the large, I don't think we are too far off-target to worry here about the fine detail. Now, one thing to notice is that when action is, as we speak today, disinterested, it scarcely makes sense to call any pleasure or delight that it gives rise to a disinterested one.[3] That phrase 'disinterested pleasure' *sounds* in order because we have got so used to it, but when we think it through it can hardly have any application at all. Of course, actions that are interested or disinterested can both give rise to pleasure on the agent's part, but our use of the terms 'disinterested' or 'interested' is exhausted by our description of the action or behaviour. Their derivative application to the pleasure itself is surd.

If Shaftesbury's second route to the idea of interest passes through consideration of motive and our own use of the pair

2. I do not think this would surprise Shaftesbury. He speaks of the love which was so remarkable between Jonathan and David as giving us 'a noble view of a disinterested friendship, at least on *one* side' (Klein, 47). 'Disinterested' here can not just mean *with no view to his (Jonathan's) own advantage*. That would have applied to both parties. Only Jonathan had any interest in dissembling in the matter, and Shaftesbury draws attention here to his not doing so.

3. Interestingly, when Kant introduces the expression 'disinterested pleasure' he does so in tow with disinterested *displeasure* ('*Wohlgefallen oder Mißfallen ohne Interesse*' is the phrase that appears in the summary of the First Moment of the Analytic of the Beautiful (*Critique of Judgement* §5 (end)). For us that poses a problem of translation, just because to talk of revulsion or distaste being disinterested doubles the absurdity of thinking pleasure might be disinterested.

disinterested/interested concerns the motivations that explain
people's actions, then it suffices to notice that our aesthetic pleasures are paradigmatically unmotivated ones, not arising as the
natural response to the satisfaction of some desire, to see that
Shaftesbury's celebrated legacy to us does very little to clarify
the nature of our contemplative delights either in the form he
bequeathed it to us or in the rather different way our later ways
of speaking might encourage us to understand it.[4]

III

It would be very natural to respond to this last rather ungenerous
observation by saying that clearly what Shaftesbury is telling us,
though in a less than perfectly clear way, is that what marks out
our aesthetic interest in things is that it is an interest and attention given to them *for their own sake* rather than for some interest
or advantage to ourselves (or anyone else for that matter),[5] and
it may seem that my reservations display a hair-splitting small-
mindedness. But I think that would be mistaken, and for two
distinct reasons. The first is that there is a distinction worth preserving between the pair 'for its own sake/for some other reason'
and the pair 'interested/disinterested' in that the latter couple
offers a contrast that applies within the range of motivated
behaviour, and that neither member has significant application
outside it. By contrast, what is undertaken 'for its own sake' lies
squarely in the realm of unmotivated behaviour, or at least with
behaviour that is not oriented towards advantage or benefit, and
so its use diverges significantly from that of 'disinterested'. It
only confuses matters to assimilate them. Secondly, and perhaps
more importantly, of the pair 'for it own sake/not for its own
sake' it is the former that wears the trousers, and we have already

---

4. In essence this is the point on which George Dickie's 'The Myth of the Aesthetic
Attitude' (*American Phil. Quarterly*, 1964) turns, although he wasn't directly concerned with Shaftesbury there.

5. That Shaftesbury might himself say this is shown by his speaking in *The Moralists*
of our loving God disinterestedly, and glossing that in terms of loving God for His
own sake because of the excellency of that being itself (Klein, 269). See also the
Inquiry (Klein, 184/5), 'If it be true piety to love God *for his own sake*, the over-
solicitous regard to private good expected from him must of necessity prove a dimin-
ution of piety' (my emphasis).

seen that of the other pair it is 'interested' that does so, not 'disinterested'. The significance of this is that to observe that our aesthetic pleasures are ones we take in things for their own sake needs some positive filling before it becomes really informative, and that we cannot provide that filling by stealing the clothing from the trouser-wearing 'interested', as the conflation of the two pairs would encourage us to do.

IV

Is there anything in what Shaftesbury tells us that narrows down the range of pleasures taken for their own sake in the location of those that are properly speaking aesthetic ones? His own move in the passage I have quoted suggests that he thinks there is. For what determined that my pleasure in finding myself pleased by mathematical structures or deep chess moves was not an aesthetic one was that it had the wrong sort of object. The object wasn't adequately foreign to me. As we saw him put it before, the object of our aesthetic 'admiration, joy or love turns wholly on what is exterior and foreign to ourselves'. Strange as it may seem, and despite the baseball cap and the full-bottomed wig, there is something quite right about this, though Shaftesbury did not express it well and (as Glauser points out) it can't be the whole story anyway.

For better or for worse, Narcissus certainly admired Narcissus, so attention given to oneself can well be aesthetic attention contrary to what Shaftesbury suggests. Is that not the end of the matter? Surely not. Let us distinguish on Shaftesbury's behalf (and in Ovid's wake) between the thought that Narcissus admired Narcissus and the thought Narcissus admired himself. Then the kernel to be saved from Shaftesbury's exclusion of the self will be that attention given to something for its own sake under a thought that introduces it in terms of the thinker first personally (as myself, as my wife, as my saviour) cannot generate a genuine (i.e. potentially well-founded) aesthetic satisfaction.

If we ask why not, the most plausible answer consonant with Shaftesbury's general aesthetic realism, which we can accept without thinking of beauty as anything akin to a primary quality, would seem to be that it is because the domain of the aesthetic is essentially a public domain.[6] Our aesthetic pleasures have to be responsive to something that is theoretically accessible to the world at large, and only Narcissus can have the pleasure in himself, thought of thus reflexively. The rest of us are restricted to finding Narcissus beautiful, thought of in terms that can be accessed by others, typically of course as Narcissus, which is of course one way in which Narcissus could have thought of himself, although most certainly he didn't.[7]

Is that doctrine plausible though? Do not the vain have an genuine aesthetic appreciation of themselves, and yet think of themselves first-personally as they do so? We may not like the phenomenon, but it does undoubtedly occur. The existence of this kind of vanity would only be a decisive counter-example to the realism that Shaftesbury endorses if a vain pleasure could be derived from the contemplation of an object generating an aesthetic judgment that was both true and well-founded. Now, there may well be situations in which Narcissus says truly that he is beautiful, thinking of himself in the first person. Only he may not be displaying vanity in doing so, but be viewing himself quite dispassionately, with a view maybe to making up his mind whether to go for a part in the new Lloyd-Webber musical, *Metamorphoses*. ('Shall I audition for Narcissus?', he wonders, 'No problem on the beauty front, but maybe my voice isn't quite up to it.') However, in any case like this, the occurrence of the first person is eliminable. Narcissus could equally well have said 'Narcissus is beautiful enough for the part' and simply drawn on the ineliminably reflexive information that he is Narcissus in deciding to give the auditions a miss.

What would make the pleasure he finds in his own beauty a vain one, or better perhaps narcissistic, I think is that the fact that the person viewed is himself enters essentially into the

6. My use of the term 'realism' would commit Shaftesbury to no more than that judgments of an aesthetic character are assessable as true or false independently of the opinion of one who makes them.

7. The poignancy of Ovid's fable consists in Narcissus's coming to realise why the figure he sees in the water cannot be possessed: the realisation that it is he himself kills him, as Tiresias had dimly foreseen it would. Before that point in the story, the first person is absent. Only, of course, Narcissus wouldn't then have thought of that figure in the pellucid water as Narcissus, but as that ravishingly beautiful and distressingly elusive youth.

reasons he has for finding himself beautiful, a reason that is not available to the rest of us.[8] Now a realist of Shaftesbury's stamp will say that there is something illegitimate about this, and he might put his hesitation about it in either of two ways. First, he could say that we expect that the reasons for which we find something beautiful must be rooted in something that is open to experience. What it is about the object that justifies the claim that it is a beautiful one must itself be something that determines how the object appears. But for Narcissus to identify Narcissus as himself is not to identify him in terms of anything that impinges on his appearance; nor for that matter is 'being mine' in any of the various ways we use that expression (possession [my cat], causation [my seducer], close relation [my nephew]) cut out to mark any particular experienceable aspect of things. Hence it could not introduce a way of thinking about things I judge to be beautiful that underwrites a claim that I, or my garden, or my grand-daughter is beautiful.

In the end I believe that this thought is correct, but it would take a considerable amount of argument to defend it properly. The difficulty is that it is anything but clear what features of things we can allow to be experienceable in an understanding of that notion that coincides with the field of the aesthetic. For instance, we would not normally say that being a moral monster is an experienceable feature of someone, but it makes good sense to think that to view someone in the light of a belief that a moral monster is what they are makes a significant difference to the way that we experience them and to the aesthetic judgments that we think it right to make about them.[9] If this is true then if we are to rule out 'being me' or 'being mine' as introducing no experienceable feature of myself or things that are mine, we

8. This is not the situation of Ovid's figure at *Metamorphoses* III, 461–2, for the aesthetic judgment that he makes about himself after his recognition of his situation is supported in exactly the same way as it had been beforehand. The original Narcissus was no narcissist, the first-personal element in his appreciation of himself being straightforwardly eliminable.

9. I have used this thought elsewhere to argue that the Sirens' song must have been cacophonous, whatever Ulysses thought about it. See 'The Sirens' Serenade' in R.I.P. Lectures, 1999–2000, A. O'Hear (ed.), CUP (2000). It is along these lines that I think we might introduce the idea of the beauty of virtue that so mattered to Shaftesbury: a person's virtue is manifest in their bearing or in the way their behaviour lends itself to be perceived. Compare here *Critique of Judgement* §17.

would need to supply reasons why they cannot be brought in, in the way that moral monstrosity can be.[10]

Without pursuing that issue, let us then suppose that at least for the person who sees something as themselves or as theirs there is a difference to the way in which they experience these objects—whether or not they are correct in their belief (Narcissus might have taken Echo for himself, or have confused Echo's reflection with his own). Can that justify the claim that they make that the object, thought of in those terms is truly a beautiful one? The answer must be 'No', for while we can easily enough introduce a difference between getting it right and getting it wrong with regard to whether the reflection Narcissus takes to be his own is so in fact, what cannot be done is to find a difference between Narcissus thinking that the reflection's being his really makes a contribution to the appearance of the reflection that renders it beautiful and its merely seeming to him to make such a difference. At the point we might say, with Kant, that Narcissus would be confusing the beautiful with the merely subjectively agreeable (cf. *Critique of Judgement* §7). Furthermore, if the possession of the putative reflexive property were to have evidential weight, just because it is a property possessed by all, there would have to be an explanation of how its recognition could reasonably weigh favourably in some cases but not in others. The only plausible answer would be one that made appeal to the differing aesthetic characters of the property's bearers when considered entirely impersonally and non-reflexively. But then the reflexive property would function evidentially completely idly.

What then are we to say of the truly beautiful Narcissus who vainly judges himself to be beautiful? Certainly his judgment is true, but given that his vanity is at work, the ground for his judgment must be that Narcissus is him. Hence he is making his true judgement on grounds that do not support it. Curiously, his judgement is based on an insensitivity to the beauty that is his

10. For the record, the point echoes the kind of criticism that George Dickie made of Jerome Stolnitz's claim that the introduction of disinterestedness into our understanding of the aesthetic brought with it as consequence a detachment of the objects of our attention from their causal and moral relations. Since for Shaftesbury our disinterested love of God was grounded in His excellence, that could hardly have been an idea that would have appealed to him, however attractive it seemed to later writers.

own in that it is open to him to appreciate Narcissus for exactly the reasons that the rest of us do, but instead he turns to something quite private to do so. In that case Narcissus has what is a necessarily flawed line to the truth of the matter, and his vanity is occluding his beauty from him rather than revealing to him a beauty that eludes poor Echo and his other admirers.[11]

My conclusion on Shaftesbury's behalf then is that pleasures that are aesthetic must have as their object things that are thought of in terms that are not irreducibly first-personal. Now we are in a position to see why Shaftesbury's second-order pleasures having the self as their object are not aesthetic ones, and we can do that without drawing on the notion of attention not being given to the object for its own sake or through lack of disinterestedness. It is that in those second-order cases my pleasure is to notice that I have a certain pleasure. For me just to notice that Anthony Savile takes a pleasure in mathematics will not standardly give rise to any pleasure on my part. If I am looking for an aesthetic pleasure in reading through Hardy's papers, say, then when my desire is satisfied I am most unlikely to experience a second-order pleasure unless I know that the person so raptly reading through those papers of Hardy's is me. First personal reflexivity is effectively ineliminable here. So the pleasure in question cannot be a genuinely aesthetic one. To say that 'The admiration, joy or love turns wholly on what is exterior and foreign to ourselves' enjoys a measure of plausibility when taken like that, not as proscribing any particular range of objects though, but rather as banning a way of conceiving of them.

V

Does Shaftesbury have anything else to tell us about the specific nature of the pleasure which he gives some indication of thinking of as *sui generis*? Indeed he does, for not only does he delimit its way of specifying its objects in the way I have suggested we might most generously read him, but in addition he indicates the

11. If the vanity manifests itself as such in the subject's behaviour and appearance that could lead to the thought that it would be bound to undermine the outsider's tendency to judge the subject beautiful. It would be a pleasing conceit to say that a vain person could not possibly be truly beautiful, but hard to make out in full generality.

activity from which that pleasure arises in his very asking of his question. The delight he has in mind is of course the delight that arises from *contemplation*, and let me now just add contemplation of something viewed *in person-neutral non-reflexive terms*. And, from Shaftesbury's general aesthetic, we know also that contemplation in his mind is activity that is especially appropriate to that feature of things that he identifies with their beauty, namely their 'harmony, order, and proportion', something found in natural forms, in moral behaviour, and acknowledged in our natural love of God.

For two reasons, though, we are bound to part company with Shaftesbury here in matters of detail. First, it is generally recognised that the attention we give to the things that strike us as of aesthetic interest is not restricted to benefits that are yielded by contemplation alone, and Shaftesbury's own writing makes it clear he is aware of this. Anyway, although the passage on which I have focused asks the question specifically about contemplative pleasure, the real core of Shaftesbury's discussion is wider than that and aspires to capture the general nature of that sort of attention. Second, however attaching we find harmony to be, there are clearly other values that we are sensitive to in the aesthetic mode, and disvalues too, not all of which can be understood in terms of disharmony. Shaftesbury himself speaks of finding something 'shocking and offensive on first acquaintance and it taking practice and skill to come an appreciate the real beauty of that same thing'.[12] A false judgement of some painting as offensive (e.g. Rembrandt's *Anatomy Lesson*, or Caravaggio's *Dentist's Surgery*) or a true judgement to the same effect (e.g. items in the Royal Academy's recent *Sensation* exhibition) are clearly both aesthetic in nature and both rooted in specifically aesthetic experience, and there is absolutely no reason to suppose that Shaftesbury would deny it. It is not realistic to say that as we make such judgements we are simply alert to harmony, the real or apparent absence of which grounds our judgement.[13]

These are details though, and I believe that if we pay attention to the broader picture we can learn from Shaftesbury rather more

12. Klein, 320.

13. By contrast, Hutcheson's inner sense detects nothing other than unity amidst variety, so his 'empiricisation' of Shaftesbury narrows down the domain of the aesthetic in quite an unacceptable way.

than he explicitly tells us. I hope that what I shall now say would be something with which he would find every reason to sympathise, or at least would give him scant pause. First, when we account for a work's beauty by reference to its harmony, the wheels of thought are not turning idly, for harmony is not identical with beauty.[14] Rather we are saying why the work has one property (beauty) by finding some other property (harmony) which makes the piece in question a beautiful one. Indeed, speaking in the person of Theocles, Shaftesbury mentions 'shades and masterly strokes that the vulgar understand not, but find fault with; in architecture there is the rustic; in music the chromatic kind and skilful mixture of dissonances'),[15] which properties, he makes clear, can all be invoked to explain why the works bearing them are beautiful ones. To my mind this suggests that beauty itself might helpfully be thought of as a second-order property, viz., the property things are liable to have of possessing to a marked degree some discernible first-order property that we value—harmony, order and proportion being but a small selection of these. The general tendency of theorists of earlier times to think of beauty as the prime aesthetic quality stems surely from its being that term which always seemed in place when we had found something sufficiently valuable aesthetically to be really attaching. Only it was not realised at all sharply that this was not because beauty is one peculiarly salient first-order aesthetic property and that a better explanation of the phenomenon treats it as a second-order property of the sort described. That then is the first idea the admirer of Shaftesbury might consider adopting.

Of course this does not at all tell us what makes for plausible membership of the range of first-order properties which are loosely called aesthetic ones, and that is what Shaftesbury the aesthetician is primarily interested in. Now let us suppose for his sake that contemplation is indeed the apt activity in regard of harmony. What we want is some characterisation of the range of activities that are appropriate to it and those other first-order properties that determine whether something is beautiful, or on

14. Stolnitz recognises that Shaftesbury ignored, or failed to understand, the difference between the 'is' of identity and the 'is' of predication.

15. Klein, 321.

the other hand that it is not beautiful (assuming here that that negative description of something is also an aesthetic appreciation of the thing in question, and not just some property compatible with beauty but different from it, such as being possessed of eight legs, but one that is incompatible with beauty, a contrary falling within the same category).

Shaftesbury does not tell us, but from my concessive remark we can see that contemplation, specifically attached to harmony as I am supposing it to be, must share that general structure. Secondly, Shaftesbury generally thinks of contemplation as a mode of perceptual experience, one he likes to render on the model of vision. That then suggests the following: the range of first-order aesthetic properties will be those that are discernible in experience and which reveal some value (or disvalue) perceptibly manifest in individual things to which we give our attention. That, I suggest, is a second thing that would give him no immediate reason to protest.

If the idea is found to be at all plausible, it will have the benefit of allowing us to understand something that Kant said ninety years or so after Shaftesbury was writing and which has often seemed puzzling. Talking of pleasure or displeasure without interest (*Wohlgefallen oder Mißfallen, ohne Interesse*) Kant does so saying that we are not interested in the existence of the object, and one wonders how that could be. Our aesthetic gaze is after all only rarely fixed on illusions. It is often found useful to say here that we are concerned for the existence of an object when we are thinking that we need it as a means to satisfy some desire we have, and hence are motivationally 'interested' in it. While this may well be part of what Kant had in mind, I do not think it is all. (He does, after all, insist that we have an interest in things that are good in themselves as well as good as means (*Critique of Judgement* §5), and in terms of the present discussion that rather negative idea isn't the most important thing.) What he may well otherwise have meant, and far more positively, is that our aesthetic delights are different from other pleasures, which latter are not dependent on our experiencing their objects at the time we have the pleasure. In their case it may be sufficient that the objects be known to exist for us to be pleased. By contrast, aesthetic pleasure is essentially pleasure in the way things appear to us in our experience of them, and that pleasure cannot outlast

the experience itself. Our aesthetic pleasures do, of course, sometimes 'live on', as we say, in memory, but that is memory of the
absent pleasure, not the continuation of it without the experience. Putting these things together, then, we can say that if we
generalise from Shaftesbury's close concentration on the beauty
of harmony and our contemplative attention that is supposedly
proper to that, the broader idea he seems to be on the track of
is that the pleasures we have of an aesthetic nature are ones
which are internal to our experience of objects, and in particular
derive from our experience of them from an impersonal standpoint, as notable manifestations of values of one kind or another
which we affect, or (to take in the Kantian enlargement) notable
manifestations of what is contrary to them and which we naturally disaffect.[16]

Returning now to Shaftesbury's conception of the aesthetic in
terms of a disinterested attitude and a *sui generis* pleasure, and
asking how my own modest suggestions to bear on that, I should
say that if there were anything *sui generis* about this sort of pleasure it would have to be located in the activity that properly gives
rise to it. Let us then take the expression 'disinterested attitude'
as a loose way of talking about the activity undertaken for its
own sake and which can in favourable circumstances give rise to
the responses that Shaftesbury variously cites as delight, love,
relish, joy, wonder, transport, ecstasy or rapture. Such activity
would be *sui generis* only if there were some special mode of
experiencing the world that on occasion elicits these responses
and their kin from us. We have already seen that contemplation
is not a good candidate, and my attempt to generalise from that
in a way that does not exclude responses of disfavour from the
aesthetic canon while embracing the favourable ones, suggests
that there is no such privileged mode of experience. The most we
can say is that our aesthetic responses to things arise out of the
attention we give to them in our experience of them, and the
ways in which we may do that vary not just according to the
sensory modality that is involved in the particular case but also
in the various ways in which those modalities are explored from

16. George Dickie claimed that once *distancing* and *disinterestedness* are purged (in
favour of something like *attention to something for its own sake*) the notion of the
aesthetic attitude is just vacuous (op. cit., 37–8). The formulation I am offering Shaftesbury is an attempt to swallow the purge without losing all the weight.

time to time. If Shaftesbury were to find this way of putting it acceptable, he should view the attribution to him of commitment to a *sui generis* pleasure with some suspicion. And if we, the inheritors of what Shaftesbury has to teach us, think about the matter, we ought to view it askance too. To do that, I have suggested, would not be to throw his real legacy to us away.

VI

A notable feature of the systematic character of Shaftesbury's thought that Glauser has brought into sharp focus is his presentation of our natural pleasures in forms (the die, the sphere), in nature (brooks, streams and the heavens) and in minds, above all the Divine mind, as different cases of the same contemplative or more broadly, aesthetic, delight. We should ask whether that is really an option open to him, or whether his neo-Platonically inspired thought breaks down at that point, stretched beyond the limits of the ideas he is using. The point on which the answer turn is whether God is a possible object of aesthetic contemplation. It seems to be agreed by Shaftesbury that that involves something akin to perceptual experience, since as Glauser points out elsewhere,[17] he speaks in the *Letter on Enthusiasm* of our contemplation of God in terms of *vision* rather than *possession*. Only that is metaphorical, not literal. Initially, I am inclined to say that while the verb 'contemplate' has a well-established broad use (as witnessed by Cicero's '*id contemplare animo*')[18] which can be well applied to God, as Shaftesbury uses it more narrowly in an aesthetic role, it must designate some specification of experience. (There is no need to introduce any ambiguity here though, since we may be speaking of no more than different species of the same thing, giving close attention to something in one way or another.)

Shaftesbury is naturally enough anxious to avoid accusations of being pagan, so he certainly doesn't want to identify the natural and perceptible world with God in the manner of his near

---

17. cf. R. Glauser, 'Shaftesbury: Enthousiasme et Expérience Religieuse', forthcoming.

18. *Pro rege Dejetaro*, 40.

contemporary Spinoza.[19] God is the Creator, and Shaftesbury thinks that because God is the ideally harmoniously ordered subject of contemplation, it must be right to say that he is supremely beautiful. The price to pay is that the activity in question has to be regarded as closely analogous to that of perceptual experience. Now clearly one can give one's attention to God for his own sake on account of 'the excellence of the object',[20] but that would only be a truly aesthetic matter if one could be presented with that object in appearance. Once one declines to say that one contemplates the beauty of God by admiration of his beautiful works and one attempts to say the more ambitious thing (using the metaphor of vision), then the specifically aesthetic nature of the matter is all but lost (except of course metaphorically). Here I am sure Shaftesbury would demur, but it is arguable whether he has a right to do so. The shift to the contemplation of God has to be an intellectual and not a sensory matter; then contemplation operates in a different way—rather like reflection or meditation, and even if that does in the end come down to a reflection about the harmonious working of God, it is only the tacit identification of harmony and beauty which we have rejected above that Shaftesbury can rely on to introduce God's beauty. One might of course contemplate (*animo*) with wonder properties of God that one couldn't experience, such as a harmony that gives rise to beauty that other heavenly creatures could experience—think of Dante's experience at the end of *Paradiso*—but that contemplation of ours wouldn't be aesthetic experience.[21] Rather it would be wondering at the fact that God is so beautiful, not a rapt appreciation of His beauty. (Compare

19. As comes out plainly in the rapturous apostrophe of the sun in *The Moralists* (Klein, 309): 'Prodigious orb! Bright source of vital heat and spring of day!—Soft flame, yet how intense, how active! ... Mighty being! *Brightest image and representative of the Almighty*! Supreme of the corporeal world!' (my emphasis).

20. Klein, 269.

21. Dante cannot endure the sensible vision, but it's clear that other inhabitants of the spheres can. So within the poem, the model of vision is apt and Dante knows there is aesthetic experience to be had, only not by him. The poem itself, however, is offering a story of purely intellectual contemplation at that point presented metaphorically in terms of vision. Dante later gets to the point where the vision cannot be captured by concepts at all (not just Beatrice, the purity of whose smile is initially too dazzling for him to bear (at *Par.* XXI, 4)—though no longer so after the necessary spiritual improvement, see *Par.* XXIII, 46–69) but of God and the essentially ineffable Trinity at *Par.* XXXIII, 69 ff. In that last case though one might think that there would be rather limited scope for intellectual contemplation either.

Adam after the Fall and cast out from the *eccelso giardino*: looking back on his days in Eden with regret and remorse, he still
takes a meditative pleasure in what had once been.)[22]

Although he does not notice the Procrustean way he is treating
the notion of contemplation, there is a possible line of reply to
this obstacle that Shaftesbury might consider investigating. Our
paradigmatic objects of aesthetic attention are, as he notices,
given to us visually, but he might perfectly reasonably ask
whether we do not enjoy aesthetic pleasures when we recite a
poem though to ourselves in our heads, or silently work through
a mathematical proof that we admire, or try to solve a tricky
chess problem. Surely these are aesthetic endeavours all right,
and they don't depend on the external senses. So why shouldn't
our contemplation of God's harmony be like them, awareness of
his beauty in the mind's eye, as we like to put it?

There are two questions here. The first is whether this sort of
example is torturing the idea of the aesthetic beyond endurance,
and the second is, if it isn't, whether that kind of experience can
be extended to our contemplation of the one true living God.
The answers to these questions seem to me to be 'No' in both
cases. As for the first, the crucial point will be whether the appeal
to experience that I have taken to be so central to our aesthetic
engagement with things can be retained while freeing it from the
close connection with perception that Shaftesbury assumes it
must have. To eighteenth century minds like Hutcheson's it
might seem that this transition can be made quite easily because
for them the notion of a novel 'inner sense' stood ready to hand
and could be turned to advantage. Or so it might have seemed.
However, to us it would just be unrealistic to move in that direction, since either there is no such inner sense, or else it enjoys the
wrong sort of sensitivity for the job, as do our propriocentric or
our kinaesthetic sensibilities.

There does remain however another avenue for a Shaftesbur-
ian to explore. When I recite a poem to myself, I make the poem
present to myself in my experience by thinking it through. The
activity of thinking itself is what performs the office of inner,
reflective, experience here. Similarly in the case of my working
through the mathematical proof or the chess problem. And these

22. *Paradiso* XXVI, 109–112.

thinkings can surely be akin to experiences of objects that have aesthetic properties which provide us with the sort of delight that occupies Shaftesbury. This is in all likelihood the kind of thing that we are going to have to say anyway when we address the question of what is it that makes our experience of a poem read from the printed page an aesthetic one, for what our experience is addressed to is not the perceptible page, but the poem which the page prompts us to conjure up in thought as we read the lines of the open book before us.

So yes, the notion of aesthetic experience can be, indeed must be, freed of any essential tie to perception *stricto sensu*. And the appeal to the experience of thinking seems to be just what is needed to secure that freedom, for we can say of it that the pleasure it gives rise to lies not in the existence of the thought, but in the very thinking of it. So I might take (non-aesthetic) pleasure in the knowledge that you are next door now reciting lines of Milton to yourself, which would be a pleasure at the present existence of those magnificent thoughts that you are thinking, whereas my own aesthetic pleasure in the thinking those same thoughts myself is, in Kantian terms, a pleasure I take in the thoughts' appearance, in the way they move me as I think those lines through.

As Shaftesbury contemplates God's beauty as something quite distinct from the beauty of His works, he has a thought of God as harmonious, orderly and perfectly proportioned, and that thought that he thinks is undoubtedly thought with love. But God is not identical with that thought, but is its extramundane internal object. Were Shaftesbury's contemplation of God to be a truly aesthetic one, God would have to appear to Shaftesbury in the thoughts that he thinks, and that God surely does not do. The situation is rather that if there is an aesthetic pleasure in the contemplation of God it is a pleasure not so much in God's beauty but in the thought of God and *its* beauty, the beauty of a thought about God that you or Shaftesbury might share with me. Alternatively, Shaftesbury would be considering a pleasure he has in the meditative, reflective, contemplative realisation that God is the perfectly ordered intelligence that our religion teaches us, and that is a pleasure he has in God's *existence*, and one that would on that score count (for Kant at least) as an uncontroversially 'interested' pleasure, not truly aesthetic at all.

Does this imply then that God isn't beautiful? Only if he isn't a possible object of experience. Reflecting on the case of Narcissus, we might say that we have no compelling reason to suppose God might not appear in one way or another to himself (thought of course not in any essentially first personal way). Or thinking back some centuries before Shaftesbury, we might suppose, with Ovid, that we could indeed experience God perceptually—mustn't God's omnipotence allow Him to bring that about?—but that, lest we suffer the fate of Semele, He takes good care that we don't.[23] Alternatively, moving forward again, we might suppose, with Dante, that the stain of sin so muddies our souls that, quite contingently, we cannot achieve the experience. These reflections would all offer Shaftesbury something that he dearly wants, although certainly not enough, but they do all turn on the thought that God is a possible object of experience. Someone who finds that difficult to accept on account of a close connection between experience and perception, and who does not claim to understand the alluring idea of intellectual intuition either, will find at this point how hard it is to keep Shaftesbury company.

23. Cf. *Metamorphoses* III, 254.

INTENSIONALITY

by Graeme Forbes and Jennifer Saul

I—Graeme Forbes

ABSTRACT   In I, I summarize the semantics for the relational/notional distinction for intensional transitives developed in Forbes (2000b). In II-V I pursue issues about logical consequence which were either unsatisfactorily dealt with in that paper or, more often, not raised at all. I argue that *weakening* inferences, such as 'Perseus seeks a mortal gorgon, therefore Perseus seeks a gorgon', are valid, but that *disjunction* inferences, such as 'Perseus seeks a mortal gorgon, therefore Perseus seeks a mortal gorgon or an immortal gorgon', are invalid. Since 'a gorgon' and 'a mortal gorgon or an immortal gorgon' are extensionally and intensionally the same quantifier, it is not completely trivial to arrange the semantics of intensional transitives so that this classification of the inferences is obtained. (This paper is an abridged version of Forbes (2001a); the latter will be incorporated into a forthcoming monograph, *Attitude Problems*.)

One subset of psychological verbs can be used to ascribe mental attitudes towards propositions. Another subset, overlapping the first, can be used to make what are, *prima facie*, ascriptions of mental attitudes towards *objects*, that is, to make *objectual* attitude ascriptions. The 'intensional transitive' verbs (ITVs) that figure in such ascriptions include desire verbs such as 'want', 'wish', 'hope', 'be hungry', evaluative verbs such as 'fear', 'despise' and 'worship', and search verbs such as 'seek', 'hunt' and 'rummage about'. Perhaps unsurprisingly, ITVs display one or both of the characteristic features of propositional attitude verbs: (i) the contexts they create can be inhospitable to substitutivity, and (ii) quantified noun phrases (QNPs) in those contexts can be subject to an ambiguity between 'relational' and 'notional' senses.[1] To illustrate (i): if you agree that the joint truth of 'Lex believes that Superman is nearby' and 'Lex fears Superman' has the capacity to explain Lex's furtive behaviour, and that such a capacity does not survive substitution of 'Superman' by 'Clark' in the propositional ascription, you should also think that it does not survive substitution in the objectual ascription instead. To illustrate (ii): 'Lois seeks an extraterrestrial' can

---

1. The terminology is that of Quine 1955.

be understood in two ways: there may be a *particular* extraterrestrial she seeks, or she may just be an enthusiast for the SETI
project, seeking *no particular* extraterrestrial.

The class of ITVs is usually widened to include verbs that are
not necessarily used to ascribe mental states, but show some of
the same behaviour as those which are. For instance, depiction
verbs such as 'sketch', 'draw' and 'caricature' may be included,
since we can distinguish Jekyll-caricatures from Hyde-
caricatures,[2] and we can discern the relational-notional ambiguity in 'Guercino drew a dog.'[3] With this and other groups of
verbs, only one of the two puzzling types of behaviour may be
present, and in the case of the relational-notional ambiguity,
there may be a sensitivity to which quantifiers are used. For
example, 'need', transaction verbs ('owe', 'wager', 'trade') and
verbs of absence ('omit', 'lack') generate the relational-notional
ambiguity, but at least some of these never block substitution of
different terms for the same object or property in the way that
'want' can; for instance, if you need/lack water you need/lack
H_2O, though it is likely that there is no *particular* quantity of
water you need/lack. Depiction verbs only allow the relational-
notional ambiguity for existential quantifiers: if we say that
Guercino depicted most or all unicorns, there must be particular
unicorns he depicted. And arguably, evaluative verbs allow only
relational readings for existential QNP-complements: if you
worship a goddess, there must be a specific goddess you
worship.[4]

In this paper I focus on logical aspects of notional readings,
and ignore substitution-resistance. This is possible because the
mechanism that explains the relational-notional ambiguity must
be independent of the one that explains substitution-resistance,
given the behaviour of 'need' and 'lack' just noted. But even

2. Cf. Peacocke 1987, 399– 400.

3. Aware of this, the curators at the Norton Simon Museum have mounted a wall-
label for Guercino's *The Aldrovandi Dog* which disambiguates by stating 'this must
be the portrait of a specific dog'.

4. I am ignoring 'generic' readings of indefinites. You may worship a Greek goddess
in the generic sense in which you may enjoy a good mystery story, but this is not the
missing notional reading, which would have no restriction to the typical. The existence of notional readings for *universal* QNPs was suggested to me by Michael Jacov-
ides with the example 'Perseus worships every god who lives on Mt. Olympus'. A
non-relational, non-generic, reading does seem to exist.

restricting our attention so narrowly, there are some puzzling phenomena to be accounted for.

I

The DGM Semantics. Investigating logical consequence in some fragment of natural language goes hand-in-hand with developing a semantics for that fragment—each project constrains the other. To get us off the mark, I will briefly rehearse the outlines of a higher-order semantics for ITVs which is based on ideas of Davidson, Goodman and Montague.[5] The semantic problem characteristic of these verbs is that of representing the notional reading of an objectual attitude ascription such as

(1) Perseus seeks a gorgon

in a formalism for which a compositional semantics is available. The relational reading, true in the Greek myth because Perseus seeks Medusa, is straightforward:

(2) $(an \; x: gorgon(x))[Perseus \; seeks \; x]$.

But for the notional reading (suppose Polydectes challenged Perseus simply to bring him the head of some gorgon or other), we face the difficulty that there is no alternative position for the quantifier. So either we must go beyond a first-order framework by allowing higher-order terms to figure as arguments to 'seek', or else we must uncover more elaborate structure than (2) displays, structure which reveals the position the indefinite in (1) occupies when (1) is understood notionally.[6]

In pursuit of the first strategy, the core idea I employ is from *Languages of Art*, where Goodman suggests that the notional reading of 'a man' in 'picture of a man' arises when we are merely

---

5. See Forbes 2000b, §§5–7, for detailed development.

6. The main alternative to a higher-order approach is the 'propositionalist' account, according to which intensional transitives only superficially have an NP-complement. In fact, it is claimed, there is covert extra material which allows the full syntactic complement to be associated with a complete proposition. This idea is familiar from the Quinean suggestion that (1) means 'Perseus tries to find a gorgon', in which there are two possible positions for 'a gorgon', heading the entire statement (relational) or just the infinitival clause (notional), as it were 'Perseus tries to make it true that for at least one gorgon, he (himself) finds it'. Recent interesting elaborations of propositionalism are to be found in den Dikken *et al.* (1996) and Parsons (1997). For critical discussion of these, see Forbes (2000a).

classifying the picture according to the kind of pictorial content it has.[7] 'Picture of a man' may be understood as 'a-man picture' according to Goodman,[8] so we can distinguish 'a picture of one man' and 'a picture of two men' as 'a one-man picture' versus 'a two-men picture'. There is undeniable appeal in the idea that for depiction verbs, notional readings of complement QNPs arise when we are simply classifying. But to turn this idea into a complete account of notional readings, we have to extend it to other groups of intensional transitives; and we have to give a compositional semantics for such phrases as 'a two-men picture' in which the functioning of 'two-men' is not implausibly distant from the functioning of those words in, say, 'two men are running towards us'. I take these problems in turn.

What is it that the notional reading of (1) might be said to classify? Search verbs are action verbs, and according to Davidson (1967), action verbs involve quantification over events. In Parsons's (1990) development of this idea, the relational reading of (1) could be represented as

(3) $(some\ e\colon search(e))[agent(e) = Perseus\ \wedge$
     $(an\ x\colon gorgon(x))\ [theme(e,\ x)]].$[9]

That is, 'some search's agent is Perseus and there exists a gorgon that is its theme'. (3) and (2) are related as 'sub-atomic' to 'atomic' in Parsons's approach, and (3), like (2), can be true only if there is a gorgon in the domain. But once we are being explicit about searches, we can formulate a Goodmanian account of the *notional* reading of (1), using the apparatus of (3):

(4) Perseus is the agent of a some-gorgon search.

Here we are merely classifying the search according to the goal it has, which is in turn settled by the agent's intentions: to ascribe a goal to a search is not to say that there is, in the domain, an

---

7. 'The simple fact is that much as most pieces of furniture are readily sorted out as desks, chairs, tables, etc., so most pictures are readily sorted out as pictures of Pickwick, of Pegasus, of a unicorn, etc., without reference to anything represented.' Goodman (1976, 21).

8. Ibid., 22.

9. A typical definition of 'theme' is 'entity undergoing the effect of some action' (Radford 1988, 373), though this is keyed towards extensional transitives.

entity that the search is *for*, just as to say that a picture is a two-men picture is not to say that there are, in the domain, two men whom it represents.

There remains the second question, of how to use a QNP to classify a search *e*: what exactly is the semantics of 'a some-gorgon search'? In Montague grammar, the difference between relational and notional readings of (1) is captured in part by allowing QNPs to occupy term position, as higher-order terms for properties of properties. Adopting this treatment of QNPs here allows us to introduce a third-order relation '(search-)kind' between events and properties of properties. Suppose we simply *identify* kinds of search with the meanings of the QNPs that specify them: to say that a search *e* is of the some-gorgon kind to say that *e* stands in the kind relation to the meaning of 'some gorgon'. And let us simplify Montague's semantics by modelling properties extensionally, as sets, so that the property of being a property of a gorgon is the set of all sets that contain a gorgon.[10] Then '*e* is a some-gorgon search' is '*kind*(*e*, {*X*: (*some x*: *gorgon*(*x*))[*x* ∈ *X*]})': *e* is a search of the kind which is (associated with) the set of all sets that contain a gorgon. The notional reading of (1) emerges from this as

(5) (*some e*: *search*(*e*))[*agent*(*e*) = *Perseus* ∧
         kind(*e*, {*X*: (*some x*: *gorgon*(*x*))[*x* ∈ *X*]})].

(5) classifies a certain search in terms of what it is for, as fixed by the intentions of its agent, in the same way that on Goodman's account of its notional reading, 'Guercino drew a dog' classifies a certain drawing by what it depicts, as fixed by the lines and shapes Guercino put on paper (and also, perhaps, his intentions in putting them there).

Two comments on (5) are in order. First, the extensional treatment of properties as sets will eventually have to be abandoned, though not in favour of Montague's possible-worlds alternative.

---

10. The treatment of a QNP as a set of sets is the standard Generalized Quantifier account. A sentence consisting in a QNP (e.g., 'every untrained dog') followed by a VP (e.g., 'bites its owner') is processed semantically by assigning a set (i.e., a property) to the VP and a set of sets (property of properties) to the QNP. The sentence is true iff the VP-set is an element of the QNP-set. Thus 'every untrained dog bites its owner' is true iff the set *X* of things which bite their owners is an element of the set *Z* of all sets *Y* such that *Y* contains every untrained dog; i.e., iff *X* ∈ {*Y*: every untrained dog is in *Y*}, iff {every untrained dog} ⊆ *X*.

Second, the use of a set abstract in the semantic representation (5) of (1) is for perspicuity only. In a type-theoretic setting, to which we will ultimately move, the very same lambda term, $\lambda X.\text{some(gorgon)}(X)$, would figure in the derivation of both the notional and the relational readings of (1). But even as things stand, 'a gorgon' receives the same semantic value, a set of sets, in both (3) and (5). If this does not satisfy our constraint that the meanings of QNPs in the two uses not be 'implausibly distant' from each other, nothing does.

In the contrast between (3) and (5) we capture an elusive aspect of the difference between relational and notional readings of the likes of (1). In the case of a relational reading, there is something in the domain of individuals that the search is for, while in the case of a notional reading, a normal understanding of 'for' dictates that there need be no entity at all that the search is for. One unsettling aspect of Montague's own semantics (strictly, an improved variant of it with flexible types) is that on the notional reading, it seems that the agent of the search is said to be searching *for* a property of properties, in that the property-of-properties term occupies the very same position occupied by the relational reading's term for the individual sought. Our classificational analysis of notional readings avoids this awkwardness: there is no entity of any type at all that (5) says the search is for. The price, obviously, is that the difference between (3) and (5) is no mere scope-ambiguity. But that, I think, is a price worth paying.

II

Weakening Inferences. With the DGM semantics as background, I turn to issues about logical consequence in a language with ITVs, focussing initially on search verbs. There is a sort of argument in which the conclusion seems to weaken or reduce the information given in the premise that classifies the search by kind. Conclusions obtained by simply deleting information from a premise follow from that premise, but when intensional transitives are used it can be hard to tell if information-deletion or weakening is all that is going on.[11] Some examples:

> (6) Perseus seeks a mortal gorgon. Therefore, Perseus seeks a gorgon.

11. This was brought home to me by the variety of objections I received to the examples to follow, especially the objections of R. Thomason.

(7) Perseus seeks every gorgon. Therefore, Perseus seeks every mortal gorgon.

(8) Perseus seeks at least two gorgons. Therefore, Perseus seeks at least one gorgon.

On the face of it, for each of (6)–(8), what the premise says includes what the conclusion says, so the former ought to entail the latter. And while there is nothing in our semantics for notional readings that in and of itself guarantees the entailments, a simple admissibility-condition on models guarantees them, that the kinds to which searches belong be closed under including kinds:

(9) If e satisfies a search-verb predicate, then if $\langle e, X \rangle$ is in $[\![kind]\!]$ and $X \subseteq Y$, then $\langle e, Y \rangle$ is in $[\![kind]\!]$.

Thus, since the set of all sets containing every gorgon is a subset of the set of all sets containing every mortal gorgon, then if a certain search falls under the former kind, it falls under the latter. Hence admissible models verifying the premise of (7) must verify its conclusion. The inferences also seem to work with 'want' or 'need' or (with existential QNPs) 'sketch'; thus, if, to satisfy Polydectes, Perseus needs every gorgon's head, he needs every mortal gorgon's head for the same end. So more admissibility-conditions in the style of (9) are motivated (though not for absence verbs such as 'lack' and 'omit').

Nevertheless, inferences (6)–(8) may be contested. We are bracketing issues about substitutivity, so it is irrelevant that the conclusions may not reflect how Perseus thinks of his project (perhaps he thinks 'mortal gorgon' is like 'toy spear', perhaps he lacks the concept of mortality, perhaps he cannot subtract one). What is at issue is whether, if Perseus's search is of the kind specified in the premise, it follows that it is of the kind specified in the conclusion. But it may be objected that if the premises of (6)–(8) are true, then their conclusions are *false* if the kind in the conclusion strictly includes that in the premise. If Perseus seeks a mortal gorgon, he doesn't seek a gorgon: a gorgon, as such, may not be good enough, since he is looking for a mortal one. But this objection justifies the conjunction

(10) Perseus seeks a mortal gorgon and does not seek a gorgon

which should seem contradictory if we are careful to avoid interpreting the 'not' as 'metalinguistic' negation[12] and do not supplement the second conjunct with hypothetical elided material:
Perseus seeks a mortal gorgon, so, he does not *merely* seek a
gorgon, he does not seek *just any old* gorgon. Counterexamples
to the arguments require situations in which their premises are
true and their conclusions false, not ones in which the conclusions are merely less than the *whole* truth: 'not' in (10) has to
be truth-functional.

But the same challenge to the arguments can be made while
being careful about negation. When intuitions about logical
consequence are uncertain or contested, questions may be answered by finding paraphrases for the problematic sentences which
make their logical relations less opaque. It appears that objectual
attitude ascriptions using search verbs, desire verbs, and 'need',
may be paraphrased in terms of 'ending-conditions'. Searches,
needs and desires may end for all sorts of reasons (say, death of
the agent), but an objectual attitude ascription states an ending
condition which, at least partially, characterizes the *identity* of
the search, or need, or desire. Searches can end by *concluding
successfully*, needs can end by being *met*, desires can end by being
satisfied. The QNP in an objectual attitude ascription says something about how such endings could or must come about, something which distinguishes one objectual attitude from another.
For searches, the QNP characterizes a state or event of finding,
and for needs and desires, a state of having or getting. And the
logical status of the weakening inferences turns on exactly how
this is spelled out.

It might be proposed that Perseus is searching for some gorgon
iff finding some gorgon is *enough* for his search to end successfully; similarly, he is searching for every gorgon iff finding every
gorgon is *enough* for his search to end successfully. If this is correct, (6)–(8) are all invalid. The problem is evident with (7):
clearly, it may be enough for his search to end successfully that
he find every gorgon (Euryale, Medusa, and Stheno) without it
being enough that he find every mortal gorgon (Medusa). But
this objection to the weakening inferences turns on interpreting
their premises and conclusions as stating *sufficient* conditions for

12. See Horn 1989.

successful ending. The first move in defence of the inferences is to insist on paraphrases that state *necessary* conditions. Thus, the premise of (6) is true iff it is *necessary* for Perseus's search to end in success that he find a mortal gorgon. And then the conclusion follows, for a mortal gorgon is found only if a gorgon is found; so it is also necessary for the search to end in success that a gorgon is found, which is what (6)'s conclusion, we are now supposing, says. Similarly, if it is necessary for Perseus's search to end successfully that he find every gorgon, then it is necessary that he find every mortal gorgon, so (7) is justified as well.

If these two types of paraphrase are the only options on the table, the weakening inferences win easily, since the sufficient-condition paraphrases validate the clearly incorrect *strengthening* inferences, the converses of (6)–(8). If it is sufficient for a search of Perseus's to end successfully that he find every mortal gorgon, then it is also sufficient that he find every gorgon, since finding them all entails finding every mortal one. But certainly it does not follow from Perseus's seeking every mortal gorgon that he seeks every gorgon.

In addition, a defender of weakening inferences can plausibly resist *biconditional* paraphrases, for the following reason. In claiming that Perseus seeks a mortal gorgon, we do not seem to commit ourselves to the view that, say, he is indifferent between mortal gorgons of human origin and those of divine origin. Our justification for the claim may simply be that we have observed him making preparations appropriate for hunting mortal gorgons—we may have no evidence one way or the other about possible preferences with respect to origin. But by sufficiency, finding a mortal gorgon, period, is enough for his search to end successfully: origin does not matter. It is implausible that we commit ourselves to such indifference in asserting 'Perseus seeks a mortal gorgon'. Those who favour a sufficient-condition clause in the paraphrase might modify the account to say that finding a *satisfactory* mortal gorgon is sufficient; but this threatens triviality. Alternatively, the modification might be that *absent other requirements*, finding a mortal gorgon is sufficient. But there are always other requirements on successful ending, for instance, that $2 + 2 = 4$. Necessary condition paraphrases, which validate weakening inferences, appear to be preferable, unless there are other considerations which favour a sufficiency clause.

III

Disjunction Inferences. There are such considerations. Quantified NPs can be co-ordinated with 'and' and 'or', and some other boolean connectives, to provide more complex complements to ITVs than we have hitherto considered. Using 'and', we have

(11) Perseus seeks a sword and a shield.

This example presents no special problem for the DGM semantics, since we can interpret its notional reading as ascribing a single activity to Perseus ('and' has narrow scope with respect to 'seek') which is classified as belonging to the kind determined by the meaning of the co-ordinated NP 'a sword and a shield'. Standardly, this use of 'and' is interpreted as intersection, so on our current extensional approach, the search kind is the set of all sets that contain at least one sword and at least one shield.

Let us use the phrase 'happy-outcome paraphrase' for reformulations of objectual attitude ascriptions in terms of successful ending of searches, satisfaction of desires, meeting of needs, and so on. If (11)'s happy-outcome paraphrase is that finding a sword and a shield is necessary to end Perseus's search in success, then both 'Perseus seeks a sword' and 'Perseus seeks a shield' follow, since finding each will be individually necessary. Perhaps we have come too far to claim a 'pre-theoretic intuition' supporting this result, but if we wish to provide for the entailment, it is easy to add a clause to our definition of 'admissible model' that guarantees it.

It is co-ordination with 'or' that is a serious problem for simple necessary-condition paraphrases. A contemporary at the Battle of Bosworth might have said

(12) Richard III needs a horse.

But it does not seem to follow from (12) that

(13) Richard III needs a horse or a donkey.

More carefully, the co-ordinator in (13), like the one in (11), can be given a narrow-scope or a wide-scope reading with respect to 'needs'. As Partee and Rooth point out,[13] the wide-scope reading

13. Partee and Rooth 1983, 374–5.

is preferred when we append something like 'he isn't sure which'. But without such an epistemic coda, the narrow-scope-'or' (or 'non-distributive') reading will be the preferred one. And the reason we are inclined to say that (13) fails to follow from (12) is that on this reading, (13) apparently has the happy-outcome paraphrase (or a paraphrase entailing) that his need will be met *if* he gets a horse *or* he gets a donkey. By truth-functional logic, this means in turn that his need will be met if he gets a horse *and* his need will be met if he gets a donkey; cf. $(A \lor B) \to C \dashv\vdash (A \to C) \land (B \to C)$. The claim that getting a donkey is sufficient is not justified by (12). So a sufficient-condition paraphrase explains the invalidity of the inference.[14] But a necessary-condition paraphrase does not. One who gets a horse thereby gets a horse or a donkey. So if it is necessary to meet Richard III's need that he gets a horse, then it is necessary to meet it that he gets a horse or a donkey. Since the latter is the necessary condition paraphrase of (13), that analysis incorrectly predicts that (13) follows from (12) after all.[15]

In the terminology of von Wright (1963), the disjunction in the interderivability mentioned in the last paragraph 'distributes conjunctively' (call this '$\land$-distribution'). So

(14) If he gets a horse or gets a donkey then his need will be met

has conjunctive force: *each* type of animal has the capacity to meet his need. (In (14), if necessary, give 'or' what Jennings (1994, 128) calls 'a good intonational thump'.) But $C \to (A \lor B) \nvdash (C \to A) \land (C \to B)$, and from

(15) If his need is met then he got a horse or got a donkey

we can infer only that at least one type of animal had the capacity to meet his need. (15) follows from (12), so (15) cannot be a

14. (13) may somehow convey that he does not need both, but here and elsewhere I read 'or' in the usual inclusive way. The conjunctive force of the happy-outcome paraphrase is still present if 'or' means 'xor', though the point is clearer with 'looks for': 'he is looking for a horse xor a donkey' has the narrow-scope 'xor' paraphrase 'he is the agent of a search of the kind that ends/can end in success if he finds a horse but not a donkey and ends/can end in success if he finds a donkey but not a horse'.

15. This difficulty arises for Moltmann's (1997) account of disjunctive co-ordination; see p. 38.

correct paraphrase of (13), which is not a consequence of (12) on the intended reading.[16]

Thus the defender of weakening inferences requires happy-outcome paraphrases of their premises and conclusions which agree with the necessary condition versions in justifying the inferences *and* with the sufficient-condition versions in blocking the inference from (12) to (13). One candidate is that these objectual attitude ascriptions make claims about *potential* ways of producing happy outcomes. For (12), 'Richard III needs a horse', we can express such a claim as

> (16) Richard III has a need that can be met by his getting horse

and then (13) with the narrow-scope construal of 'or' is paraphrased by

> (17) Richard III has a need that can be met by his getting a horse or a donkey.

The natural reading of (17), because of its 'can', is ∧-distributive (see also (29) below). And to say that a need *can* be met by such-and-such is not to say that such-and-such is or would be sufficient, but only that in certain circumstances it is sufficient. (17) unfolds into

> (18) Getting a horse can meet his need and getting a donkey can meet his need.

(18) does not follow from its own first conjunct, so (13) does not follow from (12), the right outcome. But the weakening inferences stand. For instance, if finding a mortal gorgon can end Perseus's search successfully, then finding a gorgon can end Perseus's search successfully.

But (18) has a serious flaw as a paraphrase of (13). (18) entails the result of replacing both occurrences of 'his need' in it with 'some need of his', which is a conjunction whose first conjunct is the paraphrase of 'Richard III needs a horse' and whose second

---

16. Even if (15) has a reading that Richard III's need for a horse or a donkey was satisfied only if he got a horse *and* only if he got a donkey, which I doubt, that would not be an accurate paraphrase of (13), though it might be of 'Richard III needs a horse and a donkey'.

is the paraphrase of 'Richard III needs a donkey'. Therefore (13), explained as (18), turns out to entail

(19) Richard III needs a horse and needs a donkey.

But (19) is clearly not a consequence of (13). For if Richard III's only need is for a horse or a donkey, and he gets a satisfactory horse, then he has no unmet needs; while according to (19), he will still have an unmet need for a donkey. This also shows that (12), 'Richard III needs a horse', is not a consequence of (13) either.

Apparently, the paraphrase of (12) as 'getting a horse can meet his need' omits some information that (12) contains and (13) does not. According to (13), there is more than one way of meeting the need. If (12) is consistent with the possibility of other ways of meeting the need, it would be unclear why it should fail to follow from (13). It is more plausible that there is something in the content of (12) that makes it flat-out inconsistent with the availability of alternatives. For example, there might be a necessary condition as well. So for (12), we are led to:

(20) Getting a horse can meet his need and his need is met only if he gets a horse.

(20) goes with the following account of (13), which generalizes to multiple-disjunct disjunctions:

(21) Getting a horse or a donkey can meet his need, and his need is met only if he gets a horse or a donkey.

As with our first try, (18), we still correctly predict that (12) fails to entail (13), since (20) does not entail (21). But now we also have the result that (13) fails to entail (12), since (20)'s second conjunct cannot be derived from (21)'s. The strengthening inferences still fail. Concomitantly, the weakening inferences hold. For instance, for any search e, (i) if finding at least two gorgons can end e in success, then so can finding at least one; and (ii) if it is required for e to end in success that Perseus find at least two gorgons, then it is required that Perseus find at least one gorgon. Thus, searching for at least two implies searching for at least one.

Our use of happy-outcome paraphrases as a control on the logic of intensional transitives requires further comment. One issue is how close to the meaning of the original objectual attitude ascription its happy-outcome paraphrase really is. But a more pressing question here concerns what we mean by '*can* produce a happy outcome'. We have the conception of a sequence or course of events in which, or whose outcome is that, a certain search ends in success, or a certain need is met, or a certain desire is satisfied. But if 'can' ranges over only *possible* courses of events, then ascriptions of impossible needs, goals, and desires, have necessarily false paraphrases. Yet someone, having dreamed the impossible dream, may want to live it. One way round this problem, which we will adopt here to avoid a substantial digression, is to distinguish ways *for* things to be or go from ways things *could* be or go.[17] We will allow 'can' to range over the former, not necessarily metaphysically possible, courses of events; and in paraphrases, we will employ explicit quantification over individual events and ways for things to go, using the analogue of possibilist quantifiers. Thus 'Perseus seeks a sword' gets an informal paraphrase which includes

> (22) There is some way for things to go in which Perseus's search concludes successfully in his finding a sword.

Let us use $\bar{e}$ to range over ways for things to go (total courses of events, including impossible ones) and write (i) '$SC(e', e, \bar{e})$' to mean that e' successfully concludes e in, or as part of, $\bar{e}$; and (ii) '$e \approx_a e'$' to mean that e and e' have the same agent ('agent of e'', like 'finding', 'sword', etc., we assume for simplicity to be rigid). Then the full paraphrase of 'Perseus seeks a sword', incorporating (22), is

> (23) (some$_@$ e_1: search(e_1) $\wedge$ agent(e_1, Perseus))[(some $\bar{e}$)
> (some e_2: $SC(e_2, e_1, \bar{e})$)[finding(e_2) $\wedge$ $e_1 \approx_a e_2 \wedge$
> (some x: sword(x))[theme(e_2, x)]] $\wedge$
> (any $\bar{e}$)(any e_2: $SC(e_2, e_1, \bar{e})$)[finding(e_2) $\wedge$ $e_1 \approx_a e_2 \wedge$
> (some x: sword(x))[theme(e_2, x)]].

'some$_@$' means 'some actual'; and the second conjunct of (23) says that in any way for things to go in which Perseus's search is concluded successfully by some event, that event is a finding of a sword by Perseus. If only certain ways for things to go are

17. See Salmon 1989.

relevant to the truth-value of 'Perseus seeks a sword' we may assume a contextually given restriction on the range of '$\bar{e}$'.

To formulate a paraphrase involving conjunctive co-ordination, as in (11), we could just add to (23) that some shield is also a theme of e_2 (we assume that 'theme' is a relation and that two things may be found in a single finding, perhaps simultaneously). But since the limitations of first-order notation prevent us from employing the co-ordinated quantifier 'a sword and a shield', which classifies the search in (11), we allow ourselves the resources of type-theory and represent both the ascription (11) and its paraphrase in parallel. For our original (1), the type-theoretic semantics is

(24) **some(search)λ e$_1$.agent(e$_1$)(Perseus) and kind(e$_1$)(some(gorgon)).**

In general, where t is either the type i of individuals or the type e of events, a *basic* QNP is of type $(t \Rightarrow bool) \Rightarrow bool - (tb)b$ for short—so that a truth-value is produced by applying it to an argument of type tb.[18] '**kind(e$_1$)**' is of type $((ib)b)b$, since it outputs a truth-value (for example, the truth-value of '**kind(e$_1$)** (some(gorgon))' relative to an assignment to 'e$_1$') when applied to a QNP. Therefore '**kind**' itself is of type $e(((ib)b)b)$.

For (11) in the same notation we would have

(25) **some(search)λ e$_1$.agent(e$_1$)(Perseus) and kind(e$_1$)(some(sword) and some(shield)).**

The type of '**and**' in (25), is raised from $b(bb)$ to accept inputs of type $(ib)b$ (e.g. '**some(shield)**') and produce outputs of type $((ib)b)((ib)b)$.[19] (25)'s paraphrase is

(26) **some$_{@}$(search)λ e$_1$.agent(e$_1$)(Perseus) and [(some)λ $\bar{e}$.(some(rel(sc($\bar{e}$)(e$_1$))(finding)))λ e$_2$.e$_2 \approx_a$e$_1$ and (some(sword) and some(shield))λ x.theme(e$_2$)(x)] and [(any)λ $\bar{e}$.(any(rel(sc($\bar{e}$)(e$_1$))(finding)))λ e$_2$.e$_2 \approx_a$e$_1$ and (some(sword) and some(shield))λ x.theme(e$_2$)(x)].**[20]

18. For example, in '**some(sword)λx.rusting(x)**' ('some sword has the property of rusting'), 'λ**x.rusting(x)**' is a function of type ib from individuals to truth-values (it is the characteristic function of the set of rusting things); so '**some(sword)**' must accept inputs of this type, and output a truth-value from them; therefore its type is $(ib)b$.

19. '**some(sword) and some(shield)**' is infix for '**and(some(shield))(some(sword))**'.

20. **rel** corresponds to relative pronouns such as 'which'; see Carpenter (1997, 200–206). In (26), **rel** is of type $(eb)((eb)(eb))$. The input eb is the property of successfully concluding e_1 in $\bar{e}$. The output is the property 'which successfully concludes e_1 in $\bar{e}$'. It is of type $(eb)(eb)$ and, given the property of being a finding as input, produces the property 'finding which successfully concludes e_1 in $\bar{e}$' as output.

This says that some actual search e_1 by Perseus is successfully concluded in some way for things to go by Perseus's finding of a sword and a shield, and in any way for things to go, any finding which successfully concludes e_1 is a finding of a sword and a shield by Perseus.

In view of our concern that 'Perseus seeks a sword' not entail 'Perseus seeks a sword or a shield', we cannot paraphrase the latter simply by replacing the quantifier co-ordinator '**and**' with '**or**' in (26); for the result *would* be something entailed by 'Perseus seeks a sword', in fact, it would be a paraphrase appropriate for the wide-scope reading of 'or'. Instead, we need to develop a general account of the conjunctive force of 'or' that we can apply to happy-outcome paraphrases in a principled way.

IV

When Good 'or'*s Go* 'and'. The conjunctive force of 'or' generates a clear difficulty for the DGM semantics, or for any semantics that interprets 'or' by a union-like operation and imposes some kind of closure-under-inclusion condition such as (9) to validate weakening inferences. For in view of (9), a disjunction inference such as 'Perseus seeks a sword, therefore he seeks a sword or a shield' will hold in the DGM semantics. This is because $\{X:$ a sword is in $X\}$ is a subset of $\{X:$ a sword is in X or a shield is in $X\}$, so a need belonging to the kind determined by the first set is thereby a need belonging to the kind determined by the second. Thus (9) denies 'or' conjunctive force.

Capturing the conjunctive force of 'or' is a problem that arises in many kinds of case—with 'prefers x to y or z', with permission statements, and in the following:

(27) Perseus seeks a sword or a shield.
(28) Perseus's sword is heavier than his shield or his helmet.
(29) Perseus could have been a swordsman or a shield-bearer.
(30) If Perseus were to find a sword or a shield, he'd be pleased.

(28)–(30) all have readings (preferred ones, in the absence of epistemic codas) in which 'or' is $\wedge$-distributive.

In the range of approaches to the phenomenon of $\wedge$-distribution, there are two extremes. At one we find the postulation of two senses of 'or'. But postulating a lexical ambiguity is usually a last resort, especially when the same ambiguity appears in other languages.[21] At the other extreme, only a single sense of 'or', the boolean one, is admitted, and each of (27)–(30) is held to express just one proposition, the one where 'or' distributes *dis*junctively.[22] How a proposition with conjunctive force gets conveyed in uses of the sentences is explained by pragmatic, broadly Gricean, considerations.[23]

But while context surely has a role in determining which proposition is associated with a given use of one of (27)–(30), a third account lies between these two extremes. On this account, these sentences can literally express a proposition with conjunctive force as well as one in which 'or' distributes disjunctively. Context can favour one rather than the other disambiguation of literal sense just as it can favour one rather than another resolution of a sentence with $\forall\exists/\exists\forall$ ambiguities.

In view of $(A \lor B) \to C \dashv\vdash (A \to C) \land (B \to C)$, the $\land$-distributive behaviour of 'or' in (28)–(30) is explained if in the interpretations of those readings, the disjunction is raised to a position semantically akin to that of the antecedent of a conditional, say, the restriction of a restrictive universal quantifier.[24] Interpretations in standard higher-order intensional logic appropriate for the $\land$-distributive readings of (28)–(30) are:

(28)′ (Any x: x = Perseus's shield $\lor x$ = Perseus's helmet) [Perseus's sword is heavier than x].

(29)′ (Any F: $F = {}^\land\lambda x.\text{swordsman}(x) \lor F = {}^\land\lambda x.\text{shieldbearer}(x))$ $[\Diamond^\lor F(\text{Perseus})]$.[25]

---

21. The French, German, Italian, Swedish and Finnish words for 'or' manifest the ambiguity. But there is also a version of the 'two senses' view to which this objection may not apply immediately, namely, the idea that there is one 'or' which is a negative polarity item and another which is not (see Larson 1988, 10–11). I discuss this view in greater detail in (Forbes 2001b), but for the moment: negative polarity items are supposed to be licensed only by downward-entailing contexts; but it is not difficult to see that neither phrasal comparatives (insert 'is heavy' in (28)—$\land$-distributive 'or' is still preferred) nor the 'could have been' of (29) create downward-entailing contexts; e.g., $p \land \neg p \vDash q$ but $\Diamond q \nvDash \Diamond(p \land \neg p)$.

22. See Follesdal and Hilpinen (1981, 22–3), Stenius (1982).

23. As in Kamp (1979, 259), Loewer (1976, 535–7).

24. Although I decided on this approach independently, I was not surprised to find it already in the literature; see Makinson (1984).

25. The modal examples have a *de re/de dicto* ambiguity, which I have resolved in favour of the (strongly preferred) *de dicto* readings.

(30)′ (Any $\mathfrak{Q}$: $\mathfrak{Q} = {}^\wedge\lambda F$ (some x: sword(x))[Fx] $\vee \mathfrak{Q} =$ ${}^\wedge\lambda F$(some x: shield(x))[Fx]) [$^\vee\mathfrak{Q}(\lambda x.$Perseus finds x) $\square\!\!\rightarrow$ Perseus is pleased].

This simple proposal leaves many interesting questions unanswered.[26] But for our present purposes, the main issue is whether the quantificational analysis of (28)–(30) sheds any light on how (27) is to be prevented from following, by (9), from 'Perseus seeks a sword'. Suppressing irrelevant detail, the interpretation of the happy-outcome paraphrase of (27)'s non-distributive reading can be expressed informally as follows, split into two parts (27)′ and (27)″ corresponding to the possible sufficient condition and the necessary condition respectively:

(27)′ For some actual search e_1 of Perseus's, and any $\mathfrak{Q}$ which is either the property of being a property of a sword or of being a property of a shield (i.e., $\mathfrak{Q}$ is the meaning of 'at least one sword' or of 'at least one shield'): there is an $\bar{e}$ and an e_2 which successfully concludes e_1 in $\bar{e}$ such that e_2 is a finding by Perseus and $\mathfrak{Q}$ ($\lambda x.$theme(e_2)(x)).

(27)″ For any $\bar{e}$, any e_2 which successfully concludes Perseus's search e_1 in $\bar{e}$ is a finding by Perseus of a sword or of a shield.

The DGM semantics for (27) is (25) with 'or' for the second 'and'. For (27)′ we have

(31) **(some(search))λe_1.agent(e_1)(Perseus) and (any)$\lambda\mathfrak{Q}$. if $\mathfrak{Q}$ = (some(sword)) or $\mathfrak{Q}$ = (some(shield)) (some)$\lambda\bar{e}$.(some(rel(SC($\bar{e}$)(e_1))(finding))) $\lambda e_2.e_2 \approx_a e_1$ and $\mathfrak{Q}(\lambda x.$theme(e_2)(x))]]].**

Neither (27)′ nor (31) will follow from the interpretation of the happy-outcome paraphrase of 'Perseus seeks a sword,' (23), since

26. For example: does the analysis work for co-ordinated quantifiers of different sorts? Why does the ∧-distributive reading of (29) disappear if 'could have been' is replaced with 'must have been' or 'will be' or 'is going to become'? Why is it unavailable (I think) if 'is heavier than' in (28) is replaced by 'is hidden in the same cave as'? Why in every case is the reading incompatible with an epistemic coda such as 'no-one knows which', or, as Andrew Pavelich pointed out to me, 'and I know which'? And how are we to respond to Jennings's objection (1994, 166–7) that quantificational analyses provide representations without explanations? I pursue these questions in Forbes (2001b).

the latter does not say that finding a shield can conclude the search successfully. This is the desired result.

Curiously, though the meaning of 'a sword or a shield' is a constituent of the meaning of the non-distributive reading of (27), it does not appear as a constituent in the meaning of the happy-outcome paraphrase partially represented in (31). This is the opposite of what happens with the distributive reading of (27) (wide-scope 'or') on the plausible assumption that this reading involves ellipsis of 'seeks': the meaning of 'a sword or a shield' is not a constituent of the reading, but it is a constituent of the reading's paraphrase, (= (26), with **'or'** for the co-ordinating **'and'**).

V

Structural DGM Semantics. The general approach to ∧-distributive 'or' sketched in IV seems to have provided us with happy-outcome paraphrases that block disjunction inferences yet preserve the weakening inferences. But we have now arrived at a serious difficulty, which can be brought out by the sentences in (32):

(32) (a) Perseus seeks a mortal gorgon; (b) Perseus seeks a gorgon; (c) Perseus seeks a mortal gorgon or an immortal gorgon.

The following logical relations hold between (a), (b) (= (1)), and the narrow-scope 'or' reading of (c): (a) entails (b) but not vice-versa, (c) entails (b) but not vice-versa (if (b) is true because (a) is true, (c) need not be true); and neither (a) nor (c) entails the other. It is straightforward to check that these relations are exactly those predicted by the happy-outcome paraphrases of the sentences in (32). The paraphrases also predict, correctly, that with wide-scope 'or', (c) is entailed by (a) and is equivalent to (b).

But the DGM interpretations of these sentences do not make the correct predictions. In particular, the DGM semantics as we currently have it makes (b) equivalent to (c) when (c) is read with *narrow*-scope 'or'. Their semantics are, respectively, (24) and

(33) **(some(search))λe_1.agent(e_1)(Perseus) and kind(e_1)(some(mortal(gorgon)) or some(immortal(gorgon)))).**

(24) and (33) are equivalent because, for any event e, if e is a search of the a-gorgon kind, it is *ipso facto* a search of the a-mortal-gorgon-or-an-immortal-gorgon kind. In turn this is because we are using the meanings of QNPs to classify searches and we are taking these meanings to be (the characteristic functions of) sets of sets. Clearly, the set of all sets that contain a gorgon is identical to the set of all sets that contain a mortal gorgon or an immortal gorgon. Concomitantly, the happy outcome 'paraphrase' of (32c) and (32c)'s semantics in (33) fail to match in the most crucial respect, that of being indistinguishable by the entailment relation.

This is the kind of extensionality problem that can often be avoided by possible-worlds semantics. But it is equally clear that in any model, the function which, for each w as argument, has the set of all sets that contain a gorgon as value, is identical to the function which, for each w as argument, has the set of all sets that contain a mortal gorgon or an immortal gorgon as value. So in this case, nothing would be gained by a move to intensions.

The problem may be thought to lie in taking (33) to be the DGM semantics for the narrow-scope reading of (32c). We treat the QNP as contributing its meaning as a unit to the meaning of (32c), even though, as observed at the end of Section IV, it does not show up that way in the happy-outcome paraphrase. But it is hard to see how this is to be avoided, in view of the association of the wide-scope reading, the one demanded by epistemic codas, with 'seeks a mortal gorgon or [seeks] an immortal gorgon', and the naturalness of the terminology 'wide-scope/narrow-scope' to capture the different roles of 'or'.[27] The line of thought I will pursue here is rather that the problem lies in the use of a semantics for quantifiers that identifies the meanings of '**some-(gorgon)**' and '**some(mortal(gorgon)) or some(immortal(gorgon))**'. For although there are no independent entailment-based grounds for distinguishing their meanings, there are *structural* grounds: our

---

27. Kamp (1973, 70) proposes that we should use a 'focus' operator '↑' to capture the wide-scope/narrow-scope difference. In the present context, this would mean that (33) is incomplete; for the narrow-scope, non-distributive reading, we should have '(↑**some(mortal(gorgon)) or** ↑**some(immortal(gorgon)))**' and for the wide-scope reading, '↑**(some(mortal(gorgon)) or some(immortal(gorgon)))**'. '↑' corresponds directly with '𝒬 =' in paraphrases; see (31). But we still have the problem of characterizing the intrinsic difference between the two 'marked up' quantifiers truth-conditionally (Kamp gives a 'dynamic' characterization).

two quantifiers differ in complexity and constituents, and they may have a difference in meaning resulting from this, even if, as functions, they produce logically equivalent outputs when applied to the same argument.

Obviously, then, the outputs in question cannot be truth-values or possible-worlds propositions. But we can get what we need by adapting the 'intentional logic' of Thomason (1980). Thomason observes that some of the problems that possible worlds semantics has with propositional attitudes (more generally, with hyperintensionality) can be eliminated if the type of propositions is taken as *primitive* instead of being *analysed* as the type of functions from worlds to truth-values. A variant of this exactly captures the level of 'granularity' we need for our purposes.

The idea is to take the type of *states of affairs* (SOAs) as primitive and let it play a role at the level of meaning that the type of truth-values plays at the level of extension. At the level of extension, a monadic predicate is a function of type ib and a QNP is a function of type $(ib)b$. Suppose that at the level of meaning, the type σ of SOAs replaces the type b of truth-values. Then if there are enough SOAs, QNPs with the same extension, or even intension, can have different meanings. All that is required is that we distinguish necessarily co-obtaining SOAs if they involve different properties or have different logical structure. In particular, we distinguish, say, the SOA of *some gorgon looking Perseus in the eye* from that of *some mortal gorgon or some immortal gorgon looking Perseus in the eye*. A QNP, at the level of meaning, is a function from properties to SOAs. So the QNP 'some gorgon' is a different function from the QNP 'some mortal gorgon or some immortal gorgon', precisely because, in terms of our example, the former produces a different state of affairs from the property of looking Perseus in the eye than the latter.

'some(gorgon)' and 'some(mortal(gorgon)) or some (immortal (gorgon))' are different functions of type $(i\sigma)\sigma$, according to this account. Hence the function 'kind(e)', of type $((i\sigma)\sigma)\sigma$, produces different states of affairs when applied to these two inputs, SOAs which need not even be necessarily equivalent: the SOA of a search e's being of the a-gorgon kind may hold while the SOA of e's being of the a-mortal-gorgon-or-an-immortal-gorgon kind does not hold (say, because finding an immortal gorgon is not a way of concluding e successfully). Yet we have preserved the intuition that the meaning of 'a mortal gorgon or an immortal gorgon' is a unitary constituent of the meaning of (32c), since its interpretation (33) still stands.[28]

Though this is as much as we need to say to resolve the problem raised by (32), we also want to explain why weakening inferences hold. Previously, we did this in terms of the postulate (9), which introduces a notion of kind-inclusion, and, exploiting the extensional semantics of QNPs, explains it as set inclusion. For completeness, we need to do something comparable for the SOA framework.

One approach would be to redefine the notion of kind-inclusion in terms of functions of type $(i\sigma)\sigma$ in place of functions of type $(ib)b$. However, to get the right results *vis à vis* disjunction, we would have to characterize kinds in terms of happy outcomes, so that, for instance, a search is of the a-sword-or-a-shield kind if and only if finding a sword can conclude it successfully and finding a shield can conclude it successfully and any successful conclusion of it involves finding a sword or a shield. But in assembling the materials to define inclusion for this notion of kind, we would quickly be in a position to get the same result by the more orthodox route of meaning-postulates, so for the sake of reaching a speedy conclusion, we use these.

We want to allow arbitrary co-ordinations of quantifiers in which '**and**' or '**or**' have multiple occurrences, for instance 'Perseus seeks some gorgon or every unicorn, and, three centaurs or two mermaids'. Any such co-ordination of quantifiers is logically equivalent, by familiar distribution principles, to a co-ordination in a *normal form* that consists in an alternation of conjunctions. For the example just given, one normal form would be 'some gorgon and three centaurs, or, some gorgon and two mermaids, or, every unicorn and three centaurs, or, every unicorn and two mermaids'. The meaning postulates we want are the instances of a schema for kind-classifications in this normal form. They allow

---

28. We now regard interpretations such as (33) as formulae of a formal language $\mathscr{L}_\sigma$ in which there are two sets of logical constants, the boolean ones *not*, *and*, *every*, etc., and meaning-sensitive counterparts **not**, **and**, **every**, etc. We include in $\mathscr{L}_\sigma$ a function $^\cup$ of type σb, which provides each state of affairs with a truth-value. Following Thomason, we then formulate meaning-postulates that use the extensional connectives to impose the correct behaviour on the meaning-sensitive connectives; for example, we would require: **every(thing$^\sigma$)**$\lambda x^\sigma.^\cup$**not(x)** $= not(^\cup x)$. The definition of model and consequence is straightforward; for details, see Forbes (2001a).

us to replace any kind-classification of the form

(34) **kind(e)((QNP$_{1_{i_1}}$ and ... and QNP$_{1_{i_j}}$) or ... or (QNP$_{n_1}$ and ... and QNP$_{n_{i_n}}$))**

in an objectual attitude ascription with a generalization of the style of paraphrase illustrated in (31):

(35) **(any)$\lambda \Omega$. if Ω = (QNP$_{1_1}$ and ... and QNP$_{1_{i_j}}$ or ... or Ω = (QNP$_{n_1}$ and ... and QNP$_{n_{i_n}}$) [(some)$\lambda \bar{e}$. (some(rel(ψ ($\bar{e}$)(e))(θ)))$\lambda e'.e' \approx_a e$ and $\Omega(\lambda x.theme(e')(x))$] and [(any)$\lambda \bar{e}$.(any(rel($\psi(\bar{e})(e))(\theta)))\lambda e'.e' \approx_a e$ and ((QNP$_{1_1}$ and ... and QNP$_{1_{i_j}}$)$\lambda x.theme(e')(x)$ or ... or (QNP$_{n_1}$ and ... and QNP$_{n_{i_n}}$)$\lambda x.theme(e')(x))$].**

ψ and θ are determined by the restrictive predicate φ corresponding to the intensional transitive verb. For example, if φ corresponds to a search verb then ψ will be 'SC' and θ will be 'finding'; if φ is 'need' then ψ will be 'meet' and θ will be 'getting'. For any objectual attitude ascription that uses a search verb, a desire verb, or 'need', and a quantifier with zero or more occurrences of 'and' and 'or' and no other co-ordinators, (35) suffices to relate it, *via* a normal-form equivalent, to an appropriate happy-outcome paraphrase. The premise of a weakening inference will entail its conclusion if and only if the (35)-defined paraphrase of a normal-form equivalent of the premise entails the (35)-defined paraphrase of a normal-form equivalent of the conclusion. Inference (6), for example, goes through so long as we can move from 'some(mortal(gorgon))$\lambda x.theme(e)(x)$' to 'some(gorgon)$\lambda x.theme(e)(x)$'. Intuitively, this is guaranteed by the intersectivity of 'mortal', but has to be explicitly stated for 'mortal'. The latter is of type $(i\sigma)(i\sigma)$, so let 'mortal†' be of type $i\sigma$. Then we define 'mortal' by '$\lambda P.\lambda x.mortal^\dagger(x)$ and P(x)'. This, along with meaning-postulates that let us trade instances of (34) for corresponding instances of (35), secures all weakening inferences in the style of (6)–(8).[29,30]

29. Matters that ought to be addressed from this point include the exact interpretation of wide-scope 'or' ascriptions, the treatment of other co-ordinators such as 'neither ... nor ...', the treatment of the ambiguity of 'or' in *relational* readings, and the question of how well the happy outcome paraphrase approach to logical consequence generalizes to other groups of intensional transitives.

30. In writing this paper I have been helped by Bob Carpenter, Mark Crimmins, Keith DeRose, Kit Fine, Risto Hilpinen, Hans Kamp, Terence Parsons, Mark Richard, Ted Sider, Richmond Thomason, Johan van Benthem and Achille Varzi.

References

Carpenter, B. 1997. *Type-Logical Semantics*, Cambridge, MA.: MIT Press.

Davidson, D. 1967. 'The Logical Form of Action Sentences', in Rescher, N. (ed.) *The Logic of Decision and Action*, Pittsburgh: University of Pittsburgh Press.

den Dikken, M., R. Larson and P. Ludlow, 1996. 'Intensional 'Transitive' Verbs and Concealed Complement Clauses', *Rivista di Linguistica* 8, 331–348; also in P. Ludlow (ed.), *Readings in the Philosophy of Language*, Cambridge, MA: MIT Press, 1041–1053.

Follesdal, D. and R. Hilpinen. 1981. 'Deontic Logic: An Introduction', in R. Hilpinen (ed.) *Deontic Logic: Introductory and Systematic Readings*, Dordrecht: Reidel, 1–35.

Forbes, G. 2000a. 'Intensional Transitive Verbs: The Limitations of a Clausal Analysis', *unpublished ms.*, www.tulane.edu/forbes/preprints.html.

Forbes, G. 2000b. 'Objectual Attitudes', *Linguistics and Philosophy* 23, 141–183.

Forbes, G. 2001a. 'The Logic of Intensional Transitives, Part I: Weakening and Disjunction', forthcoming.

Forbes, G. 2001b. 'When Good "Or"'s Go "And".'

Goodman, N. 1976. *Languages of Art*, Indianapolis: Hackett Publishing Company.

Horn, L. 1989. *The Natural History of Negation*, Chicago: Chicago University Press.

Jennings, R. E. 1994. *The Genealogy of Disjunction*, Oxford and New York: Oxford University Press.

Kamp, H. 1973. 'Free Choice Permission', *Proceedings of the Aristotelian Society* 74, 57–94.

Kamp, H. 1979. 'Semantics versus Pragmatics', in Guenthner, F. and S. Schmidt (eds.) *Formal Semantics and Pragmatics for Natural Language*, Dordrecht: Reidel, 255–287.

Larson, R. 1988. 'Scope and Comparatives', *Linguistics and Philosophy* 11, 1–26.

Loewer, B. 1976. 'Counterfactuals with Disjunctive Antecedents', *Journal of Philosophy* 73, 531–537.

Makinson, D. 1984. 'Stenius's Approach to Disjunctive Permission', *Theoria* 50, 138–147.

Moltmann, F. 1997. 'Intensional Verbs and Quantifiers', *Natural Language Semantics* 5, 1–52.

Parsons, T. 1990. *Events in the Semantics of English*, Cambridge, MA.: MIT Press.

Parsons, T. 1997. 'Meaning Sensitivity and Grammatical Structure', in Dalla Chiara, M. L., K. Doets, D. Mundici and J. v. Benthem (eds.), *Structures and Norms in Science*, Dordrecht: Kluwer Academic Publishers, 369–383.

Partee, B. and M. Rooth. 1983. 'Generalized Conjunction and Type Ambiguity', in Bäuerle, R., C. Schwarze and A. v. Stechow (eds.) *Meaning, Use and Interpretation of Language*, Berlin: de Gruyter, 361–383.

Peacocke, C. 1987. 'Depiction', *Philosophical Review* 96, 383–410.

Quine, W. V. 1955. 'Quantifiers and Propositional Attitudes', in Linsky, L. (ed.), *Reference and Modality*, Oxford and New York: Oxford University Press, 101–111.

Radford, A. 1988. *Transformational Grammar*, Cambridge and New York: Cambridge University Press.

Salmon, N. 1989. 'The Logic of What Might Have Been', *Philosophical Review* 98, 3–34.

Stenius, E. 1982. 'Ross's Paradox and Well-Formed Codices', *Theoria* 48, 49–77.

Thomason, R. 1980. 'A Model Theory for Propositional Attitudes', *Linguistics and Philosophy* 4, 47–70.

Wright, G. H. v. 1963. *The Logic of Preference*, Edinburgh: Edinburgh University Press.

INTENSIONALITY

by Graeme Forbes and Jennifer M. Saul

II—*Jennifer M. Saul*

WHAT ARE INTENSIONAL TRANSITIVES?

ABSTRACT This paper discusses the question of which verbs are intensional transitives. In particular, I ask which verbs Forbes should take to be intensional transitives. I argue that it is very difficult to arrive at a clear and plausible understanding of what an intensional transitive is— making it difficult to answer these questions. I end by briefly raising some questions about the usefulness of the category of intensional transitives.

W*hat are Intensional Transitives?* Some intensional constructions are easy to identify—we can tell when a sentence contains a modal operator or a report of a propositional attitude. Partly, perhaps, because they are less often discussed, it is less obvious which verbs are intensional transitives.[1] In this paper, I take up the issue of which verbs are intensional transitives, arguing that it is far from simple to answer this question. I will be focussing mainly on the question of what Forbes should say about this. But the issues that arise are mostly quite general, and pose difficulties for anyone who wishes to discuss intensional transitives. My goal here is not to argue for any one particular answer to the question of which verbs are intensional transitives, but rather to explore the implications of a variety of ways of drawing the line between intensional and other transitive verbs. I will not, of course, be surveying all the possible ways of drawing this line. Instead, I hope merely to draw attention to some unanswered questions and some tricky issues regarding the category of intensional transitives.

I

Forbes's Discussion. Although Forbes does not offer an explicit definition of 'intensional transitive' in his paper, he discusses two

---

1. Indeed, when I tell a philosopher that I am working on intensional transitives, I am generally asked 'Intensional transitives? What are those?' Non-philosophers, of course, quickly change the subject.

traits of intensional transitives which one might take to be somehow involved in a characterisation. I will begin by examining
Forbes's discussion of these traits, and exploring how they might
figure in a characterisation.

Forbes takes the most obvious cases of intensional transitives
to be those involving verbs used to report psychological attitudes
other than *propositional* attitudes. These verbs seem to display
what is often taken to be the most important characteristic of
propositional attitude ascriptions: resistance to substitution of
co-referential terms (in their complements). (1) seems as though
it might be true while (1*) is false.

   (1)   Lois likes Superman.
   (1*) Lois likes Clark.

Similarly, (2) seems like it might be true while (2*) is false, and
(3) might be true while (3*) is false. ('William Henry Pratt' and
'Boris Karloff' refer to the same person.)

   (2)   Melvin fears Boris Karloff.
   (2*) Melvin fears William Henry Pratt.
   (3)   Norma seeks Boris Karloff.
   (3*) Norma seeks William Henry Pratt.

These cases are very similar to propositional attitude reports.
After all, they are reports of psychological attitudes, even if these
are not attitudes toward propositions. However, they are also
importantly dissimilar. In particular, the lack of a *that*-clause
makes it difficult to apply standard substitution-blocking
strategies.

There are also other verbs which Forbes takes to be non-
psychological, and to generate substitution-resisting contexts,
such as 'depicts'.[2]

   (4)   Oswald depicted Superman.
   (4*) Oswald depicted Clark.

These verbs are another step removed from propositional-attitude-reporting verbs. They don't seem to involve psychological

2. My own intuitions are a bit fuzzy as to whether 'depicts' should count as
psychological.

attitudes or *that*-clauses, yet they appear to generate substitution resistance in their complement clauses.

Although substitution-resistance is the most popularly cited feature of intensional contexts, it is not the only one. Another key feature of propositional-attitude-ascribing contexts is the possibility of a relational/notional ambiguity. Sentence (5), below, has two different readings.

(5) Petunia believes that a horror movie actor is at the door.

On one reading, the relational, (5) states that there is some particular horror movie actor who is believed by Petunia to be at the door. On this reading, (5) can be true in a case in which Petunia believes William (who happens to be a horror movie actor) to be at the door, whether or not she knows him to be a horror movie actor. On the other reading, the notional, (5) states that Petunia believes that some horror movie actor (she may not know which) is at the door. These readings can be easily captured as scope ambiguities, with (5R) capturing the relational and (5N) the notional.

(5R) $\exists$x: x is a horror movie actor and Petunia believes that x is at the door.

(5N) Petunia believes that $\exists$x: x is a horror movie actor and x is at the door.

With examples like this in mind, then, Forbes takes the availability of notional and relational readings to be another trait of intensional transitives. 'Seeks' provides perhaps the standard illustration of this. (6) can be read as asserting that Quentin seeks a particular individual, who happens to be a horror movie actor; or as asserting that Quentin is seeking some non-specific horror movie actor—something that he can do even if there aren't any horror movie actors.[3]

---

3. It's not completely clear to me what the right way to formulate the notional reading of a sentence containing an intensional transitive is. There seem to be at least three options. First, the notional reading of (6) could be one which is true just in case Quentin seeks a non-specific horror movie actor. Second, one could claim that the notional reading of (6) is one which can be true even if there isn't a specific horror movie actor sought by Quentin. Finally, the widespread assumption that a reading must be either notional or relational would suggest a very simple formulation (closely related to the previous one): a notional reading of (6) is a non-relational one. Unfortunately, I do not have space in this paper to explore the question of how 'notional' should be understood.

(6) Quentin seeks a horror movie actor.

Due to the absence of a *that*-clause, it is much more difficult to make sense of the relational and notional readings of (6) in terms of scope distinctions.[4]

Forbes does not claim that intensional transitives must exhibit both substitution-resistance and relational/notional ambiguities. He writes, 'With [depiction verbs] and other groups of verbs, only one of the two puzzling types of behaviour may be present.'[5] This opens up the possibility that a verb may be considered an intensional transitive even if it exhibits only one of the two traits he discusses. The examples Forbes gives to illustrate this possibility help to reveal just how complicated these issues are. One example involves 'needs'. (7) seems to have both relational and notional readings.

(7)   Rexella needs a horror movie actor.

(8), however seems to allow the substitution which yields (8*).[6]

(8)   Rexella needs Boris Karloff
(8*) Rexella needs William Henry Pratt.

Forbes also draws attention to 'depicts'. We have already seen that 'depicts' may resist substitution. According to Forbes, 'depicts' may fail to allow for a relational/notional ambiguity: in (9), below, he claims that only a relational reading is possible.

(9)   Guercino depicted all dogs.[7]

It is important to be clear on what these examples show and don't show. Forbes notes, rightly, that some sentences involving 'depicts' do allow for a notional/relational ambiguity, as in (10).

(10) Guercino depicted a dog.

4. Some, of course, argue that sentences containing intensional transitives actually involve concealed *that*-clauses. See Quine (1966), Den Dikken et al. (1997).

5. Forbes (2002), introductory remarks.

6. Forbes's own example involves substitution of 'water' and 'H_2O'.

7. My own intuitions regarding this example are very unclear. Its success may depend on particular views about the working of 'depicts'. But my interest in the example is really an interest in working out what Forbes takes the criteria for intensionality to be, rather than in how 'depicts' works.

Moreover, one example in which 'needs' permits substitution doesn't show very much—there are plenty of examples in which 'believes' permits substitution.[8] Arguably, sometimes substitution does fail for sentences involving 'needs', as might be the case with (11) and (11*), uttered in the most likely sort of context.[9]

    (11)   Lois needs Superman.
    (11*) Lois needs Clark.

The complications over the way Forbes's examples work reveal that there are two readings of Forbes's claim that 'With [depiction verbs] and other groups of verbs, only one of the two puzzling types of behaviour may be present.'[10] He could be allowing that a transitive verb may be intensional even if it only ever exhibits one of the two types of behaviour, or he could be allowing that a transitive verb may be intensional even if it *doesn't always* exhibit both types of behaviour. On the first reading, an intensional transitive verb need only exhibit *either* substitution-resistance *or* a relational/notional ambiguity. On the second reading, Forbes might still require intensional transitive verbs to exhibit both behaviours, even though he doesn't require them to *always* exhibit both behaviours. These two readings would yield different verdicts about which verbs are intensional transitives.

We will examine the first reading first. On this reading, a transitive verb is an intensional transitive just in case it exhibits *either* substitution resistance in its complement *or* a relational/notional ambiguity. 'Seeks', 'fears', and 'likes' are all intensional transitives on this reading, for reasons that we have already seen.

On the second reading, a transitive verb is an intensional transitive if and only if we can find cases in which it shows a relational/notional ambiguity and cases on which it resists substitutivity. 'Seeks', 'depicts' and 'fears' turn out to be intensional transitives on this reading, as (6), (12), and (13) seem to admit both notional and relational readings.

---

8. Such cases have helped to motivate both Salmon and Soames's Millian semantics and contextual variation accounts like those of Crimmins and Richard. See Salmon (1986), Soames (1988), Crimmins (1992), Richard (1990).

9. Forbes has suggested that when substitution fails with 'needs' it fails in a different way from the way that it fails with verbs like 'fears'. One possibility for what the difference is will be discussed in V.2.

10. Forbes (2002), introductory remarks.

(6)   Quentin seeks a horror movie actor.
(12) Strom fears a horror movie actor.
(13) Rexella is depicting a horror movie actor.

The important difference between this reading and the previous one comes with verbs like 'likes'. Although 'likes' does display substitution resistance, it does not seem to allow for a notional/relational ambiguity. There doesn't seem to be a reading available on which (14) claims that Trigby likes a non-specific man.[11]

(14) Trigby likes a man.

So using the more stringent standard for what counts as an intensional transitive would rule out verbs like 'likes'.

II

Lack of Existential Commitment. Another trait commonly cited in discussions of intensional transitives—although not one mentioned by Forbes in Forbes (2002)—is lack of existential commitment. This trait is another which sentences containing intensional transitives are taken to share with propositional attitude reports. Propositional attitude reports are standardly taken to display a lack of existential commitment. Sentence (5) seems as though it might be true even if it turned out that in fact all apparent horror movie actors were really cunningly generated animations—that is, even if there were no horror movie actors. (5), then, does not seem to entail (5G).

(5)   Petunia believes that a horror movie actor is at the
       door.
(5G) There is a horror movie actor.

With this in mind, lack of existential commitment has also been taken to be a characteristic of intensional verbs. (This feature is often taken to be an especially important trait of intensional transitives. In den Dikken, Larson and Ludlow (1997) it

---

11. Similarly, it doesn't seem that 'Trigby likes all men' or 'Trigby likes most men' could be made true by Trigby liking non-specific men. It just doesn't make much sense to talk about someone liking non-specific men. Working with a different understanding of 'notional' (see footnote 3), it also seems wrong to suppose that (14)—or any of the variants suggested in this footnote could be true without there being a particular man that Trigby likes.

is clearly taken to be a sufficient indicator that a transitive verb is an intensional transitive.) 'Seeks' provides a nice example of lack of existential commitment. (6) does not seem to entail (6G).

(6)   Quentin seeks a horror movie actor.
(6G)   There is a horror movie actor.

There are (at least) two obvious ways that we might add this trait to our means of determining which verbs are intensional transitives. The first would be to add it to (potentially) loosen still further the looser standard, so that a transitive verb is an intensional transitive just in case it displays *either* a relational/notional ambiguity *or* substitution failure *or* lack of existential commitment. The second would be to (potentially) tighten still further the stricter standard, so that a transitive verb is an intensional transitive just in case there are occasions on which it displays a relational/notional ambiguity, occasions on which it displays substitution failure, *and* occasions on which it displays lack of existential commitment.

It seems likely that in most, possibly all, cases, lack of existential commitment and availability of a notional reading will go together. We have seen that the notional/relational ambiguity is present with 'seeks', 'fears', and 'depicts', and that 'seeks' displays lack of existential commitment. 'Fears' and 'depicts' do as well. (12) does not seem to entail (12G), and (13) does not seem to entail (13G).

(12)   Strom fears a horror movie actor.
(12G)   There is a horror movie actor.
(13)   Rexella is depicting a horror movie actor.
(13G)   There is a horror movie actor.

The notional/relational ambiguity does not seem to arise with 'likes', and sentences with 'likes' also seems to make existential commitments to their complements. (14) does seem to entail (14G).

(14)   Trigby likes a man.
(14G)   There is a man.

I have by no means established that verbs will exhibit the notional/relational ambiguity iff they exhibit lack of existential commitment. But if this claim is true—as it looks like it is—

then the alterations to our criteria suggested above will make no difference whatsoever. Any transitive verb which displays a relational/notional ambiguity will also display a lack of existential commitment, and any transitive verb which does not display a relational/notional ambiguity will not display a lack of existential commitment.[12] Accordingly, it seems harmless to add them to the two standards in the ways suggested above.

III

Summary of Options. We have, then, two different standards for what counts as an intensional transitive, which give different results. I will name them 'The Strict Standard' and 'The Loose Standard', and present them here for easy reference.[13]

> *The Strict Standard*: a transitive verb is an intensional transitive just in case there are occasions on which it displays a relational/notional ambiguity, occasions on which it displays substitution failure, *and* occasions on which it displays a lack of existential commitment.

> *The Loose Standard*: a transitive verb is an intensional transitive just in case it sometimes displays *either* a relational/notional ambiguity *or* substitution failure *or* a lack of existential commitment.

---

12. Dominic Gregory has suggested a potential counterexample to this hypothesis: 'I remember a man' seems as though it may display a relational/notional ambiguity. However, if 'remember' is factive, then 'I remember a man' cannot be true unless there is a man. If this example is right, then there are sentences which display the relational/notional ambiguity but do not display a lack of existential commitment. This would substantially complicate my formulation of the options available for defining 'intensional'. However, I do not think it would affect the main points of this paper.

13. Another standard is, it seems to me, also available. This would be the one most obviously suggested by standard characterisations of intensionality for constructions other than intensional transitives, what one might call 'The Substitution Failure Standard'.

   The Substitution Failure Standard: a transitive verb is an intensional transitive just in case it displays substitution failure.

   The Substitution Failure Standard seems to yield different results from The Strict Standard since 'likes' seems to exhibit substitution failure yet does not count as an intensional transitive under The Strict Standard. However, it will yield the same results as The Loose Standard if any verb which exhibits either a relational/notional ambiguity or resistance to existential generalisation also exhibits substitution failure. I have not found any cases to disconfirm this hypothesis, and this is why I don't discuss this standard explicitly in the paper.

IV

The Strict Standard, The Loose Standard, and Forbes.
IV.1. *The Strict Standard.* We have seen that adopting The Strict Standard has the result that 'likes' is not an intensional transitive while 'fears' and 'seeks' are. This seems odd. Moreover, if one thinks—as some do—that genuine substitution failure can occur only in intensional contexts, this yields the counterintuitive result that the substitution inference from (1) to (1*) must succeed while that from (2) to (2*) may fail.

(1)   Lois likes Superman.
(1*) Lois likes Clark.
(2)   Melvin fears Boris Karloff.
(2*) Melvin fears William Henry Pratt.

For those who accept that genuine substitution failure only occurs in intensional contexts, this will be a very undesirable consequence of the Strict Standard.[14] One way of avoiding this consequence, and of classifying 'likes' and 'fears' together—as seems intuitively desirable—is to adopt The Loose Standard. Under The Loose Standard, as we have seen, 'seeks', 'fears', and 'likes' are all intensional transitives. But adopting The Loose Standard would have some striking consequences for Forbes, as we will see below.

IV.2 *The Loose Standard and Forbes.*
IV.2.1. *Forbes and Simple Sentences.* Forbes takes there to be genuine substitution failure in certain sentences of a sort that I have called 'simple sentences'.[15] I defined these as sentences lacking propositional attitude, modal, or quotational constructions, or other constructions generally taken to block substitution. Some of them, I suggested, nevertheless provoke anti-substitution intuitions. Imagine, for example, that (15) provides a true description of what took place one eventful day in Metropolis.

(15) Superman saved 20 people from a train wreck, then Clark came and interviewed them.

---

14. One might, of course, avoid this consequence by abandoning the view that genuine substitution failure only occurs in intensional contexts.
15. Forbes (1997), (1999); Saul (1997a), (1997b).

Substituting co-referential names gives us (15*).

> (15*) Clark saved 20 people from a train wreck, then Super-
> man came and interviewed them.

Intuitively, in the situation described, (15*) is false. But (15*)
simply results from the substitution of co-referential names.

It turns out to be rather easy to construct simple sentences like
(15) and (15*), which evoke anti-substitution intuitions. (16), for
example, seems like it might be true.

> (16)   Superman wears more capes than Clark does.

(16*) certainly cannot be true.

> (16*) Clark wears more capes than Clark does.

We don't need fiction to produce anti-substitution intuitions
about simple sentences either. (17) seems like it might be true
while (17*) must be false.

> (17)   I visited St Petersburg once, but I never made it to
> Leningrad.
> (17*) I visited St Petersburg once, but I never made it to St
> Petersburg.

We can even get anti-substitution intuitions about sentences
involving verbs which seem as though they should be paradigms
of extensionality—'goes' and 'hits'.

> (18)   Clark Kent went into the phone booth, and Superman
> came out.
> (18*) Clark Kent went into the phone booth, and Clark
> Kent came out.
> (19)   I hit Clark Kent once, but I never hit Superman.
> (19*) I hit Clark Kent once, but I never hit Clark Kent.

Forbes maintains that the anti-substitution intuitions generated by all these sentences should be taken seriously, and he does
so by providing a semantics which allows substitution to be
blocked in all these cases.[16]

IV.2.2. *Forbes, Simple Sentences and The Loose Standard.* If
Forbes adopts The Loose Standard, then any transitive verb

16. Forbes (1997), (1999).

which exhibits genuine substitution failure in its complement is an intensional transitive. According to Forbes, 'hits' exhibits genuine substitution failure. 'Hits', then, would count as an intensional transitive. Given the ease with which apparently substitution-resistant simple sentences can be constructed, it seems likely that we can find cases of apparent substitution failure for all transitive verbs. If that is right, then all transitive verbs would be intensional transitives for Forbes, under The Loose Standard. This seems a problematic consequence. At the very least, it diminishes the interest for Forbes of the category of intensional *transitives*.

IV.2.3. *Further Potential Consequences of Forbes's Adopting The Loose Standard.* If Forbes adopted The Loose Standard, then the intensional constructions would for him include modal operators, propositional attitude reports, and transitive verbs. The latter category would be included because (it seems) substitution may, for Forbes, genuinely fail in the complement clause of any transitive verb. It is hard to see, though, how Forbes could justify stopping here. After all, Forbes also thinks that substitution may fail in sentences containing no transitive verbs, like (20), below.[17]

(20)   Superman is better-looking than Clark.
(20*) Clark is better-looking than Clark.

If substitution-failure is sufficient for a *transitive* verb to be intensional, why shouldn't it be sufficient for other verbs? The consequence of allowing that it is, for Forbes, would be that most, and possibly all, verbs would be intensional. All sentences containing verbs—which is to say, all sentences—would then be intensional sentences. This would surely be unacceptable to anyone who wants to maintain the interest of intensionality.

One alternative might be to abandon the focus on intensional *constructions*. It has long been accepted that context (in a broader sense than sentential context) is extremely important to substitution-resistance, even with widely accepted intensional verbs like 'believes'. If Forbes is right, there is potential for substitution-resistance in just about every sentence. With this in mind, one might focus instead on what sorts of *conversational contexts*

17. And in locations other than the *complement* of a transitive verb, as in (16) and (16*).

produce intensionality, rather than on isolating particular *constructions* as intensional ones. While this strategy might be an interesting one, it would certainly be a hugely revisionary one, which Forbes would probably wish to avoid.

V

Rejecting The Strict Standard and The Loose Standard. As I noted earlier, Forbes does not offer a definition of 'intensional transitive'. He certainly does not commit himself to either The Strict Standard or The Loose Standard. We have now seen good reason for Forbes to reject each of these standards. This leaves us with the unanswered question of what an intensional transitive is. Here I review some further options.

V.1. *Negative Characterisations.* It is reasonably common to take intensional constructions to be all those constructions which are not purely extensional. I will call such characterisations of intensional constructions 'negative' characterisations, and I will examine two negative characterisations.[18] These characterisations differ in how they define 'extensional', and this leads to a difference in what counts as intensional. I am not to attempting to provide a full menu of options for defining 'intensional' negatively, but rather to point to some complications of what might seem initially appealing definitions.[19]

18. I thank Chris Hookway for suggesting the contrast between 'negative' and 'positive' characterisations of 'intensional'.

19. There is actually a complication which arises rather quickly when dealing with these definitions of 'intensional'. They give necessary and sufficient conditions for a *sentence* to be intensional, rather than a construction. It's pretty easy to use these definitions to recognise certain sorts of constructions as intensional. If we start with an intensional sentence like 'Petunia believes that there is a horror movie actor at the door' and remove 'Petunia believes that' we get an extensional sentence. This kind of thing gives us (at least) very good reason to suppose that *A believes that* is an intensional construction. But if we start with a sentence like 'Strom fears a horror movie actor', and then remove 'Strom fears' we don't get any sentence at all. (We could, of course, compare the intensional status of a sentence with 'fears' as its verb and one with a known non-intensional verb substituted in for 'fears'. But we could only do this if we had already identified some verbs as non-intensional, and such identifications are precisely what is at stake here.) So turning these definitions of 'intensional sentence' into definitions of 'intensional construction' or 'intensional transitive verb' would take a bit of work. I won't attempt to do this work here. Instead, I want to see what the prospects are for these definitions doing the job Forbes needs them to do, even if we don't worry about this problem. I will assume, then, that a verb counts as intensional if it is *involved in the right way* in an intensional sentence—leaving the right sort of involvement to be defined by those who want to defend this way of identifying intensional transitive verbs.

V.1.1. Definition 1. The first negative definition is of an extremely common sort. I have taken my formulation of this definition from the *Oxford Dictionary of Philosophy.*

> A sentence puts a predicate or other term in an extensional context if any other term or predicate with the same extension can be substituted without it being possible that the truth value changes— Other contexts—may not allow substitution, and are called intensional contexts.[20]

According to this characterisation, a context is intensional just in case substitution of co-extensional terms or predicates fails to preserve truth value. On this understanding, then, substitution failure is sufficient for intensionality. This will not, then, help Forbes out of the difficulty discussed above: simple sentences still turn out to be intensional.

V.1.2. Definition 2. Our next negative definition does not make explicit reference to substitution, but consequences regarding substitution seem likely to follow.[21]

> A sentence is extensional if and only if its truth value is determined solely by its structure and the extensions of its parts (when fully analysed). Otherwise, it is intensional.

The most important difference between this formulation and the previous one is the reference to the fully analysed form of the sentence. On this definition, the substitution of co-extensional terms which is relevant to extensionality will be substitution that takes place *at the level of the fully analysed sentence.* That is, this definition would require us—when testing for intensionality— to hold fixed the extensions of any elements which appear *in the analysis* other than the substituted ones.

We can see how this difference matters by looking closely at what Forbes says about simple sentences. Forbes analyses (19) as, roughly, (19F).[22]

(19)   I hit Clark Kent once, but I never hit Superman.

20. Blackburn (1994), 133.

21. I thank David Braun for suggesting this sort of definition to me.

22. Here I am focusing on a substitution-resistant utterance of (19). Forbes actually holds that (19) (like any other simple sentence) can express either a proposition which makes reference to modes of personification or one which does not, depending on the context in which it is uttered (Forbes 1999). Substitution may only fail when (19) expresses the former sort of proposition.

(19F)   I hit Clark Kent, in his so-labelled mode of personifi-
         cation, once, but I never hit Superman, in his so-
         labelled mode of personification.

Both 'Clark Kent' and 'Superman' in (19F) pick out the individual Superman/Clark Kent. The 'so' in the first 'so-personified'
refers to the name 'Clark Kent'; the second refers to the name
'Superman'. Since the 'Clark Kent'-labelled mode of personification is different from the 'Superman'-labelled mode of personification, (19) may be true. It is the 'so-labelled's, then, which do
all the work of blocking substitution for Forbes.

To test for intensionality, we substitute 'Clark Kent' for
'Superman' while holding fixed the extensions of all other
elements of the fully analysed sentence (19F). If doing this produces a change in truth value, then (19F), and hence (19), is
extensional. But doing this fails to produce a change in truth
value. Recall that what we must do is to hold fixed the extensions
of all terms other than 'Superman' and 'Clark Kent' in (19F).
This means that we hold fixed the extensions of the two 'so's.
But if those extensions are held fixed, there is no substitution
failure, as changes in the extension of 'so' are wholly responsible
for the substitution failure from (19) to (19*).

(19*)   I hit Clark Kent once, but I never hit Clark Kent.

(19) is not intensional, under this definition of intensionality.
Simple sentences, then, will not be intensional for Forbes if this
understanding of 'intensional' is adopted. So far, it looks like
this definition might be a good one for Forbes to use.

However, sentences with intensional transitives also turn out
not to be intensional on this understanding of 'intensional'. The
reason is that Forbes's semantics for such sentences involves the
same sort of structural features that rendered simple sentences
extensional. Forbes accounts for the substitution failure from (2)
to (2*) by analysing (2) as, roughly, (2F); and (2*) as, roughly,
(2*F).

(2)   Melvin fears Boris Karloff.
(2*)   Melvin fears William Henry Pratt.
(2F)   Melvin fears Boris Karloff, under Melvin's so-lab-
         elled way of thinking of Boris Karloff.
(2*F)   Melvin fears William Henry Pratt, under Melvin's so-
         labelled way of thinking of Boris Karloff.

In (2F), 'so' refers to the name 'Boris Karloff', and in (2*F) 'so' refers to the name 'William Henry Pratt'. 'Boris Karloff' in (2F) and 'William Henry Pratt' in (2*F) both refer to the individual Boris Karloff/William Henry Pratt. Once more, then, the substitution failure is due solely to a shift in the reference of 'so'. Substituting 'William Henry Pratt' for 'Boris Karloff' while holding the reference of 'so' fixed will preserve truth value. (2), then, also fails this test for intensionality.[23] We cannot yet conclude that 'fears' must be extensional for Forbes on this understanding of 'intensional'. The reason is that some sentences containing 'fears', such as (12), below, also seem to exhibit a notional/ relational ambiguity.

(12) Strom fears a horror movie actor.

Forbes (2002) offers an analysis of the notional readings of sentences involving (at least some) intensional transitives. On this analysis, the notional readings of such sentences are intensional by the current standard.[24] The verbs for which this analysis

23. In his (1989, 121), Forbes discusses the sentence 'Giorgione was so-called because of his size', and concludes that—due to the demonstrative nature of 'so', and the sorts of concerns discussed above, this sentence does not exhibit genuine substitution failure. It is clear, however, that Forbes does take there to be genuine substitution failure in both simple sentences and those involving intensional transitives. This might seem initially puzzling, but Forbes has told me in correspondence hat he no longer holds the (1989) view regarding the 'Giorgione' example. (Neil Feit (1996) also argues, for the same reasons, that 'Giorgione was so-called because of his size' fails to exhibit genuine substitution failure.) The view of intensionality discussed in the text above is actually silent on the issue of whether the apparent substitution failures in the 'Giorgione' sentence, sentences involving intensional transitives, and simple sentences, should be taken as genuine on Forbes's account. This is because its subject matter is extensionality/intensionality rather than substitution failure. But for Definition 2 to have any appeal to Forbes, it would have to be combined with the claim that these substitution failures are genuine (since Forbes does take the substitution failures to be genuine). Thus, it would require commitment to the idea that there can be genuine substitution failures outside intensional contexts.

24. To see that Forbes's analysis of notional readings yields sentences which are intensional, consider sentence (21).

    (21)   Perseus is seeking a gorgon.

Forbes's semantics yields (21F) as his understanding of (21).

    (21F)   some search λe_1.agent(e_1)(Perseus) and kind(e_1)(some(gorgon)).

Sentence (22) results from substituting the extensionally equivalent 'a mortal or immortal gorgon' for 'a gorgon' in (21).

    (22)   Perseus is seeking a mortal or an immortal gorgon.

Forbes's semantics yields (22F) as his understanding of (22).

    (22F)   some search λe_1.agent(e_1)(Perseus) and kind(e_1)(some (mortal (gorgon)) or some (immortal(gorgon))).

works, then, are intensional. But, problematically, it is not so clear that Forbes's analysis works for 'fears'. Forbes's analysis can easily be applied to verbs like 'seeks' and 'needs', for which it is clear what a happy outcome paraphrase would be. But there is no happy outcome paraphrase available, it seems to me, for sentences containing 'fears'. If this is right, then Forbes's analysis will not work for the notional readings of sentences containing 'fears'. So Forbes cannot show 'fears' to be intensional, on this understanding of 'intensional', by pointing to his analysis of notional readings of sentences containing it. However, if Forbes develops an analysis of the notional readings of sentences containing 'fears', and if 'fears' is intensional on this analysis, he will be able to do so. At this point, then—while 'fears' remains, for Forbes, a verb with an as-yet-unanalysed notional reading—Forbes should (on this understanding of 'intensional') refrain from judgement as to whether 'fears' is intensional.

The line suggested above—finding an intensional analysis of the notional reading—is clearly not available for verbs without notional readings. It cannot, then, even be tried for 'likes'. Since there is no notional reading for sentences containing 'likes', and since Forbes's substitution-blocking mechanism for 'likes' is the same as that for 'fears' and 'hits', 'likes' cannot be intensional on this understanding of 'intensional'.

It's worth reflecting for a minute on the point we have come to here. If Forbes accepts the understanding of 'intensional' suggested in this section, then the verbs involved in simple sentences are not intensional. In fact, no transitive verbs which exhibit only substitution failure will be intensional—as Forbes's mechanism for dealing with substitution failure is the same for verbs like 'hits' and those which are generally called 'intensional transitives', and it is not one which involves intensionality. The only transitive verbs which may turn out to be intensional for Forbes will be those which display a notional/relational ambiguity—as Forbes's analysis of the notional reading in some cases does, and in other cases may, render these verbs intensional. Availability of a notional reading thus turns out to be a necessary condition

We can get from (21F) to (22F) by substituting extensionally equivalent expressions while holding the extensions of all other expressions fixed. Yet (21) and (22), for Forbes, have different truth conditions. So Forbes's analysis of notional readings yields sentences which are intensional by the standard under consideration.

for a transitive verb's intensionality, if Forbes adopts this understanding of 'intensional'.

V.2. *A Positive Characterisation?* We have just looked at attempts to define 'intensional' by contrast with 'extensional'. One can also define intensional sentences as those which, when fully analysed, say something about certain sorts of entities—intensional ones. In particular, Forbes might point to a potentially significant difference between his analyses ((19F) and (2F)) of (19) and (2).

> (19)   I hit Clark Kent once, but I never hit Superman.
> (19F) I hit Clark Kent, in his so-labelled mode of personification, once, but I never hit Superman, in his so-labelled mode of personification.
> (2)   Melvin fears Boris Karloff.
> (2F)   Melvin fears Boris Karloff, under Melvin's so-labelled way of thinking of Boris Karloff.

(2F) makes reference to one of Melvin's ways of thinking of Boris Karloff. (19F) does not make reference to any ways of thinking. Forbes might argue that reference to a way of thinking is what makes (2F), unlike (19F), intensional. The intensionality could be due to the mental nature of ways of thinking, or to their representational nature more generally.[25] To make this line work, one would need to provide a full list of intensional entities. Moreover, in order for this definition to succeed for Forbes, this list would have to be such that modes of personification are not intensional entities. I am genuinely uncertain what the prospects are for doing this.[26]

VI

Why Intensional Transitives? We've seen many difficulties with attempts to delineate which verbs are the intensional transitives.

25. Forbes has suggested to me in correspondence that this approach holds some appeal for him.

26. Steve Laurence has pointed out an potential interesting consequence of this sort of line: propositional-attitude-reporting sentences might count as intensional for Nathan Salmon if we are loose enough about what counts as involvement of ways of thinking. After all, Salmon does take what is said by such reports to involve quantification over something very like ways of thinking. However, Salmon denies that there is any substitution failure in such sentences (Salmon 1986). So, on this view, there may be the potential for intensionality and substitution failure to come apart.

These difficulties seem to be due largely to two factors. The first is differences in behaviour between the standardly accepted intensional transitives—some exhibit notional/relational ambiguities and some not, some exhibit failure of existential generalisation and some not. The second is similarities in behaviour between these standardly accepted intensional transitives and verbs which are not thought to be intensional—both seem to exhibit substitution failure, the one trait which *does* seem common to all the standard intensional transitives. The nature of these difficulties seems to me to at least suggest that perhaps the reason it is hard to say which verbs are the intensional transitives is that this is not really a unified category. These difficulties alone don't of course show this—it might be that at some deeper level intensional transitives really are like each other and different from other verbs. But, for Forbes at least, this doesn't seem to be so—simple sentences and those involving intensional transitives have structurally parallel analyses (in contexts in which substitution fails), while different intensional verbs will require very different analyses for their notional readings (those which don't admit of happy ending paraphrases can't be dealt with as suggested in the paper which precedes this one). This leaves me wondering whether it is a good idea to have a category of intensional transitives at all. One alternative would be to simply group verbs by their behaviour, leaving us with substitution-resistant verbs, verbs which generate notional/relational ambiguities, and so on. It would then be an open question whether these verbs exhibiting different puzzling behaviours had anything significant in common. Another alternative would be to group verbs by the sorts of analyses they call for. In both cases, different theorists would undoubtedly end up with different groupings from one another, but at least we would be clear on what criteria were being used to group verbs together. I am not sure what purpose is served at this point by the rather disparate category of *intensional transitive.*[27]

27. I have received a great deal of generous help in writing this paper. I am very grateful to Albert Atkin, David Braun, Ray Drainville, Graeme Forbes, Dimitris Galanakis, Dominic Gregory, Chris Hookway, Rob Hopkins, Rosanna Keefe, Steve Laurence, Teresa Robertson, Ian White, and Harry Witzthum for reading and commenting on drafts of this paper, and for extremely helpful discussion of the material in this paper and related matters.

References

Blackburn, S. 1994. *The Oxford Dictionary of Philosophy*, Oxford: Oxford University Press.

Crimmins, M. 1992. *Talk About Beliefs*, Cambridge, MA: MIT Press.

den Dikken, M., R. Larson and P. Ludlow. 1997. 'Intensional 'Transitive' Verbs and Concealed Complement Clauses', in P. Ludlow (ed.) *Readings in the Philosophy of Language*, Cambridge, MA: MIT Press, 1041–1053.

Feit, N. 1996. 'On a Famous Counterexample to Leibniz's Law', *Proceedings of the Aristotelian Society* 96, 381–386.

Forbes, G. 1997. 'How Much Substitutivity?', *Analysis* 57: 2, 108–113.

Forbes, G. 1999. 'Enlightened Semantics for Simple Sentences', *Analysis* 59: 2, 86–90.

Forbes, G. 2002. 'Intensionality', this volume.

Quine, W. V. 1966. ' Quantifiers and Propositional Attitudes', in his *Ways of Paradox*, Cambridge, MA: Harvard University Press, 185–196.

Richard, M. 1990. *Propositional Attitudes*, Cambridge: Cambridge University Press.

Salmon, N. 1986. *Frege's Puzzle*, Cambridge, MA: MIT Press.

Saul, J. M. 1997a. 'Substitution and Simple Sentences', *Analysis* 57: 2, 102–108.

Saul, J. M. 1997b. 'Reply to Forbes', *Analysis* 57: 2, 114–118.

Saul, J. M. 1999. 'Substitution, Simple Sentences and Sex Scandals', *Analysis* 59: 2, 106–112.

Soames, S. 1988. 'Direct Reference, Propositional Attitudes, and Semantic Content', in N. Salmon and S. Soames (eds), *Propositions and Attitudes*, Oxford: Oxford University Press.

EPISTEMIC CONSEQUENTIALISM

by Philip Percival and Robert Stalnaker

I—Philip Percival

ABSTRACT I aim to illuminate foundational epistemological issues by reflecting on 'epistemic consequentialism'—the epistemic analogue of ethical consequentialism. Epistemic consequentialism employs a concept of cognitive value playing a role in epistemic norms governing belief-like states that is analogous to the role goodness plays in act-governing moral norms. A distinction between 'direct' and 'indirect' versions of epistemic consequentialism is held to be as important as the familiar ethical distinction on which it is based. These versions are illustrated, respectively, by cognitive decision-theory and reliabilism. Cognitive decision-theory is defended, and various conceptual issues concerning it explored. A simple dilemma suggests that epistemic consequentialism has radical consequences.

I aim to do for epistemic consequentialism what others have attempted recently on behalf of virtue epistemology:[1] expound and explore an epistemic analogue of an ethical theory. Though sympathetic, my exposition is not a defence: others may find commitments I expose unpalatable.[2]

I

Epistemic consequentialism is an epistemic analogue of ethical consequentialism. Since ethical consequentialism connects moral act-evaluations (in terms of 'right/wrong', and 'ought' etc.) extensionally with evaluations of 'consequences' according to their relative 'goodness', epistemic consequentialism connects epistemic evaluations of cognitive acts (in terms of 'epistemic justifiedness', or 'rationality', etc.) extensionally with evaluations of

---

1. See Axtell (2000), especially the editor's introduction. It is generally recognised that virtue ethics/epistemology is consistent with 'consequentialist' ethics/epistemology. My terminology concurs: some virtue ethics/epistemologies are species of ethical/epistemic consequentialism. (Whether some are not is moot.)

2. In the draft on which Bob Stalnaker based his contribution to this session, I gave greater attention to the question of epistemic consequentialism's commitments than space now permits. My discussion survives only as the 'dilemma' with which the paper ends.

'consequences' employing an evaluative concept, 'cognitive value',[3] analogous to 'good'. But it does not claim more of an analogy than this. In particular, it no more presupposes that cognitive acts are *acts*, or that options to cognitive acts are *optional*,[4] than it presupposes that epistemic norms are appropriate vehicles of praise and blame:[5] it is therefore neutral regarding cognitive voluntarism and epistemic deontology.[6] And it is no more meta-epistemology than ethical consequentialism is meta-ethics: it is neutral vis-a-vis the semantic or metaphysical status of evaluations of cognitive acts in terms of e.g. epistemic justification, and/or the evaluation of consequences in terms of cognitive value.

Without further qualification, ethical consequentialism—and hence epistemic consequentialism too—is extremely weak. The characterisation just given offers no account of 'consequences', and places no formal or substantive constraints on 'good', or on how moral act-evaluations are connected extensionally with evaluations of consequences. Ethical consequentialism is thereby allowed to take many forms. It is not restricted to the strict causal consequences of an act: it may utilise 'consequences'—or 'outcomes' as they are commonly termed—which include not only the act itself, but the act's historical setting.[7] It can connect moral act-evaluations 'indirectly' with evaluations of causal

3. I prefer 'cognitive' value to the common alternative, 'epistemic' value, because using it to signify an evaluation of *consequences* better emphasises the contrast with an evaluation of cognitive *acts* according to their 'epistemic justifiedness' etc.

4. It might construe 'cognitive acts' as transitions in an agent from one cognitive state to another, and a cognitive act of kind K with content p as being 'optional' for S at t iff S can grasp p and enter into cognitive states of kind K. Two examples of the notion of a 'kind' of cognitive act I am employing here are 'accepting p' and 'giving p credence to degree r'. How or whether these acts relate to acts which fall under the folk-concept of belief is controversial.

5. If the propriety of praise or blame is a necessary condition of normativity, this has to be made out.

6. Epistemic deontology is the view that it is appropriate to evaluate cognitive acts in terms of such deontological concepts as 'ought' and 'obligation'. I take it that epistemic deontology is equivalent to the view that it can be appropriate to praise or blame an agent for his cognitive acts. Some hold that epistemic deontology presupposes cognitive voluntarism. But they may be wrong about this even if an agent is only properly praised or blamed for acts for which he is responsible: we might be responsible for that over which we have 'direct control', with the realm over which we can exert direct control extending beyond the realm of voluntary acts (see Owens (2000)).

7. As in Sosa (1993).

consequences other than of the act itself and the options to it,[8] and/or via non-optimising principles such as 'satisficing'.[9] It has no commitment to the impartiality or absoluteness of 'good': it may rank consequences in a partial, agent-relative way, or hold 'good' itself—and hence the ranking of consequences—to be relative to agents and/or times.[10] And it allows moral act-evaluations to be connected with goodness of consequences *and more besides*: so it has 'subjective' versions in which moral act-evaluations are connected with the various consequences which the agent *believes* might ensue from his various optional acts, as ranked according to their relative goodness *and according to his subjective probabilities*.[11]

Thus characterised, ethical consequentialism is consistent with just about any first-order moral theory. This much is obvious in the case of 'indirect' species of the doctrine.[12] To see that just about any first-order theory can be framed as a *direct* ethical consequentialist theory, consider Kantianism as a(n extreme) test case. With a view to finding a ranking of the consequences of acts and the optional alternatives to them with respect to which the consequence of violating a Kantian duty is bound to be worse than the consequence of performing it, suppose that good/bad consequences (of acts) include the acts themselves—and so are 'outcomes'—and that either the only property which is bad is non-universalisability of acts (or whatever Kant's account of the duty-making property of acts is), or that non-universalisability (or whatever) 'trumps' other bad properties. For convenience, suppose further that promise-breaking is the only non-universalisable act. Then, with a single proviso, if my options are to keep my promise or break it, the outcome of breaking it must be worse than any outcome of keeping it. The proviso is this: the outcome of keeping my promise must not include the breaking of further promises that would otherwise be kept. For if e.g. keeping my promise will cause five others to break theirs, keeping

---

8. As in Hooker (2000).

9. As in Slote (1984).

10. As in Sen (1982) and Broome (1991).

11. As in Jackson (1991).

12. Even so, an indirect ethical consequentialist version of a first-order moral theory will embody an empirical claim regarding how certain rules/faculties/motives/beliefs or whatever would promote good. This claim might be implausible and/or false.

it will have a worse outcome than will breaking it. However, agent-relative ranking accommodates this difficulty. If goodness of outcomes is relative to agents, it can be supposed that *relative to me*, it is the badness of *my* broken promises that trumps anything else bad, including promise breaking by others. A final problem stems from the fact that the outcome of my promise-keeping now might be that *I* break five promises tomorrow. But moment-relative ranking accommodates this difficulty. If goodness of outcomes is relative not just to agents, but to times, it can be supposed that relative to me, now, the badness of my breaking a promise overrides any amount of promise-breaking on my part subsequently. Relative to the present moment, and me, keeping my promise now and breaking five promises tomorrow is a better outcome than is breaking my promise now and keeping five promises tomorrow.[13]

Influenced by this consideration, perhaps, many authors qualify ethical consequentialism further so as to give it first-order import: they confine it to what I call 'direct' ethical consequentialism, and/or to rankings of consequences that are impartial, and/or agent-neutral, and/or non-relative.[14] I once thought to follow suit: I ruled out moment-relative rankings, and took so doing to render direct ethical consequentialism incompatible with Kantianism at least.[15] But I now think a ban on moment-relative rankings arbitrary.[16] I no longer consider it vital that ethical

13. Broome (1991: 11–16) seems to think that there are first-order moral theories which cannot be reconciled with direct ethical consequentialism under the present characterisation. Observing that 'at least as good as' is a transitive and reflexive relation which (at least) quasi-orders consequences, he maintains both that if right depends on good, this ordering will be transferred to acts, and that there are first-order moral theories with respect to which acts are *not* ordered in this way. Perhaps he means to invoke moral theories according to which e.g. the comparative 'ought to A rather than B' is not transitive, with a view to suggesting that even the relativisation of rankings to agents and moments will fail to reconcile theories of this kind with direct ethical consequentialism. If so, I agree: under the present characterisation, direct ethical consequentialism is not *completely* neutral with respect to first-order moral theories.

14. His earlier implementation of this policy in his own work notwithstanding, Scheffler's (1988) collection *Consequentialism and its Critics* favours a very broad spectrum of papers. It is especially noteworthy that his editorial introduction does not contain a definition of '(ethical) consequentialism'.

15. It is with this proposal, and with my presumption regarding it, that Stalnaker takes issue in his footnote 4.

16. I must confess that I now realise that such a ban is also inconvenient. Without moment-relative rankings, the classification of Bayesian cognitive decision-theory as a species of epistemic consequentialism is undermined. See below, Section II.i.

consequentialism should be given first-order import. If it is characterised so as to lack such import, what was once an issue over whether ethical consequentialism is correct becomes an issue over which species of ethical consequentialism is correct. So what? Either there is an alternative framework in which to approach moral evaluation of acts which might sensibly be thought superior, or there is not. If there is, the worry over vacuousness is misplaced: ethical consequentialism in my sense is substantive after all. If there is not, the framework is vindicated, and we are free to proceed.

Leaving ethical consequentialism weak renders epistemic consequentialism weak and encumbered with many variants. The most important sub-classifications of it include analogues to those already mentioned: direct vs. indirect; optimising vs. satisficing; objective vs. subjective; agent-neutral vs. agent-relative; and rank-absolute vs. rank-relative. They also include the sub-classification externalist vs. internalist, an 'externalist' version of epistemic/ethical consequentialism being one whose ranking of consequences gives weight to properties which, typically, are extrinsic to acts and uncertain to agents.

II

The idea of a 'consequentialist' epistemology bearing some analogy to ethical consequentialism is not new, and it has several advocates. But to my knowledge no one has pursued the analogy to quite the lengths to which I have just pursued it. So the question arises as to whether my *specific* notion of 'epistemic consequentialism' is of any interest. I think it is. With a little effort, two influential approaches to epistemology—cognitive decision-theory and reliabilism—can be profitably subsumed under it. I will focus on cognitive decision-theory. I do so in part because cognitive decision-theory is the poor relation: it is less familiar than reliabilism, and Goldman himself is somewhat dismissive of it.[17] But I do so mostly because cognitive decision-theory's central concept—its own notion of 'consequence'—is fundamental to epistemic consequentialism. Standard characterisations of reliabilism mask this fact by masking their employment of this concept.

17. Goldman (1986).

II.i. *Cognitive Decision-Theory*. Cognitive decision-theory is a cognitive analogue of practical decision-theory. Versions of it have been developed for at least two kinds of cognitive act— 'acceptance', and, perhaps more surprisingly, 'credence' ('partial belief', or 'subjective probability'). For the moment, versions pertaining to acceptance suffice to illustrate the principles involved.

Bayesian decision-theory holds that, tacitly at least, a rational agent employs a utility-function defined over consequences of practical acts, and a credence-function defined over these consequences conditional upon performances of the acts, with respect to which his acts maximise expected utility. Similarly, Bayesian cognitive decision-theory holds that a rational cogniser employs a cognitive utility function defined over possible consequences of cognitive acts, and a credence function defined over these consequences conditional upon performances of the acts, with respect to which his cognitive acts maximise expected cognitive utility. Importantly, the 'shape' of an agent's cognitive utility-function reflects his cognitive values: it reflects what he values cognitively, just as, in the practical case, the 'shape' of his utility function reflects what he values practically.

That the 'consequences' in question are not *causal* consequences of cognitive acts is vitally important. An example will help bring out what they are. Let p be the proposition that a certain chasm in the Negev is 2 metres wide, and let $p \pm n$ be the proposition that this chasm is $2 \pm n$ cms metres wide. Let '$\{Xp; q\}$' be the 'consequence' of effecting the cognitive act Xp when q is true. For all I know, the consequence of Bp—my believing that p—might be any of:

$\{Bp; p\}$
$\{Bp; p+1\}, \{Bp; p+2\} \dots \{Bp; p+n\} \dots$
$\{Bp; p-1\}, \{Bp; p-2\} \dots \{Bp; p-n\} \dots$

These possible consequences of Bp do not depend causally upon it, and they depend upon it counterfactually only in the trivial sense that for all truths p and q, had p not been the case p&q would not have been either. Yet, in an obvious sense, they are possible consequences nevertheless. Were I to believe that p, the result, or 'outcome' of my believing it would include not only my belief that p and whatever states of affairs are counterfactually dependent upon this belief, but actual states of affairs which are counterfactually independent of it. To call possible outcomes in this sense 'consequences' does not preclude an analogy with ethical consequentialism. As in Jackson (1991) and Sosa (1993), it is increasingly common for ethical consequentialists to identify a 'consequence' of an act with an 'outcome' thus construed.

It is outcomes of cognitive acts which are the primary bearers of cognitive value. Cognitively speaking, it would be natural to suppose that $\{Bp; p+n\}$ has the same value as $\{Bp; p-n\}$, but that for all $m < n$, $\{Bp; p+m\}$ has higher value than does $\{Bp; p+n\}$.[18] However, there is as yet no *requirement* to value outcomes in this way, and all manner of alternatives are possible. Someone else might insist that there are just two possible consequences which differ in their cognitive value, namely $\{Bp; p\}$ and $\{Bp; not-p\}$. An attitude to error of this kind would be a sort of cognitive perfectionism, in that it holds that from a purely cognitive point of view, if a belief is in error, it does not matter by how much it is in error—a miss is as good as a mile. Any dispute of this kind will be reflected in the 'shape' of the various cognitive utility functions employed. Formally, of course, the possibilities are legion: a cognitive utility function may take myriad shapes.

What then does Bayesian decision-theory have to say about the epistemic evaluation of cognitive acts? Primarily, it imposes a necessary condition which must be met if a cognitive act—in the specific case under consideration, an act of acceptance—is to be 'rational'. In Maher's version of the theory,[19] the condition imposed is this:

> S's cognitive act of accepting K as corpus is rational only if it maximises S's (subjective) expected cognitive utility (in comparison with optional alternative acts of acceptance).

'Accepting K *as corpus*' is a matter of accepting K *and nothing else*. In practice, accepting K as corpus is a matter of modifying the existing corpus by adding some proposition p (which may be as 'big' as a scientific theory) and/or deleting some proposition

---

18. *Non-cognitive* evaluations of these outcomes will give them radically different utilities. While $\{Bp; p+50\}$ includes nearby possible worlds in which I leap and fall to my death, the companions to these worlds included in $\{Bp; p-50\}$ are worlds in which leaping across the chasm is easier than I feared.

19. Maher (1993).

q.[20] The agent's expected cognitive utility of the act of accepting K as corpus is defined in the standard way as the sum of the products comprising, for each (subjectively) possible outcome O of accepting K (such as {AK; K}, and {AK; not-K}), the agent's credence c(O|AK) in O conditional on performing the act AK, and his cognitive utility u(O) for O. (What outcomes have to be considered depends on what the agent values cognitively. If he deems the difference between the outcomes O and O* irrelevant to cognitive evaluation, only the outcome OvO* need be considered.)

Is Bayesian cognitive decision-theory a species of epistemic consequentialism? Having classified reliabilism as a 'consequentialist' theory, Goldman[21] is somewhat reluctant to classify cognitive decision-theory similarly. He says that 'If [cognitive decision-theory] is a consequentialist view at all, it should be classed as a different variety: a 'subjective' consequentialism.' But while this remark reflects the fact that cognitive decision-theory appeals to something else besides (the cognitive value of) outcomes and consequences—namely, the agent's *credences* in outcomes (conditional on acts)—from my point of view this feature is immaterial. For Jackson's 'subjective' ethical consequentialism makes such an appeal too,[22] and does so while making a claim to being 'classical'. On the other hand, classifying cognitive decision-theory as a species of epistemic consequentialism is problematic even so. For the way in which it ranks outcomes is disanalogous to the way in which classical ethical consequentialism ranks consequences. The latter connects the moral evaluation of an act with a single ranking of consequences according to their relative goodness, the origin of this ranking depending on meta-ethics: the ranking is provided either by the nature of 'good' itself (if the extension of 'good' is objective), or by the evaluator (if the extension of 'good' is subjective). The *agent's* opinions about good don't come into it. In contrast, Bayesian cognitive decision-theory connects the rationality of a cognitive act not just with the

20. If acceptance came in degrees, there would be more to accepting K as corpus than this. But Maher holds that acceptance does not come in degrees.

21. Goldman (1986: 102).

22. Jackson (1991).

agent's credences about outcomes, but with *the agent's own cognitive valuations.* This is why the evaluation is (typically) described as being couched in terms of (the agent's) cognitive 'utility', rather than cognitive 'value'.

Since epistemic consequentialism is defined as a doctrine which connects the epistemic normativity of cognitive acts with the cognitive 'value' of consequences, Bayesian cognitive decision-theory can only be a species of epistemic consequentialism if its talk of 'cognitive utility' amounts to talk of 'cognitive value'. The only way for it to do so would be for cognitive utility to *be* cognitive value. This a tall order. An identity between cognitive utility and cognitive value would have to be approached in two stages. At the first stage, cognitive value must be held to be relative, not absolute, and relative not just to agents, but to times. That it must be held relative to agents is obvious: different agents are allowed to have—and are typically given—different cognitive utility functions. But it must be held relative to times too because Bayesian cognitive decision-theory does not require an agent's cognitive utility function to take account of the causal consequences of cognitive acts *for his own subsequent cognitive acts.* Suppose that a causal consequence of my act AKT of accepting theory T into my existing corpus K is that in three year's time I accept another theory T* into my then corpus K*. Bayesian cognitive decision-theory does not require my current cognitive utility function to discriminate between the consequences {AKT; not-T & T* & 3 years later (AK*T*)}, and {AKT; not-T & not-T* & 3 years (AK*T*)}. However, in three years time my cognitive utility function will certainly discriminate between {AK*T*; not-T & T* & 3 years earlier (AKT)}, and {(AK*T*; not-T & not-T* & 3 years earlier (AKT)}. Accordingly, if talk of cognitive utility is to amount to talk of cognitive value, cognitive value must first be expressed by a triadic predicate relating outcome, agent, and time. It must then be held to be entirely subjective, in that the cognitive value relating outcome, agent, and time is identical to the cognitive utility for the agent of that outcome at that time.

Of itself, for Bayesian cognitive decision-theory to identify cognitive utilities with agent- and moment-relative cognitive value no more precludes an analogy with ethical consequentialism than does its essential employment of subjective probabilities: just as some ethical consequentialisms employ subjective probabilities, so too do others relativise good to agents,[23] and even times. However, the 'subjectivisation' of cognitive value which results from equating $cv\langle O, S, t\rangle$ with S's cognitive valuation of O at t (as reflected in his cognitive utility function at t) does not have an ethical analogue represented in the literature. This wouldn't be too damaging if a similar subjectivisation of 'good' were merely unattractive. But subjectivising in this way a notion of good that is already relativised to agents and times might be incoherent. If so, the proposed categorisation of Bayesian cognitive decision-theory as a species of epistemic consequentialism would face a dilemma: either equating $cv\langle O,S,t\rangle$ with S's cognitive valuation of O at t is incoherent too—in which case the classification fails, or else it is not—in which case the classification succeeds, but the doctrine classified has no ethical analogue.

In the final analysis, the classification of Bayesian cognitive decision-theory as an epistemic analogue of ethical consequentialism might not be possible. Suppose that it is impossible. In that case the culprit is not the relativisation of cognitive value to agent or times (or both), but the proposed subjectivisation of cognitive value. The solution is obvious. We have only to modify Bayesian cognitive decision-theory, first by postulating that S's cognitively valuing O at t to degree r does not guarantee that $cv\langle O, S, t\rangle = r$, and then by concerning ourselves not with the expected cognitive utility of an act, calculated in terms of the agent's own cognitive valuation of the act's possible outcomes, but with the expected cognitive *value* of the act, calculated in terms of the cognitive value of the outcomes (relative to agent and time).[25] A non-Bayesian rule of maximising expected cognitive value might then be formulated, either as a competitor to the claim that it is a condition of an act of acceptance being 'rational' that it maximise expected cognitive utility, or else as an account of a related, but (perhaps) more objective notion of 'rationality$_O$' of acts of acceptance. Invoking a non-Bayesian cognitive decision-theory in this way so as to classify (a species

23. Sen (1982).

24. Broome (1991).

25. A theory of this kind would be the explicit analogue of Jackson's (1991) 'subjective' direct ethical consequentialism. The calculation of expected cognitive value would remain based on the agent's (subjective) probabilities.

of) cognitive decision-theory as a species of epistemic consequentialism is not *ad hoc*. The cognitive value cv⟨O, S, t⟩ might well have an objective source.[26] If so, a competitor to Bayesian cognitive decision-theory which appeals to objective cognitive values distinct from the agent's own cognitive utilities enjoys the same status as does a competitor to Bayesian practical decision-theory which appeals to (objective) probabilities and utilities distinct from the agent's (subjective) probabilities and utilities.[27]

If 'cognitive value' has a degree of objectivity which prises apart talk of the cognitive value of an outcome, for an agent, at a time, from talk of the agent's cognitive utilities at that time, representing an agent's cognitive valuings by a utility function, rather than a credence (or acceptance!) function, is problematic. Yet the employment of a cognitive utility function might well be forced upon us. Just as representation theorems take an agent's preferences between practical acts into a unique pair comprising credence- and utility-functions, so do representation theorems take an agent's preferences between cognitive acts of acceptance into a unique pair comprising credence- and cognitive utility-functions.[28] The notion that an agent's cognitive valuings are reflected in his cognitive *utilities* is therefore not so easily dispensed with. It may be, therefore, that objective 'cognitive value' should be conceptualised not as something in virtue of which a credence regarding cognitive value might be true, but as an objectively right cognitive utility.[29]

At the very least, the relationship between the notion of 'cognitive utility' employed in Bayesian cognitive decision-theory, and epistemic consequentialism's central notion of the ranking of outcomes according to their 'cognitive value', is a delicate matter. I am afraid I gloss over it in what follows. I will try to use the expression 'cognitive value' in a manner which is neutral as to how cognitive value and cognitive utility are related.

26. See Section IV. If cognitive value is not objective, it might still diverge from the evaluat*ed* agent's cognitive utilities by reflecting the evaluat*ing* agent's cognitive utilities. The result would be an analogue of Smart's (1973) version of direct ethical consequentialism.

27. Cf. Mellor (1983).

28. See Maher (1993: ch.8). Like their practical forbears, such theorems presuppose controversial constraints on rational preferences, such as transitivity etc.

29. Cf. Mellor's (1983) comments on 'objective' utilities and probabilities in the case of practical decision-making.

II.ii. *Reliabilism.* Although it is commonly recognised that reliabilism is a 'consequentialist' epistemology, I need to dwell on the
question as to whether it is consequentialist in my sense. Viewing
it as such requires the presentation of reliabilist theories at a
greater level of generality than is customary.

A crude version of a 'process' reliabilist theory of 'epistemic
justifiedness' amounts to:

> (CRJ) A belief held at t is epistemically justified iff the pro-
> cess by which it is acquired or retained at t is reliable.

But superficially at least, the official version of process reliabilism is more sophisticated. It results from specifying a 'framework' principle that Goldman (1986: 63) characterises thus:

> (FP3) S's believing p at t is justified iff
>
> > (a) S's believing p at t is permitted by a right system
> > of J-rules, and
> > (b) this permission is not undermined by S's cogni-
> > tive state at t.

While this principle is neutral as to how the notion of a 'right'
system of J-rules is to be analysed, process reliabilism fleshes it
out in a consequentialist manner. Goldman[30] holds that:

> (ARI) A J-rule system is right iff R permits certain (basic)
> psychological processes, and the instantiation of
> these processes would [be reliable].

In subsequent writings, however, Goldman has favoured an
alternative, 'virtue', reliabilism. Goldman sums up this theory by
saying that it

> depicts justificational evaluation as involving two stages. The first
> stage features the acquisition by an evaluator of some set of intel-
> lectual virtues and vices. This is where reliability enters the picture.
> In the second stage, the evaluator applies his list of virtues and
> vices to decide the epistemic status of targeted beliefs.[31]

Here, sophisticated process reliabilism's emphasis on the
reliability of rules of belief-acquisition is replaced by an emphasis

---

30. Goldman (1986: 106).
31. Goldman (1991: 10).

on the reliability of intellectual faculties. This theory is a *consequentialist* 'virtue epistemology' of a kind favoured by several recent authors. A neat statement of a theory of this form is provided by Dancy's gloss[32] on Sosa's 'virtue perspectivalism':

A belief is [epistemically] justified if[f] it is the product of a reliable faculty.

Reliabilist theories of this ilk are united by the use they make of the notion of something's—a process, (instantiated) rule, or intellectual faculty—being 'reliable', and they are deemed 'consequentialist' in the literature because that thing's reliability turns on features of its causal consequences. However, although sophisticated process reliabilism and virtue reliabilism are often spoken of as analogues, respectively, of ethical rule and virtue consequentialism, they are not explicit analogues of these theories, nor, hence, explicit versions of epistemic consequentialism in my sense. For they make no mention of the 'cognitive value' of consequences.

Still, a little reconstruction puts these theories in proper perspective vis-a-vis epistemic consequentialism in general, and cognitive decision-theory in particular. A process/rule/faculty is said to be 'reliable' when the beliefs included in its causal consequence exhibit a high ratio of what Goldman calls 'verific value', i.e. true belief. Accordingly, if a reliabilist theory of epistemic justification is to amount to epistemic consequentialism in my sense, Goldman's gloss on reliability must be elucidated as follows (or in some such way):

(a) A process/rule/faculty is 'reliable' iff its causal consequence has sufficiently high cognitive value.

(b) The causal consequence of a process/rule/faculty is the set of the causal consequences $\{C_i\}$ of those of its tokens that are relevant.

(c) The cognitive value of a set of causal consequences $\{C_i\}$ is a function of the cognitive values of the C_i.

(d) The causal consequences C_i of token processes/rules/faculties have cognitive values which are a function of the cognitive values of the *outcomes* of the beliefs $\{B_j\}$ in C_i.

32. Dancy (1995: 77).

(e) The cognitive value of the *outcomes* of the beliefs $\{B_j\}$ is a function of the number of these beliefs, and of the ratio of those that are true to those that are false.

Viewed at this level of generality, reliabilist theories hold that whether or not the cognitive act of believing that p is epistemically justified depends on the cognitive values of the outcomes of the further beliefs which are causal consequences of relevant tokens of the processes/rules/faculties from which the belief stemmed, the cognitive value of the outcome of a belief being somewhat crudely identified in terms of truth and falsity. Thus viewed, these theories belong to a species of epistemic consequentialism which contrasts with cognitive decision-theory in the following respects: it is ranking-absolute; objective (in the sense of being independent of the agent's credences about outcomes/consequences); satisficing; and, in its ranking of consequences at least, agent-neutral.

The 'indirectness' of the species of epistemic consequentialism to which reliabilist theories belong is also a point of contrast, in that cognitive decision theory connects the evaluation of a cognitive act with the evaluation of the possible consequences not of any processes, rules, or faculties, but of the optional cognitive acts themselves. However, this contrast is in some ways artificial, in that it collapses from the perspective of the most plausible variant of epistemic consequentialism—namely, a variant which is both 'externalist', in that its ranking of consequences is sensitive to properties which are typically uncertain to agents, and 'reductive' in that it holds that the evaluation of consequences according to their cognitive value *grounds* epistemic evaluations of cognitive acts.[33] Consider what an externalist epistemic consequentialist might deem to be the ground of the requirement that *expected* cognitive value be maximised. He cannot deem it to be

---

33. Similarly, a species of ethical consequentialism holds that moral act-evaluations are grounded in the evaluation of consequences according to their goodness. This much is evident in an 'analytical' variant of the doctrine according to which e.g. 'morally wrong' *means* 'would have an outcome ranked lower in terms of goodness than is the outcome of some optional alternative'. However, the grounding thesis need not take this analytical form. Even if moral act-evaluations cannot be analysed in terms of evaluations of consequences for their goodness, it may be that the normativity of moral act-evaluations derives ultimately from the evaluation of consequences for their goodness. *Mutatis mutandis*, the same holds in the epistemic case. Skorupski (1995: 52) *defines* 'ethical consequentialism' as the view that moral evaluations of acts are grounded in the evaluation of consequences.

the fact that expected cognitive value is *itself* a cognitive value. Having introduced certain cognitive values, it would be absurd for him to maintain that uncertainty generates a higher-level cognitive value—expected cognitive value—which enhances, or even overrides, the cognitive values in terms of which expected cognitive value is defined.[34] That would be double-counting. But no other direct grounding may be available: his externalism ensures that the cognitive act which maximises expected cognitive value may have an outcome lacking cognitive value. Accordingly, reductive externalist epistemic consequentialism gives the cognitive decision theorist little option. He must take his requirement that expected cognitive value be maximised to be grounded in cognitive value indirectly—say, in the fact that the practice constituted by internalising this requirement better promotes cognitive value than would any other. *His* epistemic consequentialism is therefore no less indirect than is that of reliabilism.

II.iii. *The Relation Between Cognitive Decision-Theory and Reliabilism.* Goldman[35] dismisses the suggestion that a cognitive decision-theoretic analysis might be given of epistemic justification. His so doing does not stem from a concern to distinguish belief from acceptance: even if those who maintain that the concept of acceptance is (at least a part of) the folk concept of belief are wrong, the cognitive decision-theoretic requirement on rational acceptance is easily transferred to belief. Rather, Goldman's first objection is that no such requirement could state sufficient conditions for a belief's epistemic justifiedness: although a lunatic's credences might be such that the corpus K belief in which maximises his expected cognitive value includes the proposition that he is eighteen metres tall, his belief in this proposition would not be epistemically justified, since there is too much wrong with the credences from which that expected cognitive value derives. Clearly, maximising expected cognitive value can

---

34. Compare Jackson's (1991: 471) remark, concerning the ethical analogue of non-Bayesian cognitive decision theory that he defends, that 'The [ethical] consequentialist value function *assigns no value as such to maximising expected utility* [i.e. good] ... [Action A] is the right thing to do because [expected good] takes a maximum value [among the alternatives] ... But this fact that it takes a maximum value does not then confer *additional* value on [action A].'

35. Goldman (1986: 101–3).

only yield epistemically justified beliefs if independent constraints are placed on the credences in terms of which the expected cognitive value of a belief is calculated. But in that case, as Goldman observes, 'A new theory is required, which may have little or nothing in common with the initial, [cognitive] decision motif ... At a minimum, this supplement would destroy any semblance of a *unified* approach to doxastic justifiedness.'

Of course, even if maximisation of expected cognitive value is insufficient for epistemic justification, it might still be necessary. But Goldman has an independent argument against this possibility. Putting his argument somewhat differently, part of the point of cognitive decision-theory is that the K belief in which would maximise expected cognitive value need not be given high credence by the agent: the agent's low credence in it might be compensated for by the greater cognitive value believing K would have in comparison to believing other K*'s to which the agent gives equal or higher credence. In particular, cognitive decision-theorists often suppose that the cognitive value of the outcome of accepting truths depends on how informative those truths are. Goldman objects that this feature is in tension with epistemic justification: a belief's claim to be epistemically justified is not enhanced by the logical strength of its content.

On this score, I am inclined to agree with Goldman: if cognitive values include both truth and informativeness, maximisation of *expected* cognitive value is neither necessary nor sufficient for epistemic justification. Equally, however, as Goldman observes, this is not to say that it isn't 'appropriate for other epistemic terms of appraisal', and I think there are good grounds for thinking that it is appropriate to *scientific* norms pertaining to the acceptance of scientific theories: scientific practice suggests both that acceptance of a scientific theory does not require credence that the theory is more likely true than false, and that logical strength enhances the acceptability of a scientific theory.[36] To

36. Saying this much is neutral as to whether, as the scientific realist supposes and the constructive empiricist denies, truth beyond empirical adequacy is cognitively valuable. Nor is it to endorse Maher's (1993) theory. Maher (1993: ch. 6) defines 'acceptance of p' as the 'state expressed by sincere, intentional assertion that p'. However, coupling this definition with the cognitive decision-theoretic account of rational acceptance is untenable. It conflicts with Williamson's (1996) 'knowledge-account' of assertion on which assertion is that speech-act governed by the one constitutive rule: assert that p, only if one knows that p. (Although it is intuitive enough, some work is needed to establish this conflict. For want of space I have had to omit the argument I gave for it in the draft on which Stalnaker bases his reply.)

this extent cognitive decision-theory is bound to have a role to play in cognition broadly conceived, and in the implementation of Goldman's theory of epistemic justification in particular (if only as a 'criterion' in Goldman's sense). Imagine a (sophisticated) process reliabilist G wondering whether or not an agent S's cognitive act of believing that p is epistemically justified (S might be G himself). To establish this he has first to identify the process P which gave rise to S's belief that p. He has then to establish whether P is permitted by the right system of J-rules. Suppose his inter-disciplinary investigations have narrowed down rival hypotheses regarding human cognition to just two, T_1 and T_2, and that T_1 holds that the right system of J-rules is R_1, which permits P, whereas T_2 holds that the right system of J-rules is R_2, which forbids P. Although both theories accord with the empirical evidence pretty well, T_2 is much richer than T_1. It postulates all manner of sophisticated hidden mechanisms, and has a much broader scope, with various ramifications for non-human cognition. Because of its overwhelming logical strength in comparison to T_1, T_2 is much less likely to be true, and it is given less credence by G. In this scenario, qua scientist at least, G judges S's belief that p to be epistemically justified iff he accepts that R_1 is the right system of J-rules. And he accepts as much iff he accepts T_1 instead of T_2. Should he accept T_1? Although he gives more credence to it than to T_2, the question is not trivial. It invokes deep issues concerning the nature of science. I agree with Maher (1993) that if G has embraced the cognitive values *science* requires, G should value informativeness. That is, so to speak, to the extent that science cognitively values truth, it values it not as a quality, but as a *quantity*. By these lights, an injunction to maximise expected cognitive value enjoins G to accept T_2 rather than T_1: so doing (we can suppose) has higher expected cognitive value. G should therefore *accept* that S's belief that p is not epistemically justified, even though he (G) gives higher credence to its being epistemically justified.

Let me put the point another way, and more generally. There is such a thing as theoretical 'deliberation'. Whatever the merits of an externalist approach to epistemic justification, theoretical deliberation is largely a matter of reflecting on and weighing (what is taken to be) available evidence, and any other cognitively relevant matters. The viewpoint of epistemic consequentialism—and hence of Goldman's version of it—accords 'cognitive value' a role and significance which turns this into the pursuit of value under uncertainty (under plausible conceptions of cognitive value, and at least when one is thinking 'directly'):[37] the cognitive values of one's cognitive options' possible outcomes must be weighed against one's uncertainty regarding them. At least if cognitive voluntarism is true, the advent of decision-theoretic considerations is then inevitable: for *the agent* is left pursuing some quantity—cognitive value—under uncertainty. The situation is a little different if cognitive voluntarism is incorrect. But decision-theoretic considerations might still be expected to play a role.[38]

II.iv. *The Status of Cognitive Decision-Theory.* It follows that any threat to the application of decision-theoretic considerations to cognitive acts is a potential threat not just to cognitive decision-theory, but to epistemic consequentialism itself. Such threats exist. In particular, a 'regress' objection has recently achieved prominence. Let 'value' be neutral between 'cognitive' and 'non-cognitive value',[39] and suppose one should believe that p only if the subjective expected value of so doing meets certain conditions, and that one is considering whether or not to believe that p. Hoping to do as one should, one calculates the subjective expected value of believing that p. But having done as much one then wonders whether one should believe the result. Hoping to do as one should,

---

37. Were cognitive value construed in such a way that the evaluation of outcomes depends solely on such 'internal' characteristics of cognitive acts as e.g. simplicity, explanatory power, logical strength, consistency etc., the relevant outcomes would not be uncertain. But although e.g. Ellis (1988) seems to want to focus on such characteristics, most cognitive decision theorists have a more 'externalist' conception of cognitive value. One would pursue cognitive value 'indirectly' if one's cognitive deliberations were guided entirely by rules having an indirect consequentialist analysis. (This possibility invokes the 'two-levels' model of moral thinking, i.e. the level of moral thought depending on whether good is being pursued directly or not.)

38. The falsity of cognitive voluntarism would change the situation because the pursuit of cognitive value need not then be by the agent, but by something else—cognitive acts themselves, say. Although an agent pursuing a quantitative value under uncertainty is bound to employ decision-theory, no ground exists for saying that a cognitive act 'pursuing' a cognitive value *must* be subject to decision-theoretic norms—even if the supposition that it will in fact be subject to them is natural.

39. Non-cognitive value is any value other than cognitive value. Clearly, the outcomes—and more narrowly the causal consequences—of cognitive acts have all manner of non-cognitive value. For example, acquiring a belief can make one happy while offending someone else, or get one dinner etc.

one performs another calculation, this time of the subjective expected value of believing the result of the first calculation. But one wonders once more whether one should believe this second result. And so on. Zemach[40] claims that this regress is vicious in the case of non-cognitive value. He says it shows that 'If assessing beliefs for [subjective expected non-cognitive value] is a condition for their rational adoption no belief can be adopted rationally', and he concludes that 'No believing requires practical evaluation; the [subjective expected non-cognitive value of believing that p] is irrelevant to p's beliefworthiness.' By contrast, although Weintraub[41] disputes Zemach's conclusions in the case of non-cognitive value, she deems the regress vicious in the case of cognitive value: she takes it to show that 'The attempt to emulate practical deliberation in the cognitive realm [i.e. via cognitive value] is misguided.'

This sort of problem is long familiar from the ethical case. But so too is its solution. Weintraub and Zemach are wrong to maintain (respectively) that supposing (the outcomes of) beliefs to have cognitive or non-cognitive values best pursued decision-theoretically involves a vicious infinite regress. Only an untenable internalism gets the regress started. The supposition that there is a norm enjoining beliefs which maximise subjective expected value no more obliges agents to calculate the subjective expected value of having a belief prior to having it, or condemns as unjustified or irrational the beliefs of any agent who does not do this, than the view that belief should be in accordance with the evidence requires a rational or justified believer to believe, prior to believing in accordance with the evidence, that believing would accord with the evidence.[42]

40. Zemach (1997: 526–7).

41. Weintraub (2001: 65).

42. Owens (2000: 29) makes a similar point (though not against Zemach). In fact, even if an internalist conception of 'justification' is adopted whereby S 'is justified in believing that p only if S has a good reason q that justifies believing that p,' Zemach's claim that the inevitable regress of reasons is vicious in the case of norms relating to non-cognitive value is undermined by an objection *ad hominem*. Given such norms, all X needs to justify his belief that p is a hierarchy of beliefs: Bp has best consequences; B(Bp has best consequences) has best consequences; B(B(Bp has best consequences) has best consequences) has best consequences ... Observing that 'to have a belief one need not constantly ponder it, just be ready to avow it and act on it when appropriate,' Zemach himself allows that an agent's beliefs can be nested in this way.

Weintraub and Zemach's regress objection fails for another reason. An obvious way to halt the regress once it is started is to restrict the decision-theoretic normative requirement under consideration to a subset of beliefs. Zemach does consider exclud-

III

I remarked earlier that there are versions of Bayesian cognitive decision-theory which pertain to the cognitive value of the outcomes, not of 'acts' of acceptance, but of acts of credence. I also remarked that their existence is surprising. Certainly, if the outcomes of credences have cognitive value, and the cognitive value of the outcome of credence to degree r in p is sensitive to whether or not p (as one might expect), the relevant outcomes will be uncertain, and the pursuit of valuable outcomes appears to call for decision-theory. Yet an obvious difficulty arises. To apply Bayesian decision theory in pursuit of some value one must have the relevant credences (subjective probabilities). So it seems as if decision-theory can only apply in the case in which the prior existence of credences makes its application redundant. The situation is after all disanalogous to the paradigmatic case of action, and, for that matter, to the case of acceptance.

Yet, as it stands, this 'redundancy' objection begs the question. A norm enjoining an agent to maximise the expected cognitive value of his credences would not be redundant if some credences are 'modest' in that, calculated with respect to them, the expected cognitive value of other credences is higher than their own. The norm would then enjoin an agent to rid himself of modest credences, an injunction seemingly no less sensible than the injunction to eschew any 'modest' inductive method which says of itself

ing beliefs with a content of the form 'the expected [value] of the belief that p is such and such'. But he argues that in the non-cognitive case any such restriction would be improper because 'arbitrary'. And while Weintraub retorts that a restriction of this kind might properly be made in the non-cognitive case—on the grounds that, having imposed a decision-theoretic requirement on some beliefs, one wants beliefs about the expected non-cognitive value of those beliefs to be true—she maintains that a parallel restriction in the case of cognitive value would be improper. Yet in neither the non-cognitive nor the cognitive case need there be anything arbitrary or improper about the envisaged restriction. A 'reductive' consequentialist holds that the values of cognitive attitudes' outcomes are fundamental to any consequentialist norms which govern those attitudes: it is in virtue of these values that the norms hold. But we have seen reason to think that qua reductive theory at least, cognitive decision-theory is an *indirect* consequentialist theory: it only comes into play when one is uncertain about how to promote the value in question directly, and it can only aspire to promote it indirectly, e.g. in so far as a practice constituted by the norm of maximising subjective expected value better promotes this value than does any alternative practice. It follows that there is nothing arbitrary in the contention that a practice of maximising the subjective expected value of beliefs regarding a restricted range of propositions does best among genuine alternatives: whether this contention is true or not is an empirical matter. Indeed, the regress objection could be read as a partial explanation of why some restricted decision-theoretic practice does better in this regard than does the unrestricted one.

that in the long run it does worse than some alternative.[43] So the most the objection could be saying is that assigning cognitive values to the outcomes of credences and enjoining the maximisation of expected cognitive value is redundant if all credences say of themselves, 'immodestly', that their own expected cognitive value is no less than that of others. Yet even this claim is question-begging. While an injunction to maximise expected cognitive value could never enjoin an agent to exchange his credences for others if all credences are immodest, this needn't make the injunction redundant. For it might tell us to do something else. And according to Oddie, it does: it tells us to gather cost-free evidence.[44]

Call the norm enjoining us to gather cost-free evidence 'Evidence Gathering'. This norm has been problematic ever since Ayer objected that Carnap's inductive logic left it unintelligible. For Carnap, the inductive relation between a proposition and a hypothesis for which it is evidence is an analytic 'logical probability'. Suppose that I have total evidence E for a hypothesis H which interests me, with logical probability $p(H|E) = .6$, and that $p(H|E\&Q) = .9$ and $p(H|E\&\neg Q) = .2$, where Q is a proposition about which I have no information. In this situation it appears that I have reason to try to find out whether or not Q, and that I should find it out unless some punitive extraneous cost would be involved. Yet within Carnap's framework, finding out whether or not Q appears pointless. Being analytic, the conditional probabilities just mentioned are all tautologies. Apparently, then, e.g. credence .9 in H on the basis of evidence E&Q must have exactly the same status as, and can be no cognitive improvement on, the existing credence .6 in H on the basis of evidence E.

Oddie's grounding of Evidence Gathering builds upon a pragmatist answer to Ayer's worry given by Good (following Ramsey): if gathering evidence might result in a change in one's credences with respect to propositions such that one's choice between currently optional practical acts is sensitive to one's credence in those propositions, then, as calculated by one's current credences, the result of gathering evidence can be a raising, and can never be a lowering, in the maximising practical option's expected non-cognitive utility. The defect of Good's justification

43. Cf. Lewis (1971).
44. Oddie (1997).

is that it is ill-suited to the case of science: it only works with respect to propositions which influence our actions, whereas the interest of science, and hence the injunction to gather cost-free evidence, is not confined to propositions of this kind. In effect, Oddie extends the Ramsey-Good result to propositions having no practical bearing by assigning cognitive value directly to the outcomes of credences, thereby sidestepping the necessity for actions on which these credences bear. The Ramsey-Good technique is then employed to show that, as calculated by one's current credences, the expected cognitive value of one's credences after gathering evidence might be higher, and can never be lower, than the expected cognitive value of one's current credences. Oddie concludes that the lure of cognitive value, and hence of expected cognitive value, enjoins the gathering of cost-free evidence.

Oddie's result had been largely anticipated by Horwich,[45] and details of Horwich's treatment bear close scrutiny. Intuitively, if cognitive values are to be ascribed to the outcomes of credences, the cognitive value of the outcome of a credence $c(p) = r$ should depend both on the truth-value of p, and on the value r: the closer r is to 1 the better if p is true, the worse if p is false. How natural then to put:

$$cvH\{c(p) = r; p\} = r$$
$$cvH\{c(p) = r; \neg p\} = 1 - r$$

In effect, this is the measure of the cognitive value of a credence's outcome which Horwich employs, and with respect to it he anticipates Oddie's result: gathering evidence and updating one's credences (by conditionalising) can never reduce the expected cognitive value of one's credences, and will typically increase it. However, there is a crucial difference between Horwich's measure of cognitive value and Oddie's: with respect to Oddie's measure all credences are immodest; but with respect to Horwich's measure most credences are modest! Indeed, as Maher shows,[46] with respect to Horwich's measure the only immodest credences are the extremes $c(p) = 1$, $c(p) = 0$, or $c(p) = 1/2$. Accordingly, Horwich's use of the norm of maximising expected cognitive

45. Horwich (1982).
46. Maher (1993: 178–9).

value grounds not only Evidence Gathering but an injunction to switch whatever credence one has in p to one of these extremes. Maher takes this feature to be a reductio of Horwich's analysis.

One might have supposed that Oddie's advocacy of a measure of cognitive value with respect to which all credences are immodest—a so-called 'proper scoring rule'—takes the sting out of Maher's critique. But in fact Oddie proceeds without reference to Maher, and Maher had anticipated the possibility of a modified version of Horwich's strategy using proper scoring rules. Maher rejected[47] such a strategy on the grounds, in effect, that either it relies on a contingent fact that the cognitive utility functions of scientists are proper scoring rules, in which case it holds too much hostage to fortune, or else it stipulates arbitrarily that science measures the cognitive value of the outcomes of credences by means of a proper scoring rule. Moreover, to these complaints might be added a third: neither alternative engages with the view that switching one's credences to one of the three extreme values so as to maximise expected cognitive utility would be irrational (and not just unscientific) even if one's cognitive utility function happened to accord with Horwich's measure cvH.[48]

It is difficult to judge where such objections leave Oddie's proposal. Maher advocates[49] abandoning the idea that the outcomes of credences have cognitive value, and turning the Ramsey-Good technique upon the cognitive value of outcomes of acceptances: maximising the expected cognitive value of acceptances can then be shown to enjoin the gathering of cost-free evidence *whatever the measure of cognitive value*. However, his view that the outcomes of acceptances have cognitive value when the outcomes of credences do not is puzzling and certainly leaves some explaining to do.[50] Weintraub argues[51] that acceptances cannot have cognitive value, but that credences must have, and then argues against the decision-theoretic evaluation of credences to escape what she

---

47. Maher (1993: 179).

48. Cf. Weintraub (2001: 61).

49. Maher (1993).

50. This use of 'cognitive value' somewhat obscures Maher's views. He speaks exclusively of 'cognitive utility', of an agent's cognitive values, and of what cognitive values—and hence cognitive utility functions—science demands of scientists.

51. Weintraub (2001: 57–60).

takes to be the absurd consequences Maher derives from Horwich's measure of (the outcomes of) credences' cognitive value. But Weintraub's argument against cognitive decision-theory was seen to fail,[52] and in any case her stance leaves Evidence Gathering ungrounded. Moreover, Maher and Weintraub's criticisms of the strategy Oddie pursues run up against a twist in his development of it. Oddie does not see himself as arbitrarily selecting proper scoring rules from amongst possible measures of the cognitive value of the possible outcomes of credences. On the contrary, he regards his choice of them as forced by constraints established beforehand. Chief among these constraints is one he calls

> *Cogency*   Absent any new information, your current cognitive state is strongly self-recommending, in that it alone maximises expected cognitive value.

An independent grounding of Cogency would ground the presumption that cognitive value is measured by a proper scoring rule. Oddie offers two groundings: the principle of (only) updating credences by conditionalising on new evidence, and a weaker principle he calls

> *Conservatism*   Absent any new information you should not change your cognitive state.

As I said, Oddie writes independently of Maher and Weintraub. But even so, this manoeuvre does engage their objections to his strategy: he attempts to show why, if (the outcomes of) credences have cognitive value, their value must be measured by a proper scoring rule if they are not to flout independently motivated canons of rationality.[53] In itself this does not address Weintraub's worry that an agent who had cognitive utilities measured

---

52. See II.iv above.

53. Though his concerns are different and he writes independently, in effect Joyce (1998) takes this aspect of Oddie's strategy one step further. Joyce's concern is not Evidence Gathering, but 'probabilism's' more fundamental normative doctrine that 'partial' beliefs that are 'rational' conform to the axioms of the probability calculus (and hence are subjective probabilities, or credences). Complaining that the standard arguments for this doctrine are 'pragmatic', in that they rely on claims about the rational pursuit of non-cognitive utility, or rational preferences between non-cognitive options, Joyce attempts an alternative grounding which is based on purely cognitive considerations. He argues that (i) any reasonable measure of the 'accuracy' of a partial belief function (defined over propositions) must satisfy certain independently plausible constraints C, and (ii) for every partial belief function B which is not a subjective probability, there is a subjective probability function P which, by any measure meeting the constraint C, is more accurate than B whatever the truth values of the propositions over which B, and hence P, are defined. Joyce cannot say which

not by a proper scoring rule but e.g. by Horwich's measure would still be 'irrational' if he switched to immodest credences so as to maximise expected cognitive utility. But the answer to this worry applies to any case of this kind: if you are already in an irrational state, conforming to one norm of rationality—in this case the injunction to maximise expected cognitive value—can involve flouting others.

The dispute between Maher, Oddie, and Weintraub will strike many epistemologists as esoteric. But if my classification of cognitive decision-theory is right, their dispute goes to the heart of epistemic consequentialism. Whereas Maher holds that the outcomes of acceptances have cognitive value, but that the outcomes of credences cannot have them, Oddie holds that the outcomes of credences have cognitive value (without mentioning acceptances), and Weintraub at least maintains that acceptances cannot have them. Since epistemic consequentialism presupposes that the outcomes of cognitive acts have cognitive value, it must resolve this dispute. It cannot hope to do so without reflection on what makes a value 'cognitive'.[54]

IV

Since 'cognitive value' is the fundamental concept of epistemic consequentialism, to have said next to nothing about it, as I have, is a serious omission. The omission does not concern the semantic or metaphysical status, form, or extension of this concept: as I have explained, epistemic consequentialism is no less neutral on

functions meet the condition C, though at least one proper scoring rule does so. The result most congenial to Oddie would of course be that all and only proper scoring rules meet the conditions C.

On the other hand, Joyce (1998: 591–2) contends that his measures of the 'accuracy' of a partial belief function are not measures of 'cognitive utility/value' on the grounds that a concern that one's partial beliefs be accurate is but one part of cognitive value, the result being that a cognitive utility function will not meet all the constraints on a reasonable measure of accuracy. This contention seems self-destructive: it threatens to undermine his strategy entirely. For if cognitive utility needn't satisfy the constraints C, for all Joyce has to say it might be maximised by switching credences to partial beliefs which violate the probability axioms. The pressure the concern for the particular cognitive value of accuracy puts on non-probabilistic partial beliefs would be overridden by concerns for other elements of cognitive value in general.

54. It must also reflect on the nature and point of cognition, and in particular of credence. So doing would lead to a consideration of pragmatism, and of 'pure enquiry' in Williams's (1978) sense.

these matters than is ethical consequentialism regarding similar concerns about 'good'. The problem is the *identity* of the concept. Ethical consequentialism can work with a primitive concept of 'good' because this concept exists prior to the theory. In contrast, the concept of cognitive value is not given prior to epistemic consequentialism's employment of it. A grasp of it cannot be presupposed, therefore, and some elucidation is obligatory.

The outcomes of a cognitive attitude can be evaluated in many respects: someone might evaluate the outcomes of his cognitive attitudes according to the extent to which he feels happy. What then makes an evaluation *cognitive*? When the epistemic consequentialist ranks consequences, he is not exercising or expressing some value, and then calling this value, arbitrarily, 'cognitive'. Nor is his justification for insisting that he is ranking consequences according to their 'cognitive' value the mere fact that the position of a consequence in the ranking turns on certain features of certain cognitions occurring within it: *which* features of these cognitions the ranking turns on is crucial. Rather, the epistemic consequentialist's ranking of consequences according to their cognitive value is a measure of the degree to which the cognitions in question succeed in achieving their aim. The concept of cognitive value is the concept of that (sort of outcome) for which cognition aims. The theoretical nature of this concept does not make it more suspect than is the ethical consequentialist's construal of the concept 'good'. On the contrary, in one respect the epistemic consequentialist is probably on firmer ground than his ethical counterpart. For the idea that cognition has an *objective* aim is more plausible than is the idea that action as such does so.

Still, the idea that the cognitive value of some outcome is a measure of the extent to which the relevant aim of the relevant cognitions is achieved has to face the fact that a cognitive act can have many aims. For one thing, various aims might be imposed by the agent and his projects. Bill might aim for his cognitions to concur with those of Hilary. More respectably, he might aim for his cognitions to conform to the aim of some recognisably *cognitive* project. As van Fraassen says,[55] 'It is part of the straightforward description of any activity, communal or

55. van Fraassen (1989: 189).

individual, large-scale or small, to describe the end that is pursued as one of its defining conditions.' To engage in an activity
of a certain kind is to take on board its defining aims. To pursue
a cognitive activity, then, such as science, is to take on board the
aims which define it. Although the aim of science is controversial,
might not the epistemic consequentialist reasonably hope that a
resolution of the controversy will give him the aim (of cognitive
acts) he seeks, and hence the measure of cognitive value?

I do not think so. There is no prospect of identifying a unique
aim of cognitive acts by this route. Whatever the cognitive aims
constitutive of 'science', distinct aims will be constitutive of
activities closely related to science. In order of decreasing
ambitiousness, 'schmience' aims constitutively at theoretical
beliefs that are true, 'schmience*' at theoretical beliefs that are
empirically adequate, and 'schmience**' at theoretical beliefs
that are empirically adequate with respect to phenomena within
a billion light years of us. Whichever of these activities science is
to be identified with—and all three alternatives have advocates—
pursuit of schmiences that are non-science is a recognisably 'cognitive' activity.[56]

Since epistemic consequentialism is not committed to the
objectivity of epistemic norms, it might think at this point to
abandon the search for a unique aim of cognitive acts, and hence
for a unique and objective measure of cognitive value. Yet giving
up meta-epistemological neutrality would be unsatisfactory. Epistemic consequentialism should try to preserve its *prima facie*
neutrality in this respect by offering the prospect at least of a
unique and objective aim for cognitive acts. In this regard, its
hope must be, I think, that a unique and objective aim of cognitive acts is given by their nature qua cognitive acts.[57] This hope
might be misguided, but there is enough going for it for the requi-
site neutrality to be recovered.

On the other hand, *reductive* epistemic consequentialism must
hope for more than this. Since it claims that a connection with

56. Compare van Fraassen's constructive empiricist (1980), who argues, in effect,
that while science is schmience*, many scientists do it by doing schmience, and Maher
(1993: 243), who argues, in effect, that while science is schmience**, many scientists
do it by doing either schmience or schmience*.

57. The idea that a cognitive act has a 'nature' might be grounded in various ways.
An attractive naturalistic grounding is given by the idea that cognitions have certain
biological functions.

the cognitive values of consequences *grounds* the epistemic concepts by which cognitive acts are evaluated, the mere fact that cognition has an aim is not enough for its purposes: (the concept of) this aim must also be prior to the epistemic norms it aspires to ground.

To see that this requirement is not trivial, consider a brand of reductive epistemic consequentialism which holds that truth is the only (positive) cognitive value (with falsehood being the only negative one). This doctrine bases cognitive value in truth in just the way that utilitarians of a certain stripe base goodness in pleasure. It thereby presupposes the falsity of epistemic theories of truth! If epistemic norms are to be grounded in cognitive value, and the basis of cognitive value is truth, then these norms cannot be conceptually prior to truth. But epistemic theories of truth hold that e.g. the concept of 'true' belief just is the concept of ideally epistemically justified belief, or whatever. Still, reductive epistemic consequentialism should not be unduly troubled by this consideration. Truth transcends possible knowledge, and this goes some way towards deflating (anti-realist) arguments in favour of epistemic theories of truth.[58] So one plausible basis of cognitive value can reasonably be thought to meet the conceptual priority requirement.

Still, supposing the basis of cognitive value to be conceptually prior to the epistemic norms cognitive value is to ground falls short of supposing cognitive value itself to be conceptually prior to them. Indeed, the epistemic consequentialist who responds to the challenge that cognitive value is not conceptually prior to the epistemic norms it aspires to ground by focusing on the basis of cognitive value misses the point. When in the ethical case Foot complains[59] that ethical consequentialism errs in its presupposition that the concept of 'good' applicable to outcomes is prior to the concept of right action, it would be quite misguided for e.g. the utilitarian to insist in response that the concept of pleasure is conceptually prior to the concept of right action, and that pleasure is goodness. Indeed, he would be misguided even if, in naturalistic vein, he meant that goodness is literally identical to

---

58. Cf. Percival (1990, 1991). The variant of epistemic consequentialism thus protected contrasts with the variant advocated in Ellis (1988). Indeed, Ellis (1988: 142) defines true belief 'to be that which would maximise epistemic [i.e. cognitive] value if the matter were inquired into with perfect thoroughness by an ideally rational being'.
59. Foot (1985).

pleasure. Since Foot's point operates at the level of concepts, no reflection on the extension of goodness is relevant. She denies that the *concept* of goodness is prior to that of right action, and she might be right in this even if there is a term 'X' which expresses a concept meeting the priority requirement, and goodness is identical to X. Accordingly, the epistemic analogue of Foot's objection can freely admit that plausible bases of cognitive value are conceptually prior to epistemic norms. It objects that however things might be with the basis of the concept of 'cognitive value', the concept itself is not prior to the norms epistemic consequentialism aspires to ground.

Dancy challenges 'any introduction of consequentialism into epistemology' to answer the epistemic analogue of Foot's objection to ethical consequentialism, although he 'admit[s] that it is just not clear to me who is in the right ... at the end of the day'.[60] But I think enough has been said already to meet this challenge. The concept of the cognitive value of the outcome of a cognitive act arises from the supposition that the act has an aim. But the concept of an outcomes' amounting to this aim being achieved, or being better achieved than it would be in certain other outcomes, or being achieved to such and such degree—the concept, I have suggested, of cognitive value—does not presuppose the concepts—of epistemic justifiedness, evidential warrant, rationality etc.—that epistemic consequentialism concerns, and which its reductive variant aspires to ground.

V

In Section II.ii I argued that reliabilism can be viewed as a species of 'indirect' epistemic consequentialism, and that cognitive decision-theory can be viewed as such too. Potentially, this is a very strong result. In ethics, even indirect consequentialists acknowledge the attractions of an optimising direct consequentialism: indeed, the thought that indirect ethical consequentialist norms are but useful fictions the internalisation of which serves

---

60. Dancy (1995: 83). Dancy articulates the objection in the course of a critique of Sosa's 'virtue perspectivalism' (which he rightly classifies as a ('virtue') consequentialist theory. This might explain why he articulates the analogue of Foot's objection to ethical consequentialism somewhat differently from the way in which I have articulated it.

to promote good better than would any alternative, is a common-place. I hope that the mere *concept* of epistemic consequentialism serves to suggest that this thought might profitably be directed at reliabilist and cognitive decision-theoretic norms too. More generally, I think epistemic consequentialism faces the following dilemma:

The dilemma of epistemic consequentialism

First Horn—The cognitive act evaluative concepts ('X') in question—epistemically justified, rational, evidentially war-ranted etc.—are subject to a *direct* optimising principle to the effect that a cognitive act is X only if, among the optional alternatives, it maximises cognitive value.

Second Horn—Epistemic norms framed in terms of the cog-nitive act evaluative concepts X are but useful fictions the internalisation of which, though masking *real* epistemic reasons/norms, serves to promote cognitive value.

I think epistemic consequentialism hard pressed to escape the horns of this dilemma. Were it obliged to embrace either of them, most would hold the doctrine undermined. I wouldn't. But that story is even longer than this one.[61]

References

G. Axtell (ed.). 2000. *Knowledge, Belief and Character* , Lanham: Rowman and Littlefield.
J. Broome. 1991. *Weighing Goods* , Oxford: Basil Blackwell.
J. Dancy. 1995. 'Supervenience, Virtues and Consequences: A Commentary on *Knowledge in Perspective* by Ernest Sosa', *Philosophical Studies* 78, 189–205. Page references are to the reprinting of this paper in Axtell (2000).
B. Ellis. 1988. 'Solving the Problem of Induction Using a Values-Based Epistem-ology', *British Journal for the Philosophy of Science* 39, 141–60.
P. Foot. 1985. 'Utilitarianism and the Virtues', *Mind* 94, 196–209.
A. Goldman. 1986. *Epistemology and Cognition*, Cambridge, MA: Harvard Uni-versity Press.
A. Goldman. 1991. *Liaisons: Philosophy Meets the Cognitive and Social Sciences*, Cambridge, MA: MIT Press. Page references are to the selection reprinted in Axtell (2000).
B. Hooker. 2000. *Ideal Code, Real World*, Oxford: Clarendon Press.
P. Horwich. 1982. *Probability and Evidence*, Cambridge: Cambridge University Press.

61. I am grateful to Jim Edwards, Adrian Moore, and Tim Williamson for helpful comments, and to the Arts and Humanities Research Board for funding research-leave during which this paper was written.

F. Jackson. 1991. 'Decision-Theoretic Consequentialism and the Nearest and Dearest Objection', *Ethics* 101, 461–82.

J. Joyce. 1998. 'A Non-Pragmatic Vindication of Probabilism', *Philosophy of Science* 65, 575–603.

D. Lewis. 1971. 'Immodest Inductive Methods', *Philosophy of Science* 38, 54–63.

P. Maher. 1993. *Betting on Theories*, Cambridge: Cambridge University Press.

D. H. Mellor. 1983. 'Objective Decision-Making', *Social Theory and Practice* 9, 289–309, rpt. as ch. 16 of his *Matters of Metaphysics*, Cambridge: Cambridge University Press, 1991.

G. Oddie. 1997. 'Conditionalization, Cogency, and Cognitive Value', *British Journal of the Philosophy of Science* 48, 533–541.

D. Owens. 2000. *Reason without Freedom*, London and New York: Routledge.

P. Percival. 1990. 'Fitch and Intuitionistic Knowability', *Analysis* 50, 182–7.

P. Percival. 1991. 'Knowability, Actuality, and the Metaphysics of Context-Dependence', *Australasian Journal of Philosophy* 69, 82–97.

S. Scheffler (ed.). 1988. *Consequentialism and its Critics*, Oxford: Oxford University Press.

J. Skorupski. 1995. 'Agent-Neutrality, Consequentialism, Utilitarianism ... A Terminological Note', 7, 49–54.

A. Sen. 1982. 'Rights and Agency', *Philosophy and Public Affairs* 11, 3–38, rpt. in Scheffler (1988).

M. Slote. 1984. 'Satisficing Consequentialism', *Aristotelian Society Supplementary Volume*, 58, 139–63.

J. J. C. Smart. 1973. 'An Outline of a System of Utilitarian Ethics', in J.J.C. Smart and B. Williams (eds) *Utilitarianism For and Against*, Cambridge: Cambridge University Press, 3–74.

D. Sosa. 1993. 'Consequences of Consequentialism', *Mind* 102, 101–122.

B. van Fraassen. 1980. *The Scientific Image*, Oxford: Clarendon Press.

B. van Fraassen. 1989. *Laws and Symmetry*, Oxford: Clarendon Press.

R. Weintraub. 2001. 'A Bayesian Paradox', *British Journal of the Philosophy of Science* 52, 51–66.

B. Williams. 1978. *Descartes: The Project of Pure Enquiry*, Harmondsworth: Penguin.

T. Williamson. 1996. 'Knowing and Asserting', *The Philosophical Review* 105, 489–523.

EPISTEMIC CONSEQUENTIALISM

by Philip Percival and Robert Stalnaker

II—*Robert Stalnaker*

ABSTRACT After reviewing the general ideas of the consequentialist framework,
I take a critical look at two of the epistemic consequentialist projects that Philip
Percival considers in his paper: the first assumes that there is a notion of *acceptance* that contrasts with belief and that can be evaluated by its expected epistemic utility. The second uses epistemic utility to evaluate beliefs and partial
beliefs themselves, as well as actions, such as gathering information in the course
of an inquiry. I express scepticism about the notion of acceptance required for
the first project, and argue that the second kind of project can be fruitful only
with a richer notion of epistemic utility than has yet been developed.

Philip Percival describes his discussion of epistemic consequentialism as 'sympathetic, but not a defence'. His aim is
to clarify the project by bringing out some of its commitments,
and by showing what it might accomplish if successful. His discussion is sympathetic, since it rebuts (convincingly, I think)
some hasty arguments against the project, but it acknowledges
that some may find unpalatable some of the commitments of the
enterprise that his discussion brings out.

I hope my remarks about epistemic consequentialism will also
be seen as sympathetic, though I will express some scepticism
about the idea of acceptance that is central to one of the projects
Percival discusses, and about whether this kind of project can
yield or justify any substantive epistemic principles without a
more substantive account of epistemic value. I do think that the
attempt to frame the issues in consequentialist terms helps to
clarify some questions about rationality as a standard of evaluation for both belief and action, and about the relation between
epistemic and pragmatic justification.

I will begin, in Section I, with some remarks about consequentialism in general, as I understand it, and about the commitments
of the decision theoretic framework, emphasizing those features
of the framework that are relevant to understanding its application to epistemology. Then, in Sections II and III I will look
at two of the epistemic consequentialist projects that Percival

considers, one that takes the basic epistemic 'act' to be an act of acceptance, and the other that argues that belief functions themselves can be given a consequentialist evaluation.

I

The Consequentialist Framework. To characterize the decision theoretic framework, I will use Leonard Savage's terminology, distinguishing states, acts, and consequences, though I will follow Richard Jeffrey's formulation of decision theory in treating states, acts and consequences as *propositions.*[1] A decision problem can be modelled by a space of possible worlds, and the states, acts and consequences are three ways of partitioning the space. The agent has a set of available options, and the *acts* partition the space of possibilities by the option that is chosen in the possible world in question. So for example if the agent's options are to order the duck, the haggis, or the vegetable plate, the acts partition the possible worlds into those in which the agent orders the duck, those in which she orders the haggis, and those in which she orders the vegetable plate. The *consequences* partition the space with respect to what the agent cares about. A particular act might be realized in various different ways, and if the differences matter to the agent, then the consequence partition will distinguish between them. So, for example, situations in which the duck is ordered and is tough might be distinguished from situations in which it is ordered and is tender. The third partition, the *states*, distinguish the possibilities with respect to conditions over which the agent has no control—the facts about the world that will determine what the consequences of the act will be. David Lewis explains this notion of a state, which he calls a *dependency hypothesis*, this way:

> Suppose someone knows all there is to know about how the things he cares about do and do not depend causally on his present

1. See Savage (1972) and Jeffrey (1986). In his formal development of the theory, Savage took states and consequences as primitive, and identified acts with arbitrary functions from states to consequences. The project was then to derive probabilities defined on the space of states and utility values for consequences from a preference ordering on acts. While this kind of representation theorem has some technical interest, I don't think it provides the kind of behaviouristic foundation for the theory that was the original motivation for the project, since preferences between acts, in this artificial sense of act, are not grounded in behaviour. 'Acts', as I will use the term, refers only to the feasible actions—to what the agent has the option to choose between in the situation being modelled.

actions. If something is beyond his control, so that it will obtain—
or have a certain chance of obtaining—no matter what he does,
then he knows that for certain. And if something is within his
control, he knows that for certain; further, he knows the extent of
his influence over it, and he knows what he must do to influence
it one way or another. . . Let us call the sort of proposition that
this agent knows—a maximally specific proposition about how the
things he cares about do and do not depend causally on his present
actions—a *dependency hypothesis* (for that agent at that time).[2]

If our agent knew what the state of the world was—exactly how
the consequences of whatever action she might choose would
depend on the facts—then the problem would be simple. She
would simply choose the option with the best consequences.
Where there is uncertainty about the state of the world, the theory says that one should maximize a weighted sum of the values
of the possible consequences of a given action, weighted by the
degree of belief in the state or dependency hypothesis that,
together with the action, would lead to that consequence. One
might ask why rational decisions should be based on this particular function. The standard answer is that the principle of
expected utility is constitutive of the quantitative measures of
belief and value. The significance of the numbers that measure
degrees of belief and value—subjective probabilities and utilities—comes from their role in determining, through the principle
of expected utility, what it is rational to do.

The intuitive idea behind this three way partition of the space of
possibilities is simple: the consequences of an agent's actions
depend on the interaction of what she decides to do, with what the
world is like, independently of what she decides to do. To get clear
about what to do, it seems reasonable for the agent, first, to consider what matters—how she evaluates the various possible ways
the world might be as a result of some available action, and then
to distinguish those determinants of what matters that are under
her control from those that are not. Her *beliefs* about what she
cannot control, together with her *evaluation* of what matters will
determine what choice it is rational for her to make.

It is beliefs about dependency hypotheses, or states, that are
relevant to deliberation, but the agent's belief function may be

---

2. Lewis (1986b), 312–13.

defined over the whole space of possibilities. We have beliefs about what we will do as well as about those features of the world that are beyond our control, but beliefs that are based on our intentions and decisions do not play the same role in the evaluation of action. The rationality of a potential decision is dependent on the agent's beliefs about the state of the world, but is independent of whether that decision is taken, and so of whether the agent believes that it will be taken.

If *consequentialism* is the thesis that actions should be judged by their consequences, and consequences are defined in this purely formal way—as whatever it is that matters, or whatever has value—then consequentialism makes no substantive commitments about what the values are that should guide action. As Peter Hammond, who defends this purely formal construal of consequentialism, says: 'If regrets, sunk costs, even the structure of the decision tree itself are relevant to normative behaviour, they are therefore already in the consequence domain.'[3] Or as Philip Percival says, in his characterization of ethical consequentialism: 'According to the weak characterization I favour, ethical consequentialism ... places no constraints on how consequences are ranked according to their value ("goodness") other than that the ranking should be a quasi-ordering.'[4] This 'thin' construal of

3. Peter Hammond, 'Consequentialist Foundations for Expected Utility Theory,' *Theory and Decision* 25, 25–78.

4. Although Percival adopts this thin construal of consequentialism, he argues that even on this construal, ethical consequentialism excludes certain ethical doctrine, such as one defined by Kantian duty. I am not convinced. As Percival notes, the consequentialist framework allows for agent relative values. Nothing prevents ranking consequences, relative to an agent, by whether that agent does his duty. But Percival suggests that a consequentialist version of Kantianism might yield the wrong result in a case where I make a promise, and 'an effect of my keeping the promise is that I break two further promises subsequently', but this is not clear. There is a general problem raised by such a case about the role an agent's beliefs about his future decisions should play in his current deliberation, a problem that could be faced by a utilitarian as well as by a Kantian. Suppose I today must choose between A and B, knowing that tomorrow I will choose between C and D. The best outcome will result from AC, with BC next best, followed by AD, and then BD. Suppose I know that if I choose A, I will (irrationally) follow with D, while if I choose B, I will subsequently make the rational choice, C. What does consequentialism prescribe? If I treat my future choice as something not (now) under my control—as something to be predicted rather than decided—then B is the choice that maximizes value. But it might be better (and equally compatible with the consequentialist framework) to treat one's future actions as things that call for a plan, rather than a prediction. On this way of framing the problem, the choice that maximizes value is AC. If the actual result is AD, as predicted, then the problem was with the second choice, not the first one. Faced with such a problem, what should one do (whether one is a Kantian or a utilitarian)? If a Kantian believes that by doing the right thing today, he will become morally corrupt, and do the wrong things tomorrow and forever after, what should he do?

consequentialism has been criticized as trivial, but I think this criticism misunderstands the point of the theory, which is to provide a framework for the clarification of values, rather than a substantive theory of value. Whatever my values, if I am deciding whether to perform some action, it seems reasonable to ask, first, how would the world be different, in any ways that matter, if I perform the action, as compared with the way it would be if I performed any of the alternative actions that are available? If I am not sure, then I should consider the alternative ways in which the consequences of my available actions might depend on facts that are beyond my control. To say that the value of an action is derivative from the value of its consequences is only to say that the value of an action derives from the value of the specific way the world would be if the action were performed.

Deliberation may be a matter of calculating what the best thing to do is, given one's values and beliefs, but it may also be a way of figuring out what one's values and beliefs are. I may, for example, be strongly inclined to favour action A over action B, and then reason to the conclusion that this would be rational (given my beliefs) only if I had certain values. The framework helps to bring implicit values to the surface so that they can be examined critically. The pattern is familiar from the dialectic of discussions of decision puzzles such as the Allais paradox. A pair of decision problems—choices between gambles—is described. Then it is shown that a pattern of choices that many people find intuitively plausible is inconsistent with some formal principles of the decision theoretic framework (at least if the consequences are taken to be defined by the payoffs of the gambles). Some theorists take such examples to be counterexamples to the consistency principles of the formal theory, but a better response is to use those principles to bring out the values that are implicit in the pattern of choices. One may then respond in either of two ways: if, on reflection, one is still inclined to favour the pattern of choices that seemed initially plausible, then one learns that certain aspects of the situation matter that one did not realize mattered. Alternatively, one may decide that the values required to rationalize that pattern of choices are not values one can endorse, and so conclude that one's initial responses were mistaken. The role of the theory is to provide a framework for this kind of reflective equilibrium reasoning.[5]

5. Cf. Broome (1991), Ch. 5.

The thin conception of consequentialism is *relativistic* in this sense: actions can be evaluated as rational, relative to any values and beliefs, whatever their source or status. A person giving advice might use her own beliefs, but the addressee's values to determine what to advise the addressee to do. Or a person acting as an agent for an organization, or another person, might deliberate about what to do, given the values of that organization or person. In making contingency plans, one may deliberate about what the best thing to do would be, relative to beliefs that one does not now have, but might have later. Or one might consider what should be done from the point of view of some restricted kind of value: what would be best from the moral point of view, or considering only the interests of me and my family. If there is such a thing as purely epistemic value, then one could consider what it would be best to do from the purely epistemic point of view.

II

Acceptance and Belief. The general consequentialist framework emphasizes the pragmatic role of belief and partial belief—their role, together with values, in determining rational action. Actions are rational relative to beliefs and values, but we usually suppose that beliefs and values can themselves be judged to be rational or not, and that the rationality of belief should be evaluated independently of the values that, in general, action seeks to realize. The basic assumption of all the epistemic consequentialist projects is that there is a special kind of value—epistemic value—that motivates the disinterested inquirer. The beliefs of optimists and pessimists may be influenced, one way or another, by the way they want the world to be, and anyone's non-epistemic values may reasonably influence what questions she has reason to try to answer. But the epistemic consequentialist assumes that one can isolate a purely epistemic dimension of evaluation—the values that would guide one who sought nothing but the truth.

One question is whether there is such a kind of value, and how it is to be measured. A second question is what the *acts* (or analogues of acts) are that are to be evaluated in the way that actions are evaluated in the usual applications of the decision theoretic framework. Percival considers two answers to the latter question given by different epistemic consequentialist projects:

The first is that there is a special kind of epistemic action or quasi-action: *acceptance*, which is different from belief, but that like belief, aims at the truth, and is evaluated in terms of its success in reaching the truth. The second is that one should treat partial belief functions themselves as acts, and to compare the expected epistemic utility of one's belief function with the expected utility of alternative belief functions. One may also evaluate actions (for example decisions to gather evidence, perform experiments, ask questions) from the point of view of epistemic value. I will start with the idea of acceptance, and then look at the idea of belief as an act.

Many philosophers have contrasted acceptance and belief, but it is far from clear that they all have the same contrast in mind. Keith Lehrer takes acceptance to be a kind of meta-mental judgment about one's belief—an act of endorsement.[6] Jonathan Cohen defines acceptance of a proposition p as the adoption of 'a policy of deeming, positing or postulating that p ... whether or not one feels it to be true that p.'[7] Patrick Maher connects acceptance with assertion: acceptance is the state that is expressed in a sincere assertion.[8] In my own discussion of acceptance and belief,[9] I took acceptance to be a generic notion, treating presumption, assumption and presupposition, along with belief, as acceptance concepts. To accept a proposition (on my use of the term) is to treat it as true, to ignore, for the moment at least, the possibility that it is false, whether because one is confident that it is true, or because for the purposes at hand the possible situations in which the proposition is false do not matter.

The different conceptions of acceptance, and of the acceptance-belief distinction, differ on many dimensions, but the crucial contrast between different notions of acceptance is between a notion that takes acceptance to involve an epistemic commitment to what is accepted and notions that do not. The crucial question is this: if one accepts that p when in fact p is false, is one thereby making a mistake? It seems clear that to *believe* something false is to make a mistake (even if, in some circumstances, it is a blameless mistake), but one may reasonably *presume* that something

6. Lehrer (2000).
7. Cohen (2000).
8. Maher (1993).
9. Stalnaker (1984), 79–81.

is true, even if one believes that it will probably later be shown to be false, and no one would think that a mistake had been made because one *assumed* something that turned out to be false, or even if one assumed something that was known to be false. One may reasonably *presuppose* something one does not believe to facilitate a conversation, or *grant* something that one doubts for the purposes of the argument. In such cases, one cannot be accused of having made a mistake on the ground that what one presupposed or granted turned out to be false.

It is clear that acceptance concepts of the noncommittal kind are voluntary undertakings that contrast with belief, and that can be evaluated by their consequences. But it is equally clear that non-epistemic values are relevant to acceptance in this sense. Those charged with a crime are presumed innocent because mistaken convictions are judged to be much worse than mistaken acquittals, but that judgment is not based on an epistemic evaluation of the relative merits of the different kinds of mistake. It may be reasonable to presuppose in a conversation things that are not believed (for example by using the description 'the man drinking a martini' to refer to a man who is in fact drinking Perrier from a cocktail glass) only if the truth or falsity of the presupposition does not matter for the purposes of the conversation. In doing an experiment, one might presume certain things without being sure that they are true because one knows that if they are false, their falsity will reveal itself in the course of the experiment. But this is a good reason only if the non-epistemic costs of being wrong are not great. (One cannot presume that the drug being tested on human beings is non-lethal simply on the ground that if it is lethal we will soon find out.)

The kind of acceptance that might be judged by purely epistemic values, and that is relevant to the epistemic consequentialist projects that Percival considers, is acceptance in a committal sense. Clearly, if one *asserts* something false, one is making a mistake, and so presumably the attitude one is expressing in making a sincere assertion is mistaken when the content of the attitude is false. But I am not convinced that there is a notion of acceptance of this kind—a purely cognitive affirmation or endorsement that may be reasonable even when one withholds full belief. Like Percival, I am persuaded by Timothy Williamson's case that the norms of assertion enjoin us to assert only what we know.[10] The most straightforward explanation for the Moore-paradoxical character of statements of the form '*p*, but I don't know whether *p*' is that one is acknowledging that one is violating such a norm.

Whether or not acceptance is conceptually tied to assertion, I am sceptical of acceptance as a purely epistemic act or attitude, separate from belief. Suppose, on reflection, I decide that I believe, to degree .95, that it will not rain tomorrow. Now I ask myself, should I also *accept* that it will not rain tomorrow? If the question is whether I should ignore, for the purposes at hand, the possibility of rain, then I understand the question, but its answer will depend on my non-epistemic concerns. No, I am told, the question is whether I should *endorse* the proposition that it will not rain, whether I shall confer on it an epistemic status that will have the benefit of providing me some relief from agnosticism,[11] but that will also bring a risk of being wrong (of having endorsed a false proposition). The decision to accept or not is not to affect my degrees of belief, or to have other consequences beyond this act of endorsement. I should continue to use my degrees of belief, together with my all-things-considered utilities, to evaluate any actions that might depend on whether or not it rains. (If the picnic would be sufficiently disastrous were it to rain, we may still call it off because of the five percent chance of rain, even if I *accept* that it won't rain.) Unless acceptance has some effects, unless it guides my decisions about what to do, I don't see the point. If I maintain my .95 degree of belief in the proposition, I don't think that putting a seal of approval on it will bring either any relief from agnosticism, or any additional risk of failure. The circle here strikes me as too tight: there is a special kind of value whose role is just to assess a special kind of act, where the effect of the special kind of act is just to bring a certain amount of the special kind of value. The general shape of the practice is clear enough: accepting what is true is better than suspending judgment, which is better than accepting what is false. But unless the act of acceptance is tied to something else—to some pattern of actions—I don't see what basis there

---

10. Williamson (1996).
11. The term 'relief from agnosticism' for the benefit of acceptance is Isaac Levi's. See Levi (1967), 60–74.

could be for balancing the cost of being wrong against the benefit of having an opinion. And it is not just that I don't know how to decide: I don't understand what it is that is to be decided.

III

Credence Functions as Acts. A different epistemic consequentialist project that Percival considers—the one that begins by treating beliefs and partial beliefs themselves as acts—seems to me more promising. At first glance, this kind of project may not look at all promising for at least two reasons. First, treating beliefs as acts seems to require the implausible assumption that beliefs are under the agent's voluntary control; second, the attempt to assess a belief function by its expected utility seems to be circular, or redundant, since an agent must use her degrees of belief to determine the expected utility of having those degrees of belief. But I don't think the implausible assumption is required, and I am persuaded, with the help of Percival's discussion, that the second problem is not fatal. I will consider the two problems in turn.

I will assume that to treat a belief state, or a credence function, as an act, in the technical sense, does not require the assumption that one decides what to believe but only the assumption that beliefs and degrees of belief are subject to the same kind of rational assessment as an agent's decisions and actions. What the analogy with action does require, in the context of the decision theoretic framework, is that one have a basis for factoring the considerations responsible for the consequences into states, or dependency hypotheses—the factors that are given, and not subject to rational assessment—and acts—the alternatives that are to be assessed as rational. Just as in the ordinary application of the decision theoretic framework, the state of the world is what is counterfactually independent of what the agent decides to do, so in an application of the framework to the rational assessment of beliefs, states will be possible features of the world that are counterfactually independent of the agent's state of belief—facts that would be the same as they actually are, whatever the agent's beliefs and degrees of belief about them. In most contexts, this factoring will be unproblematic. If the subject matter of my relevant beliefs is, for example, the state of tomorrow's weather, the location of Osama bin Laden, the prospects of next year's economy, then it will be reasonable to assume that the truth about these matters would be the same, whatever I believed.[12] So in such cases, we can take the alternative hypotheses about the subject matter in question to be the relevant alternative states. There may be other reasons not to treat the rational assessment of belief as analogous to the rational assessment of action, but the fact that belief is not, in general, the result of a decision to believe is not a problem for the analogy.

What about the circularity problem? Is it reasonable to think that one can evaluate the belief function one has by comparing its expected utility with the expected utility of other possible belief functions, defining the expected utility of all the candidates in terms of one's actual beliefs? Percival gives two responses to the circularity or redundancy problem. First, the evaluation procedure, even if it does not provide a noncircular justification for a belief function, may still serve to constrain the reasonable belief functions. If a credence function judges itself the best credence function to have, that may not be a particularly impressive endorsement, but if it judges itself inferior to others, that is surely a good reason to be suspicious of it (at least assuming we have reason to trust the epistemic utility function that was used to yield the result.) This kind of evaluation procedure might provide internal constraints on credence functions that go beyond the purely formal condition of coherence. Second, even if this kind of evaluation procedure does not provide any substantive constraints on credence functions themselves, the values relative to which credence functions are assessed may help with the evaluation, from a purely epistemic point of view, of other things, such as actions taken in the course of an inquiry. Percival, following Graham Oddie,[13] argues that using this procedure, we can provide a general rationale for inquiry—for trying to learn more.

The first point—that despite the circularity, the procedure might put constraints on the admissible credence functions—is right in principle, but there is a further circularity in the way the project is carried out by Oddie that undercuts this response. The

12. The situation will be more complicated when I am assessing my beliefs about matters that may be influenced by my actions, which will in turn be influenced by my beliefs, or when I assessing my beliefs, not about what will happen tomorrow, but about what I will believe tomorrow.

13. Oddie (1997).

dialectic of Oddie's project, as I understand it, is something like this: we use the assumption that the credence function one has is the one that one ought to have—that it is the one with the greatest expected epistemic utility—to determine what the utilities should be. Oddie shows that there are ways of assigning utilities to credence functions, relative to each state of the world, such that for each coherent credence function c, the expected utility of c, relative to c, is greater than the expected utility of c' relative to c, for any c'≠c. He then argues that because any credence function ought to be 'immodest' (that is, it ought to be self-supporting), the right way to measure epistemic utility is one of the ways that yields this result. A 'proper scoring rule' is a way of measuring utility that has this feature.

There is nothing wrong with this dialectic. It is an example of the reflective equilibrium process described in Section I: one begins with one's intuitions about the 'acts' that are best, and then figures out how one must be valuing the consequences in order to rationalize the choice of that option. One decides, on reflection that a certain credence function is the one that one should have. Then one asks what the epistemic utilities would have to be in order for the expected utility of having that credence function to be greater than the expected utility of having any alternative credence function. One's evaluation procedure should be 'immodest' in the sense that one should judge that one's beliefs, whatever they are, are the best beliefs to have, relative to those beliefs. That may or may not be a reasonable assumption to make—I will question it below—but if it is reasonable, one cannot also say that the procedure provides support for having the credence function that one has. If the procedure is not to be an empty gesture, the epistemic utilities that it yields must play a role in justifying the actions that are taken in the course of inquiry. Percival's second point in defence of Oddie's project is that they can play such a role. Specifically, Percival endorses Oddie's argument that once we have used the assumption that all belief functions are immodest to determine how to measure epistemic utility, we can use that measure to get a purely epistemic justification for the gathering of additional evidence: for the thesis that one always has an epistemic motive to try to learn more.[14]

14. This thesis is taken as a datum to be explained, but one might question it. What if the evidence one might gather is misleading, or would distort the inquiry? Perhaps an ideal, perfectly rational inquirer could not *believe* that his own evidence would

I have two worries about Oddie's argument: first, I am not persuaded that the procedure for determining epistemic utility is playing any essential role in the justification for gathering evidence. Second, I am doubtful about the assumption that yields the liberal scoring rules for determining epistemic utility: that every coherent credence function ought to be immodest.

On the first point: here is a completely general abstract argument for the conclusion that one ought to gather cost-free evidence, if it might matter. Suppose there is a range of acts, A_1 to A_n, (which could be actions, or credence functions) each with an expected utility, where utility is any kind of value at all, measured any way you like. Suppose now we adds some new options—all those of the following form: one undertakes an investigation to determine whether or not some particular proposition p that one is uncertain about is true or false, and then chooses one of the original actions, A_1 to A_n, allowing that one's choice may depend on whether or not p is true. That is, the new set of available acts includes all those of the form 'Find out whether p, then do A_i if p, A_j if not-p.' Suppose further that the investigation is *cost free* in the sense that for each A_i, the expected utility of finding out whether p, and then doing A_i is the same as the expected utility of doing A_i without doing the investigation. Finally, suppose that it is relevant whether p in the following sense: The one of the original options (A_1 to A_n) that maximizes expected utility on condition p is different from the action that maximizes expected utility on condition not-p. Now it is obvious—a trivial consequence of these assumptions—that the option that maximizes expected utility will be one of new ones—one of those that includes undertaking the investigation. It doesn't matter whether the original options are epistemic or practical, or what kind of value is in question. So nothing distinctive about *epistemic* values, or the way they are determined, plays any role in the argument that one has a motive to acquire more information.

mislead him, but real rational inquirers might. Scientists doing double blind experiments go to great lengths to withhold from themselves certain information about their experimental subjects, and they do it from purely epistemic motives. Some people believe that the evidence of interviews, while relevant, tends to be given disproportionate weight in the evaluation of job candidates, and so decide to refrain from acquiring the information that interviews provide in the interest of forming more accurate beliefs about the candidate. (I am indebted here to an informal talk by Roy Sorensen at a recent conference, billed as a brief for the commercial uses of scepticism, with many such examples of the purely epistemic benefits of ignorance.)

On the second point: is it reasonable to assume that *any* coherent probability function is epistemically acceptable? One might hope for more—for scoring rules that would judge certain formally coherent belief functions to be bad, on internal grounds. One is supposed to apportion one's beliefs to the evidence, and one's evidential situation is a feature of the world that might be relevant to evaluating the utility, relative to that world, of having a particular pattern of beliefs. Consider an example: I have a lottery ticket in a lottery I believe to be fair, with the drawing in the future. The winner will get $1,000. There are a thousand tickets, each with an equal (objective) chance of winning, and I know that. But I have a hunch—I am pretty sure that I will win. More precisely, I believe to degree .9 that I will win. That is why I was happy to pay $500 for my ticket. You may think me a fool, but as it happens luck is with the fools this time, and it turns out that I win. How should the epistemic value of my belief function (relative to the actual world) be judged? If truth and closeness to the truth are all that matter, then my belief function gets high marks. On the liberal scoring rules, its actual epistemic utility is high, since I was right about the lottery procedures, right about the objective chances, and gave high credence to the true proposition about who would win. You, who had more reasonable beliefs (and who had declined the opportunity to pay the exorbitant price for my ticket), had a belief function that had, objectively, lower utility. Now we can all agree that from a practical point of view, the outcome was good for me, and not so good for you—I had a net gain of $500 that you could have had. But should I get high marks from the purely epistemic point of view? I don't think so. On reflection, it is not clear that the liberal scoring rules yield plausible results.[15]

The crucial assumption that Graham Oddie made in his defence of the liberal scoring rules was that our belief revision policies should be governed by a conservative principle: 'Absent any new information, you should not change your current cognitive state.'[16] This is a plausible maxim, assuming that your cognitive state meets whatever internal constraints it is reasonable to

15. This is an example of a violation of what David Lewis called 'the principal principle.' See Lewis (1986a).
16. Oddie (1997), 538.

impose on cognitive states, but I don't think it would be reasonable to use this maxim to limit the internal constraints that it would be reasonable to impose.

The liberal scoring rules perhaps provide a measure of a certain kind of *accuracy* of a belief function—closeness to the truth—but as James Joyce argues, there are other purely epistemic virtues that we want our beliefs to have: 'Ideally, a person will hold beliefs that are informative, internally coherent, well justified and connected by secure causal links to the world.'[17] Percival worries that if epistemic value is broadened to include such factors, it may undermine the project of using the consequentialist framework to justify acquiring more information. But I want to suggest that a richer conception of epistemic value may in fact improve the prospects for a consequentialist theory that could bring out and clarify more substantive principles of epistemic practice.

I have argued that the justification of the weak maxim—gather evidence where it is cost free, and where it might make a difference to whatever one cares about—is a relatively trivial maxim that can be justified without making any essential use of epistemic value. But the assumption that actions taken in the course of inquiry can be evaluated from a purely epistemic point of view might have other more substantive consequences for how the rational inquirer should behave. For example, time and resources are limited. One can't investigate everything. One might hope that a theory of epistemic value would provide not just a general reason to gather evidence—to learn more—but also some grounds for discriminating between different possible inquiries— for answering questions about which questions are best to try to answer, from a purely epistemic point of view. Some people spend their time memorizing the decimal expansion of pi to thousands of places. Or one might undertake to find out how many people named 'Jones' are in the Boston telephone book, and whether there are more or fewer Joneses than Smiths. If it is better to believe the truth, and more generally if it is better, all else equal, to give true propositions higher probability, then such inquiries will increase the inquirer's expected epistemic utility. One would hope, however, that more interesting inquiries would

17. Joyce (1998), 592.

increase expected epistemic utility even more. One would like an epistemic consequentialist project to help to explain why certain investigations—for example crucial experiments that decide between competing explanatory theories—would be particularly valuable, from a purely epistemic point of view. Might such distinctions be made without invoking non-epistemic values? I am not sure, but I think that the projects of epistemic consequentialism will have promise only if they can help us answer questions of this kind.

References

J. Broome. 1991. *Weighing Goods*, Oxford: Basil Blackwell.
J. Cohen. 2000. 'Why Acceptance that *p* Does Not Entail Belief that *p*', in Pascal Engel, *Believing and Accepting*, Dordrecht: Kluwer.
P. Hammond. 1986. 'Consequentialist Foundations for Expected Utility Theory', *Theory and Decision*, 25, 25–78.
R. Jeffrey. 1986. *The Logic of Decision*, 2nd edition, Chicago: University of Chicago Press.
J. Joyce. 1998. 'A Non-Pragmatic Vindication of Probabilism', *Philosophy of Science* 65, 575–603.
K. Lehrer. 2000. 'Belief and Acceptance Revisited', in Pascal Engel, *Believing and Accepting*, Dordrecht: Kluwer.
I. Levi. 1967. *Gambling with Truth*, New York: Alfred Knopf.
D. Lewis. 1986a. 'A Subjectivist Guide to Objective Chance', *Philosophical Papers II*, Oxford: Oxford University Press, 1986, 83–132. Originally published in R. Jeffrey (ed.), *Studies in Inductive Logic and Probability II*, Berkeley, CA: University of California Press, 1980.
D. Lewis. 1986b. 'Causal Decision Theory', *Philosophical Papers II*, Oxford: Oxford University Press, 1986, 305–39. Originally published in *Australasian Journal of Philosophy*, 59 (1981).
P. Maher. 1993. *Betting on Theories*, Cambridge: Cambridge University Press.
G. Oddie. 1997. 'Conditionalization, Cogency and Cognitive Value', *British Journal of the Philosophy of Science* 48, 533–41.
P. Percival. 2002. 'Epistemic Consequentialism', this volume.
L. Savage. 1972. *The Foundations of Statistics*, 2nd edition, New York: Dover.
R. Stalnaker. 1984. *Inquiry*, Cambridge, MA: Bradford Books.
T. Williamson. 1996. 'Knowing and Asserting', *Philosophical Review* 105, 489–523.

PARTICULARISM AND MORAL THEORY

by Garrett Cullity and Richard Holton

I—Garrett Cullity

PARTICULARISM AND PRESUMPTIVE REASONS

ABSTRACT Weak particularism about reasons is the view that the normative valency of some descriptive considerations varies, while others have an invariant normative valency. A defence of this view needs to respond to arguments that a consideration cannot count in favour of any action unless it counts in favour of every action. But it cannot resort to a global holism about reasons, if it claims that there are some examples of invariant valency. This paper argues for weak particularism, and presents a framework for understanding the relationships between practical reasons. A central part of this framework is the idea that there is an important kind of reason—a 'presumptive reason'—which need not be conclusive, but which is neither *pro tanto* nor *prima facie*.

I

Two Kinds of Particularism. Moral particularists and their critics debate two issues. The two are related, but not as closely as is often thought.

One issue concerns the existence and nature of moral principles. Are there any correct general principles that can serve to justify moral judgements? The kinds of moral judgements we are ultimately interested in reaching are overall verdicts about the objects of moral assessment—judgements about whether actions are right or wrong, whether a person or a way of living is virtuous or vicious, whether a state of affairs is (all things considered) good or bad, and so on. Call these 'verdictive judgements'. The question is then whether there are any general principles non-trivially linking verdictive moral properties—properties such as the rightness of an action or the viciousness of a person—to other properties. Or to put the question in a more metaphysically cautious way, we can ask whether there are any general principles linking the application-conditions of verdictive moral terms to the application-conditions of other terms.

The second issue concerns whether, if a consideration counts as a good reason for an action in one situation, it must do so in others.[1] To take the particularists' leading example, it seems that normally the fact that I would enjoy something is a good reason for me to do it, and the fact that you would enjoy doing something is a good reason for me to help you to do it. However, they maintain, this is not always true. The enjoyment of cruelty or humiliation does not count in favour of an action at all: on the contrary, it actually counts against it. The normative 'valency' of enjoyment changes from one context to another: in many contexts, it counts as a reason for action, but in some it does not.

Self-styled particularists typically make a claim about each of these issues.

(i) There are no exceptionless, finite general principles specifying the descriptive conditions under which a moral verdict is justified.[2]

(ii) At least some considerations have variable normative valency.

However, these two claims are logically independent, and it is easy to find adherents of one of them who deny the other. Roger Crisp (2000) and Joseph Raz (2000) endorse (i) while arguing against (ii). And Frank Jackson, Philip Pettit and Michael Smith (2000) reject (i) while being prepared to accept (ii).

It makes sense, therefore, to distinguish particularism about principles from particularism about reasons.[3] Each comes in different strengths. Weak particularism about principles[4] is the

1. A related but different issue is whether, if a consideration counts as a reason for a given *evaluative verdict* in one situation, it must do so in others. Jackson, Pettit and Smith (2000), pp. 96–9 and Little (2000), p. 280 discuss this further issue. Raz (2000), pp. 58–61 and Crisp (2000), pp. 32–42 discuss the one in the text. Dancy (1993), Ch. 4 and McNaughton and Rawling (2000) move between the two.

2. A proponent of (i) owes us an account of the distinction between the descriptive and the evaluative. It seems to me that a satisfactory account can be given by saying that evaluative terms are those the assertoric use of which expresses a judgement of goodness or badness, and then understanding descriptive terms by contrast. The distinction between descriptive and evaluative *properties* can then be understood derivatively.

3. Compare Crisp (2000), who also distinguishes these two views from particularism about motivation.

4. Examples of weak particularists about principles are McNaughton and Rawling (2000), Raz (2000), Crisp (2000) and Nussbaum (2000).

acceptance of (i)—the view that there is no finite list of conditions D yielding any correct general principle of the form:

Under descriptive conditions D, the correct moral verdict is V.

Someone who thinks this, however, might well think that there are principles of a less ambitious kind—principles of the form:

Descriptive conditions D always count in favour of moral verdict V.

Such principles propose that there are general, descriptively specified *pro tanto* reasons—reasons that always count in favour of a given moral verdict, although perhaps not always decisively so. A stronger kind of particularism about principles denies the existence of correct principles of this more modest form.[5] And the strongest kind of particularist about principles denies that there are any true, non-trivial general principles of the form:

The presence of R supports moral verdict V.[6]

On this view, even 'thick' moral properties such as cruelty have variable valency: it is not simply that cruel actions are sometimes right because there are stronger reasons in their favour; for some cruel actions, their cruelty does not count against them at all.

Turning to particularism about reasons, we find that this equally comes in different strengths. Weak particularism about reasons is claim (ii): the claim that there are some considerations that are reasons in some contexts but not others.[7] A stronger view is that this is true of every descriptive consideration: every descriptive consideration can be a reason, but all descriptive reasons sometimes change their normative valency.[8] And once more, there is a stronger view still: the view that all non-verdictive reasons (even those supplied by 'thick moral properties such as cruelty) sometimes change their normative valency.[9]

5. E.g. McNaughton (1988), Ch. 13, and Little (2000).

6. E.g. Dancy (1993), Chs 4–6.

7. I prefer to talk of reasons as 'considerations' rather than 'facts' because I think of them as linguistic entities, and not the states of the world these entities represent. My reason for this is that the content of a state of the world is always fully specific; but the content of a reason (as I shall argue in Section III) is not.

8. E.g. Little (2000).

9. See again Dancy (1993), Ch. 4.

These two issues are connected. One connection between them is this. Some reasons to ϕ are reasons for holding that ϕing is morally right: call these 'moral reasons'. Then for any descriptive consideration D which is a moral reason of invariant valency, there will be an exceptionless principle of the form:

D always counts in favour of the moral rightness of action.

Strong particularism about moral reasons entails and is entailed by particularism about principles.

To support their view, strong particularists about both reasons and principles commonly appeal to an argument which, in condensed form, goes as follows.[10] The evaluative is 'shapeless' with respect to the descriptive. That is, no finite disjunction of our descriptive concepts has the same extension as any evaluative concept.[11]   Wittgenstein taught us to reject the prejudice about rationality of thinking that a practice of concept-application must have an independently articulable backing rule in order to count as rationally constrained. In order for me to count as genuinely going on in the same way in applying a concept, it need not be the case that there is any way, independent of the use of that concept, of spelling out the conditions under which I count as successfully doing so. If so, we should deny that there is any reason to expect that evaluative verdicts should be backed by principles linking them to the descriptively specified conditions in which they obtain. Moreover, once we see that the evaluative and descriptive are independent in this way, we should press a further question. Why think that the contribution that any descriptive characteristic makes to the evaluative character of the situations in which it is present is independent of the rest of the context in which it is found? In the absence of any compelling reason for thinking this, we won't have *pro tanto* principles linking the descriptive and the evaluative either. That leaves us

10. See McDowell (1979) and (1981); Dancy (1993), esp. Ch. 5, Section 4; and Little (2000), esp. Section II; also, for discussion, McNaughton and Rawling (2000), Section II.

11. It is hard to see how they could have a good argument for thinking there *could not* be descriptive concepts with the same extension as any evaluative concept; but as I read it, their argument relies only on the fact that we do not in fact have such concepts. I am grateful to Frank Jackson for a very helpful correspondence on this point.

with a view on which reasons emerge holistically, from the entire conjunction of descriptive features that make up the evaluative character of a situation: the reason-giving character of a descriptive feature does not attach to it in an atomistic, context-independent way.

In this paper, I defend a version of weak particularism about reasons. I shall argue that the normative valency of some descriptive considerations varies, but others have an invariant normative valency. As far as I am aware, this view has not been defended by other contributors to the debate. This is surprising in one way, because it is such a natural thing to say about the examples I shall consider. In another way, however, the rarity of this view is not so surprising. For it requires arguing against opponents from two different directions, and that may seem to make it an unstable position. I need to respond to arguments that a consideration cannot count in favour of any action unless it counts in favour of every action. But I need to do so without resorting to a global holism about reasons, if I am to claim that there are some examples of invariant valency. Arguing against these two opposing views will occupy Sections III and IV, respectively. What will emerge from this, in Section V, is a framework for understanding the relationships between practical reasons. A central part of this framework is the idea that there is an important kind of reason which need not be conclusive, but which is neither *pro tanto* nor *prima facie*: I shall call it a 'presumptive reason'.

II

The Content of Reasons. Particularists and anti-particularists about reasons can agree about the conditions under which a person has a reason. They can agree, for example, that when an innocuous action of mine would be enjoyable, there is a reason for me to do it, and that the fact that an action would produce sadistic enjoyment does not amount to a good reason for doing it. Their disagreement concerns the *content* of the reasons that we have. According to the particularist, the content of the reason in the first, innocuous case is simply *that I would enjoy doing this*. In my innocuous circumstances, this consideration is a good reason for acting; but in the sadist's different circumstances, the same consideration is not a good reason. The anti-particularist's view, by contrast, is that the description of the reason in the first case is too simplistic. The unqualified fact that I would enjoy doing something is not enough to give me a reason: after all, if it is the wrong kind of enjoyment then I do not have a reason. In the situations where I do have a reason, the reason must be at least *that I would non-sadistically enjoy doing this*. Admittedly, it would be pragmatically odd to offer this as a reason for going to the pub. But speaking with strict accuracy is often pragmatically odd. A *complete* statement of the reason that does count in favour of my action will have to include the qualification.

Of course, qualifying the content of the reason by simply excluding sadistic motivation looks inadequate. If you do not think that there is a reason to pursue every form of enjoyment, you are unlikely to think that sadistic enjoyment is the only exception. There are forms of malice that it seems incorrect to describe as sadism; forms of enjoyment of the spectacle of harm to others that involve no malice, enjoyment of destruction which involves harm to no one, and so on. It looks as though the only succinct way to capture these exceptions will be to use an evaluative term, and say that when there is a reason, it is *that I would innocuously, or morally permissibly enjoy doing this*.

One strong-looking argument for the anti-particularist view of the content of reasons can be put like this. Surely a fact can only be a reason for a given action if the obtaining of that fact is sufficient to make it the case that there is a reason to perform that action. However, the fact that an action would be enjoyable cannot be sufficient to make it the case that I have a reason to do it, if there are kinds of enjoyment that are not reason-giving. Therefore, when there is a reason to do something enjoyable, the reason cannot simply be *that it is enjoyable*. In order to mention the whole of the reason for doing it, we need to mention the kind of enjoyment that it involves, specifying that it is one of the kinds that is reason-giving, rather than one that is not.

For a second argument to the same conclusion, we can turn to Joseph Raz.[12] Raz's argument against particularism about reasons begins with what he calls 'the intelligibility of value'— the idea that

12. Raz (2000), esp. Section 3.

there is nothing 'arbitrary' in the domain of value.... There is an explanation for everything, an explanation for why what is good is good, what is bad is bad, etc.[13]

Given this, it is not enough simply to say that the same consideration might be a reason in one situation but not in another: there must be some difference between the two situations which *explains* the evaluative difference. But that difference, according to particularists, is not itself part of the reason: if it were, that would mean there were different reasons in the two situations. The upshot is that, on their view, 'not everything relevant for the evaluation of an action is part of the reasons for or against the action.'[14] But that looks wrong, for the notion of a reason for an action just is the notion of what counts in its favour.

Roger Crisp sets out a third argument for anti-particularism about reasons.[15] He points out that it is not difficult, in the sorts of cases discussed by particularists, to give an explanation of the differences between the situations in which they claim that the normative valency of a consideration varies. In each case, a transparent explanation is given by using virtue-terms. Sometimes, doing what is enjoyable is prudent; at other times, it is cruel. Sometimes, lying is dishonest; at other times, it isn't. Sometimes, doing what is illegal is unjust; at other times, it is required by justice. But that is to say that the *ultimate* reasons for action in each of these pairs of cases are given by these evaluative considerations, the normative valency of which does not vary. It may make pragmatic sense to cite as a reason for the wrongness of an action the fact that it was a lie, but when lying is wrong an explanation is readily available of why it is wrong, and that explanation amounts to the provision of the ultimate reason why it is wrong.

III

Reasons, Motivation and Explanation. I think that these arguments fail. To show this, I shall give a three-stage argument in support of particularism about reasons; then I shall explain what

13. Raz (2000), p. 50.
14. Raz (2000), p. 60.
15. Crisp (2000), pp. 32–42.

was wrong with each of the three anti-particularist arguments just given. The first stage of my argument connects normative reasons to motivation. The second connects motivation to a particular kind of explanation: *self*-explanation. The third then connects explanations with expectations of normality.

There are various different claims concerning the conceptual connection between normative practical reasons and the motivation of rational agents that have been called 'internalism about reasons'.[16] One claim which seems correct is this: a reason for me to ϕ in circumstances C must be a consideration my rational orientation towards which could motivate me to ϕ in C, were I acquainted with the facts about C.[17] That is, my being aware of this reason and rational guidance by that awareness could explain my ϕ-ing. Given the nature of the concept of a reason, and the concept of rationality, it is hard to see how this connection could sensibly be denied. A normative practical reason is a consideration that counts in favour of my performing the action for which it is a reason: it is a consideration which makes it the case that I *ought* to do it—or, to use Allan Gibbard's phrase, a consideration which shows why my doing it *makes sense*.[18] And rationality, although it need not involve being successfully guided by the reasons for acting that apply to you (for you might be rationally mistaken about these), at least involves being appropriately guided by what you are *warranted* in treating as the reasons for acting that apply to you. If that is right, then the only way in which there could be a reason for me to ϕ that could not explain my ϕ-ing when rationally oriented towards it would be if I could not be warranted in regarding it as a reason. But how could a consideration that I could never be warranted in regarding as a reason really count in favour of my performing any action? It could never *make sense* for me to act on such a

16. For further discussion of a claim closely related to the one I concentrate on here, see Parfit (1997). For some of the others, see the taxonomy in Audi (1997); also Darwall (1983), esp. Ch. 5.

17. One kind of 'externalism' about reasons is McDowell's (1995) view that there can be reasons for me to act which are such that, given my actual motivations, there is no rational process through which I could come to be motivated to act on them. This would have to occur by a process of non-rational 'conversion'. Notice that even this view is consistent with the 'internalism' proposed in the text. McDowell's reasons are still reasons I *could* (if 'converted') be rationally motivated by.

18. Gibbard (1990), Ch. 1.

consideration, no matter how rational I was. But a 'reason' that we could never be warranted in treating as a reason looks like no reason at all. It would not be worth discussing, since it would not be something that it made sense for a rational person to care about. And if not, the claimed connection between reasons (the only reasons it makes sense for us to be concerned with) and rational motivation follows: it is a necessary condition of a consideration's being a normative reason for me to ϕ that my rational orientation towards that consideration could motivate me to ϕ.[19]

This is a conceptual, not an empirical claim. It leaves it open that there are no considerations that meet this condition, and therefore no reasons. And it leaves it open that there are reasons, but we are never rationally oriented towards them. What it claims is this: for any consideration to satisfy the concept of a reason, and for any person to satisfy the concept of a rational agent, they must meet this condition. Notice also that it does not require the principle that 'ought' implies 'can'. For it leaves it open that even when I *cannot* be rationally motivated, I ought to do the things I would do if I were rationally motivated.

Now for the second stage of the argument. When we say what motivated an action, we are offering a certain kind of explanation of it: an explanation in terms of the agent's aims in performing it. (I might explain what you are doing by saying that you're confused; but it would not ordinarily make sense to say that you were *motivated* by confusion.) Normally, specifying those aims will involve saying what the agent thought of as counting in favour of the action.[20] That is, it will involve saying what the agent regarded as the normative reasons that made the action worthwhile. Motivational explanation, then, is normally explanation in terms of the agent's judgements about normative reasons. Suppose we ask this, though: explanation by whom, to whom? The answer is: in the first instance, explanation by me,

19. 'My rational orientation towards that consideration could motivate me to act' is more awkward than, 'I would be motivated to act on that consideration if I were fully rational'. It deals better, however, with situations where I have reasons to correct my own irrationality. I would not be motivated to act on those reasons if I were fully rational. But acting on those reasons is what I will do insofar as I am rational in responding to my own irrationality.

20. I say 'at least normally' in order to allow for the possibility of the kind of counter-rationally motivated action discussed in Stocker (1979) and Velleman (1992).

the agent, to myself. If my action is motivated by the pursuit of some goal then that is to say that, at some level (the level at which I am motivated), I am seeing my action as the pursuit of that goal. At that level, I am giving an account to myself of why I am doing *this*, rather than something else. That account corresponds to the content of my goals in acting. When a third person explains my action by saying what motivates it, he is therefore giving an account of how I am explaining the action to myself.

When I say this, I am not saying that we have to privilege an agent's own reports of his motives. We can be dishonest or even self-deluded about our motives. My claim is simply that in any case of motivated action, the correct account of what motivates me takes the form of attributing to me the pursuit of a goal through the action, and that my pursuing a goal through the action amounts—perhaps subconsciously—to my giving an explanation to myself of why I am doing what I do. This may not stop me from giving other, contradictory explanations of the same action to myself and others, and from wrongly believing that it is the more palatable goals that are really motivating my action. Suppose I think I'm being kind to you, but I'm really trying to dominate you by making you indebted to me. Saying this only makes sense if the action is explained by my seeing it, at some level, as enabling me to dominate you. The claim is that, at that level, I am explaining the action to myself as an act of domination.

The third stage of the argument concerns the nature of rational explanation. Clearly, the explanation it is rational to give of any phenomenon is relative to background expectations of normality. If the trees next to the vineyard normally flower before the vintage, it may be rational to appeal to the fact that they did not in order to explain why the vineyard suffered a lot of bird damage this year; but if not, it will not. If the trees never flower before the vintage, it may be true that had they done so, there would not have been a lot of bird damage; but it does not follow that their not flowering before the vintage should be included in an explanation of the bird damage. In general, it is fallacious to reason that if A would not have happened in the presence of B, the absence of B should figure in a rational explanation of why A happened.

Putting these three stages together, we have an argument for the particularist claim about the content of reasons. A reason for me to ϕ must be a consideration my awareness of which could give a motivational explanation of my ϕ-ing, if I were rationally oriented towards that consideration and aware of the other facts. But a motivational explanation is primarily a self-explanation; so a reason for me to ϕ must be something I could invoke in explaining my ϕ-ing to myself, insofar as I am rational.[21] But the content of a rational explanation is relative to background expectations of normality. If so, the background expectations of normality it is rational to have will constrain the content of normative reasons, in the following way. The absence of those considerations that would defeat the presence of a reason will not normally be part of the content of my reason. For, in straightforward circumstances, they are not part of what I can rationally invoke in explaining my action to myself. When I have an opportunity to do something enjoyable, in a situation in which questions of permissibility do not normally arise, it will simply be the fact that the action would be enjoyable that features in a rational explanation to myself of what I am doing. It might be true that were my enjoyment morally objectionable, I would not have a reason to do what I am doing. But that does not mean that its being morally unobjectionable is part of the reason I do have. For its being morally unobjectionable will not normally be part of a rational explanation to myself of what I am doing; hence not part of the goal that motivates me; and if it could not be part of what motivates me insofar as I am rational, then it cannot be part of the reason there is for me to act.[22]

---

21. This is a necessary condition on something's being a reason; not a sufficient one. It might be rational for me to explain my action by appealing to something that is not a reason at all (as Frank Jackson pointed out in discussion).

22. My understanding of what is normal will change over time. Does that mean the content of the reasons there are for me to act will change? Suppose I begin by being sensitive to whether my enjoyment of your company is morally objectionable (I've been told you're an unsavoury character). Then, as I get to know you, the fact that this enjoyment is unobjectionable becomes part of my background expectation. Does that mean that, although the unobjectionableness of the enjoyment was part of the reason there was for me to spend time with you initially, that ceases to be true?

No. My claim is that a reason must be something I could be rationally motivated to act on, *given knowledge of the facts*. If the background facts themselves change, my reasons will change: that does not seem an embarrassing result. But this does not imply that the reasons I have will change simply because my rational expectations change. Thanks to Philip Pettit for pressing me on this.

The previous section gave three arguments for the opposite conclusion. We can now say what was wrong with them. The first maintained that the fact *that I would enjoy doing this* is not sufficient for the existence of a reason for action. There is a clear sense in which this is true: this fact is not sufficient for the existence of a reason in *all* circumstances. However, given the argument I have just presented, we should still say that this fact is sufficient for the existence of a reason for action in most circumstances, where the background is uncomplicated. We must be careful not to commit a counterfactual fallacy about practical reasons that corresponds to the fallacy about explanation identified earlier. When there is a reason for me to ϕ, but there would not have been a reason for me to ϕ had consideration C been present, it does not follow that the absence of C must be part of the reason for me to ϕ.

Raz's argument involves a dubious inference of a different kind. He begins by observing, correctly enough, that on the particularist view, if a consideration counts as a reason in one situation but not another, there must be some further feature of the situation which is not part of the content of the reason, and which explains the difference. But he moves from there to supposing that this explanation of the evaluative difference cannot be part of the reasons for and against the action for the particularist, and complaining that this drives an unsatisfactory wedge between reasons and what explains evaluative nature. This does not follow, though. The evaluative difference, on the particularist's view, lies outside the content of the reason whose variable valency is being explained. But that does not mean that it lies outside the content of any practical reason. Indeed, in the case we have been considering, we can see that this is not so. Enjoyment may fail to be a reason for an action when it is malicious. On the particularist's view, we should say that non-maliciousness is not part of the reason for doing enjoyable non-malicious things. But it still makes sense to say that their being malicious *is* part of the reason for *not* doing things that are malicious. Facts about whether something is malicious or not are not always part of the reason for doing enjoyable things, on the particularist view. But that does not mean that it has to say that the factors that explain the difference between the situations in which you ought to do what is enjoyable and the situations in which you ought not are not part of the content of practical reasons at all.[23] Crisp's anti-particularist argument was that we can make sense of cases of apparently variable normative valency by appealing to invariant ultimate reasons, expressible using virtue-terminology. But our three-stage argument shows what is wrong with this. Crisp's 'ultimate reasons' are not the reasons that motivate rational agents: my reason for going to the pub is that I would enjoy it, not that it would be prudent. Maybe it *would* be prudent, and maybe (prudent person that I am) I wouldn't go if it were imprudent. But in a situation where issues concerning its possible imprudence do not arise, my going is not explained by my seeing it as prudent. Reasons are the considerations that motivate us insofar as we are rational; so it is the simpler considerations that supply our reasons in straightforward circumstances.

IV

Resisting Holism. I have argued for the first half of my weak particularism about reasons: the claim that there are some descriptive considerations that have variable normative valency. The other half is the claim that some have invariant valency.

This second claim is one that other particularists about reasons—writers like Dancy, Little, McNaughton and Rawling—all reject.[24] Their thought is that once we notice the variable normative valency of some descriptive considerations, and once we notice the shapelessness of the evaluative with respect to the descriptive, we will see that we need to embrace the general thesis that the way descriptive considerations function as reasons

23. Raz discusses at some length a different response that particularists might make to his argument: a reason for an action must be capable of being the reason why someone acted; but no one can be guided by all the evaluatively relevant factors that are present (p. 61). He replies that if reasons are objective, one can refer to them without understanding them fully (pp. 61–9). This does not seem decisive: we should certainly agree that I can *refer* to reasons without understanding them ('the reasons set out in the book I ought to read'); but what is less clear is how I can be *guided* by them without understanding them. However, it seems unwise for a particularist to take the line Raz is considering. For although particularists about principles do want to say that there is no finite descriptive account of the evaluatively relevant factors, they allow that there are evaluative terms capturing all the relevant factors, by which we can be guided.

24. Dancy (1993), Little (2000), McNaughton and Rawling (2000). In the vocabulary preferred by the latter, the position defended here is a version of 'fat intuitionism'.

is holistic. Descriptive considerations, on this view, are of the wrong kind to have invariant normative valency: the evaluative significance of any descriptive consideration depends on the rest of the context in which it is found.

This is a surprising view, since holism's leading claim about the normative status of descriptive reasons—the claim that *every* descriptive consideration has variable normative valency—is obviously wrong. Indeed, our discussion of why enjoyment should be thought to have variable normative valency supplies us with the most obvious example of a descriptive consideration with invariant normative valency: inflicting suffering on others for your own enjoyment. This always counts against an action. Indeed, a stronger claim looks plausible: such actions are always wrong. Even if someone deserves to suffer, and even if there are further reasons that make it very important to do what makes him suffer—even if he is an evil megalomaniac who needs to be harmed in order to save the world—it is wrong to make him suffer for your enjoyment. Maybe you should make him suffer because he deserves it, or because it will save the world; but it would always be wrong to make him suffer for your own enjoyment.

Finding this descriptive property was easy. Having noticed that enjoyment sometimes counts as a reason and sometimes does not, we have simply taken one class of cases in which it does not, and noticed that when this class of cases is described in a way that includes the agent's motivation, that generates a description of invariant normative valency. This will give us a recipe for generating other descriptive reasons of invariant valency: stealing for enjoyment, annoying someone for enjoyment, forcing someone to do something so that you can enjoy feeling superior to him, and so on.

Why should it be the case that some descriptive reasons have variable moral valency while others are invariant? The core of the explanation is this. Sometimes, in stating a descriptive reason, we are referring to a state, such as enjoyment, that can have different contents. I have argued that the particularists are right that often, the correct description of the reason for doing something enjoyable takes the simple, 'content-neutral' form: *I would enjoy this.* However, one of the ways in which the contents of a state such as enjoyment can differ is that they can have different values. Many of the contents of enjoyment are not bad, but some are bad. And there are some ways of describing the content of a state such as enjoyment which make it *always* bad. If so, we can use the descriptions of those contents in order to generate further, more specific considerations—such as the consideration that this would be an action of harming someone for enjoyment—which amount to reasons of invariant valency. This is consistent with thinking that, in circumstances in which there is no reason for me to be raising the question of whether the content is bad, the reason should be stated in the simple content-neutral form.

This is suggestive; but we need to take it further. What other 'content-neutral' reasons are there? How do they relate to each other? And why should it be the case that some contents of a state such as enjoyment make it invariably bad? What I offer next is no more than a start towards answering these questions. But I think enough can be said to indicate the lines along which these questions can be answered.

V

Presumptive Reasons, Practical Norms, and Undermining. In Section III, I opposed Raz's argument for anti-particularism about reasons. However, I think he is right about what he calls 'the intelligibility of value'. It cannot simply be a brute evaluative fact that a certain consideration is a reason in one place and not in another: there must be a justifying explanation of why the two cases are evaluatively different. The idea of that which is supported by reason is to be fundamentally contrasted with the idea of that which is arbitrary.

Now we have at least the beginnings of an answer to the question why a consideration that gives a reason in one situation does not give a reason in others. 'Content-neutral' descriptive considerations refer to states that can have good and bad contents; and the difference in the values of these contents explains the difference in the normative status of those considerations in different situations. However, we cannot stop there. A concern with the intelligibility of value will resurface as the question: what explains why some contents are good and others bad?

Having opened this question, we might wonder what would count as a *complete* answer. What form must a justification of evaluative claims take, if it is not ultimately to appeal to brute evaluative facts?[25] I do not propose to offer an answer to that larger question here. But it is possible at least to make a start on explaining why some contents of 'content-neutral' descriptive considerations are bad, and thus why they fail to provide reasons when they have those contents.

In order to do this, we should start by asking which other content-neutral descriptive considerations are reasons. When a consideration provides a normative reason for an action, I shall refer to the relationship of support that exists between the consideration and the action as a practical norm. And I shall use the following arrow notation to express the existence of a practical norm:

(1) ϕ-ing would be enjoyable
$$\downarrow$$
ϕ-ing.

This is the norm we have been concentrating on so far. Other descriptive considerations that can favour an action give us other simple norms, for example:

(2) ϕ-ing would be interesting
$$\downarrow$$
ϕ-ing.

(1) and (2) are naturally thought of as non-moral norms: someone who fails to follow them, the thought goes, is failing to be properly responsive to reasons, but they are not open to *moral* criticism.[26] However, we can extend our list of descriptive reasons to cite those that seem to provide us with moral norms:

(3) ϕ-ing would get her X
she needs X
$$\downarrow$$
ϕ-ing.

25. According to one line of thought, taking this problem seriously draws us towards a Kantian position. If answers to the question 'Why?' are to avoid either resting on an unvindicated claim about brute evaluative facts or leading to an infinite, uncompletable regress, this requires us to give an account of the formal nature of reasons, and derive from this formal account substantive conclusions concerning the particular reasons we have. See O'Neill (1992) and Korsgaard (1996).

26. Can moral and non-moral reasons be clearly distinguished, and if so, is the distinction important? I am not relying on any answer to these questions here.

(4)   she wants to know whether or not P
      P is the truth
                ↓
      asserting P.

(5)   others are relying on me to φ
                ↓
      φ-ing.

(6)   φ-ing would be forcing him against his will
                ↓
      not φ-ing.

(7)   φ-ing would be lying
                ↓
      not φ-ing.

(8)   I have promised to φ
                ↓
      not φ-ing.

(9)   φ-ing would be illegal
                ↓
      not φ-ing.

In (1)–(9), we have a plausible (if not exhaustive) list of
descriptive reasons that are 'content-neutral'. In each case, the
argument of Section III supports the view that, in straightforward circumstances, good reasons for acting can have the simple,
unqualified contents just listed. However, in each case, the
descriptive consideration refers to a state whose content can be
good or bad. Often, this is because it refers directly or indirectly
to attitudes of a person that can be well- or badly-directed. We
have seen this in the case of (1). Normally, enjoyment is good;
but when it is enjoyment of what ought not to be enjoyed, it is
bad. The same general point applies to (2)–(6). If I am only interested in something as part of a bad enterprise—I am interested
in finding out more about how to harm or swindle other people,
say—then the fact that I find it interesting is not a good reason:
it is the wrong kind of interest to provide a good reason. The
same goes for needing something, wanting to know something,
or relying on me for something: these could all be serving a bad
enterprise. And likewise, if someone's will is directed towards

what is bad, forcing him to act against his will may cease to be something there is a reason to avoid.

Norm (7), concerning lying, gives us a subtler case of content-neutrality. Here, unlike (2)–(6), there is no direct reference to attitudes of another person that may be well or badly directed. However, the explanation of the variable normative valency of lying is similar. There is no reason not to lie to a murderer at the door because the evil nature of his enterprise means there is no reason not to deceive him. We have a reason not to deceive other people out of respect for their pursuit of their own ends. But sometimes, others' pursuit of their ends is not respect-worthy: indeed, sometimes we ought to frustrate it. Deceiving people in relation to *these* ends is not something there is a reason to avoid.

The reasons spelt out in (8) and (9) are content-neutral in a different way. Here, the normative variation in content is not a variation in the contents of people's attitudes or enterprises, but more directly a variation in the content of promises or laws. Promises and laws that are directed towards an evil purpose are ones that we have no reason to keep.

What we have started to compile is a list of norms associated with different virtues. In straightforward circumstances, (3) gives us the reason the recognition of which is characteristic of benefi-cence or kindness. (4) and (7) are the simplest manifestations of one sort of honesty: honesty-as-veracity. Another sort, honesty-as-fidelity, is found in (8). A reliable person is someone who often follows the norm set out in (5), a respectful person (6) and a law-abiding person (9). We might want to say that the joie-de-vivre associated with (1), and the curiosity associated with (2) are not *moral* virtues. But if we do, we should still be prepared to say that a good person—someone who is properly responsive to the reasons there are—is someone who is guided by (1) and (2), along with the other norms we have listed.

I do not want to suggest that every norm associated with a virtue contains a content-neutral descriptive reason, as (1)–(9) do. Very often, the content of the reason recognized in virtuous agency will be evaluative, even in the simplest cases. Thus a further kind of honesty involves following the norm:

(10)   φ-ing would be stealing
                    ↓
             not φ-ing.

where stealing will have to be understood as an evaluative notion, since stealing is taking from someone not simply what they possess, but what they are entitled to possess. And norms for justice, conscientiousness and public-spiritedness include these:

(11) ϕ-ing would result in distribution D of these goods
        D is the fair distribution
                    $\downarrow$
        ϕ-ing.

(12) ϕ-ing would get her X
        she has a right to X
                    $\downarrow$
        ϕ-ing.

(13) I have a duty to ϕ
                    $\downarrow$
        ϕ-ing.

(14) we all ought to be ψ-ing
        we can only ψ if people like me ϕ
                    $\downarrow$
        ϕ-ing.

These evaluative considerations can have different contents, but they do not count as 'content-neutral' in the sense employed here, since it is not natural to think of their contents as sometimes being bad.

I have said that these norms are 'associated' with virtues. But what, more precisely, is the association? Clearly, it is not that any virtue simply consists in following one of these norms. In the case of (10)–(14), we might want to say that possessing the virtues associated with them is at least in part a matter of recognizing the evaluative considerations they cite as always giving *pro tanto* reasons. However, it is not true that the considerations mentioned in (3)–(9) are *pro tanto* reasons wherever they obtain. So why think that these norms tell us anything important about the virtues with which they are (sometimes) associated?

I think that in each case there is a deep association between the norm I have indicated and the relevant virtue: each of these norms gives us the core of a virtue. To explain this, we need a term to describe the kind of reason that is provided by a consideration such as that doing something would be enjoyable, or would be the fulfilment of a promise. These considerations, I have maintained, do not always give us *pro tanto* reasons. They sometimes do, but at other times, their status as reasons is undermined by further considerations (ones that show that my enjoyment, or my promise, is bad). But it would be too weak to say that they give us merely *prima facie* reasons: considerations that on first inspection appear to be reasons. They *are* reasons, unless undermined. We can mark this special status by giving them a label of their own. These considerations are *presumptive reasons*—that is, they are *pro tanto* reasons unless undermined. Being properly responsive to reasons requires recognizing this. And being morally good requires recognizing the considerations set out in (3)–(14), amongst others, as presumptive reasons.

This allows us to say in what way norms such as (1)–(9) are central to the virtues associated with them: in each case, possessing the virtue requires recognizing as a presumptive reason the consideration picked out in the statement of the associated norm. But also, finally, it allows us to answer our question about what explains why some contents of 'content-neutral' descriptive considerations are bad, and thus to make a contribution to the intelligibility of value. The norms we have mentioned set out (some of) the considerations a good person should recognize as presumptive reasons for action. But they also tell us what is presumptively bad. It is presumptively bad to act in ways contrary to these norms—to harm people (3), to let them down (5), to coerce them (6), and so on. Again, this is only *presumptively* bad: sometimes we *ought* to coerce people to abandon evil ends. But this is enough to give us an account of when a consideration that supplies us with a presumptive reason fails to give us a good reason. Such a consideration fails to give us a good reason when its content is bad. And its content is bad when the 'normative orientation' of that content is contrary to a norm that a good person should recognize. Thus our list of norms gives us not only a list of presumptive reasons, but a list of explanations of when their status as normative reasons is undermined. The problem with malicious enjoyment is that the normative orientation of malice is contrary to (3); the problem with the enjoyment of domination is that it is contrary to (6); and the problem with vandalistic enjoyment is that it is contrary to:

(15) X is precious
      ϕ-ing would damage X
              $\downarrow$
      not ϕ-ing.

The norms associated with these presumptive reasons give the normative orientations that a good person should have. But sometimes, the considerations that give us presumptive reasons can have contents that themselves violate those normative orientations. And when they do, it makes sense for a good person to think that the presumptive reason is only presumptively a reason: its status as a good reason for action has been undermined.[27]

REFERENCES

Audi, Robert. 1997. 'Moral Judgement and Reasons for Action', in Garrett Cullity and Berys Gaut (eds), *Ethics and Practical Reason*, Oxford: Clarendon Press, 125–59.

Crisp, Roger. 2000. 'Particularizing Particularism', in Hooker and Little (2000), 23–47.

Dancy, Jonathan. 1993. *Moral Reasons*, Oxford: Blackwell.

Darwall, Stephen. 1983. *Impartial Reason*, Ithaca: Cornell University Press.

Gibbard, Allan. 1990. *Wise Choices, Apt Feelings*, Oxford: Clarendon Press.

Hooker, Brad, and Little, Margaret Olivia (eds). 2000. *Moral Particularism*, Oxford: Clarendon Press.

Jackson, Frank, Pettit, Philip, and Smith, Michael. 2000. 'Ethical Particularism and Patterns', in Hooker and Little (2000), 79–99.

Korsgaard, Christine M. 1996. 'From Duty and for the Sake of the Noble: Kant and Aristotle on Morally Good Action', in Stephen Engstrom and Jennifer Whiting (eds), *Aristotle, Kant and the Stoics: Rethinking Happiness and Duty*, Cambridge: Cambridge University Press, 203–36.

Little, Margaret Olivia. 2000. 'Moral Generalities Revisited', in Hooker and Little (2000), 276–304.

McDowell, John. 1979. 'Virtue and Reason', *Monist* 63, 331–50.

McDowell, John. 1981. 'Non-Cognitivism and Rule-Following', in Stephen H. Holtzman and Christopher M. Leich (eds), *Wittgenstein: To Follow a Rule*, London: Routledge & Kegan Paul, 141–62.

McDowell, John. 1995. 'Might There Be External Reasons?', in J.E.J. Altham and Ross Harrison (eds), *World, Mind and Ethics: Essays on the Ethical Philosophy of Bernard Williams*, Cambridge: Cambridge University Press, 68–85.

McNaughton, David. 1988. *Moral Vision* Oxford: Blackwell.

McNaughton, David, and Rawling, Piers. 2000. 'Unprincipled Ethics', in Hooker and Little (2000), 256–75.

27. Thanks to an audience at the Australian National University for very helpful comments on an earlier version of this paper.

Nussbaum, Martha. 2000. 'Why Practice Needs Ethical Theory: Particularism, Principle, and Bad Behaviour', in Hooker and Little (2000), 227–55.

O'Neill, Onora. 1992. 'Vindicating Reason', in Paul Guyer (ed), *The Cambridge Companion to Kant*, Cambridge: Cambridge University Press, 280–308.

Parfit, Derek. 1997. 'Reasons and Motivation', *Proceedings of the Aristotelian Society Supplementary Volume*, 99–130.

Raz, Joseph. 2000. 'The Truth in Particularism', in Hooker and Little (2000), 48–78.

Stocker, Michael. 1979. 'Desiring the Bad', *Journal of Philosophy* 76, 738–53.

Velleman, J. David. 1992. 'The Guise of the Good', *Nous* 26, 3–26.

PARTICULARISM AND MORAL THEORY

by Garrett Cullity and Richard Holton

II—Richard Holton

PRINCIPLES AND PARTICULARISMS

ABSTRACT Should particularists about ethics claim that moral principles are never true? Or should they rather claim that any finite set of principles will not be sufficient to capture ethics? This paper explores and defends the possibility of embracing the second of these claims whilst rejecting the first, a position termed 'principled particularism'. The main argument that particularists present for their position—the argument that holds that any moral conclusion can be superseded by further considerations—is quite compatible with principled particularism; indeed, it is compatible with the idea that every true moral conclusion can be shown to follow deductively from a finite set of premises. Whilst it is true that these premises must contain implicit *ceteris paribus* clauses, this does not render the arguments trivial. On the contrary, they can do important work in justifying moral conclusions. Finally the approach is briefly applied to the related field of jurisprudence.

One thing has become clear from recent discussions: moral particularism is not a single doctrine, but a family of doctrines. Garrett Cullity, in his contribution to this symposium, distinguishes particularism about principles from particularism about reasons; and he argues for a modest version of the latter. I want to attend to the other side of his distinction: to particularism about principles. The main argument that particularists have advanced still leaves space for a considerable role for principles; and so leaves open the possibility that principles can play an important role in justifying moral verdicts. My aim is to develop the outline of an account in which they can play such a role. It transpires that if principles are to feature in deductive arguments, they must contain implicit *ceteris paribus* clauses. I try to formulate these with sufficient precision to show that they need not lead to triviality. The result is, I think, a position which, whilst still distinctively particularist, escapes the main charges that have been raised against the doctrine.

I

Characterizing Particularism about Principles. What should particularists about principles (hereafter: particularists) say? Should they deny that moral principles are *ever* true? That is probably the standard interpretation, and it is the one taken by Cullity. On Cullity's account even the weakest form of the doctrine involves denying that there are *any* correct general principles of the form:

Under descriptive conditions D the correct moral verdict is V.

But there is an alternative way of characterizing the particularists' position. Rather than denying that principles are ever true, they could be denying that they are could ever be *sufficient*: denying that any set of principles can serve to *capture* ethics. On this second interpretation the particularists' claim is that there is no one set of principles that can be used to determine the correct moral verdict in any situation.

Which of the two interpretations is the better? It seems to me that Cullity's cannot be quite right, for particularists typically endorse the supervenience of the moral on the descriptive. That is, they accept the highly plausible thesis that any two situations that are identical in their descriptive properties will be identical in their moral properties.[1] But then if D were a complete description of a situation (including the claim that it is a complete description!), and if V were the correct verdict in that situation, then the corresponding principle would be universally true: *whenever* D were realized, V would be the correct verdict.

We can imagine various ways of amending Cullity's account to deal with this worry; indeed, Cullity himself suggests one when he says that, according to particularism, there are no 'exceptionless' principles. This seems to me to be along the right lines. One way of making it precise will become clear once we get clearer on the second, more promising, interpretation of particularism. So let us turn to that.

The second interpretation of the particularist approach involves denying that there is any set of principles which serves

---

1. I skate over the issue of whether the supervenience is inter- or intra-world. For discussion, see Frank Jackson, Philip Pettit and Michael Smith 'Ethical Particularism and Patterns', in B. Hooker and M. Little (eds) *Moral Particularism* (Oxford: Clarendon Press, 2000), pp. 79–99 at p. 84.

to capture ethics. More exactly, on this second interpretation let us take particularism to be the thesis that

> There is no finite set of finite principles that serves to axiomatize ethical evaluation: that is, no finite set of finite principles, such that, given any action fully described in non-moral terms, the principles and the description entail a given moral verdict if and only if it is true.[2]

The need for talk of a *finite* set of principles comes from the fact that, as we have seen, particularists accept the supervenience of the moral on the descriptive. Given this, it would be possible to give a consistent axiomatization of ethics by simply listing every possible action and the correct verdict. In this sense then, particularists must accept that there is a consistent axiomatization of ethics, at least in a loose sense of 'axiomatization'.[3] But since there are infinitely many possible actions, such a list would have to be infinite. What the particularist claims is that there is no *finite* set of principles that serves to axiomatize ethics. Or, more precisely, since a finite list can be packed into a single principle provided that the principle is infinitely long, particularists will have to insist that their claim is that there is no finite set of *finite* principles.[4]

Formulated in this way, particularism about principles remains a radical doctrine. It is clearly incompatible with standard 'principled' theories: Kantianism and Utilitarianism for example. It

2 This way of understanding particularism was suggested by the very similar characterization given in Jackson, Pettit and Smith *op. cit.* Two points of clarification: (i) I take it that we should interpret 'entail' in a basically syntactic sense: the particularist is denying that there is any set of principles from which we can *deduce* which action is right; the principled theorist, in contrast, wants something approaching a decision procedure; (ii) whilst this thesis denies the possibility of deducing whether an action is right given its characterization in *non-moral* terms, there is a parallel but stronger thesis denying the possibility of deducing whether an action is right given its characterization in terms of *thick ethical concepts*. What I have to say in this paper about the former thesis can be easily transferred to the stronger thesis.

3. Loose, since all that we mean by 'axiomatization' is a set of principles that, together with the descriptive facts, entail all and only the ethical truths. Standardly in logic the term is only used if that set is decidable. In this stricter sense particularists presumably deny that there is an axiomatization of ethics. (The need for talk of a *consistent* axiomatization comes from the requirement that the principles entail all *and only* the ethical truths. An inconsistent axiomatization will, of course, entail all the ethical truths; but it will entail all the falsehoods as well.)

4. Although I have expressed this in terms of finitude, the particularists' worries will still be telling if the range of possible actions is not infinite but simply unsurveyably large.

holds that any attempt to discover the principles of morality will be unsuccessful. Nevertheless, there is a sense in which it should not be so surprising. For we know from Gödel's work that a similar claim is true about first order arithmetic:

> There is no finite set of finite principles that serves to axiomatize first order arithmetic: that is, no finite set of finite principles, such that, given any sentence in the language of arithmetic, the principles entail that sentence if and only if it is true.[5]

This parallel might give pause to those who argue that particularism about principles cannot be right for ethics, since it would make ethics arbitrary or unlearnable. We do not think that Gödel's results have shown arithmetic to be so.[6] But rather than pursuing that issue here, I want to follow up another point that is suggested by the analogy.

The unaxiomatizability of arithmetic entails that there is no *one* finite set of axioms that entails all of the truths of arithmetic. It doesn't entail that there are truths of arithmetic which do not follow from any set of axioms (and hence are not formally provable). It is trivially true that any sentence can be proved from some set of axioms, provided we are liberal enough in what will count as an axiom: simply add the sentence itself to the axioms. Indeed, the unaxiomatizability result doesn't obviously rule out the possibility that any truth of arithmetic can be given an *interesting* proof; although here we obviously need to make precise just what it is for a proof to be interesting.

A parallel for the particularist view of ethics should be evident. Interpreted in the second way, particularists are committed to thinking that there is no one set of true principles that entails, and hence justifies, each true moral verdict. But they are not thereby committed to thinking that there are true moral verdicts

5. Second order arithmetic is axiomatizable, but only if 'entail' is read semantically. There is still no finite set of axioms from which the theorems of second order arithmetic can be deduced.

6. Jackson, Pettit and Smith make the unlearnability point. Of course, there is much that we would need to get clear on if we were to make the parallel stick. Let me just mention one point at which it might seem to break down. Gödel has shown that an axiomatization of arithmetic will be, at best, partial; whereas it might be thought that particularists think that any attempted axiomatization of ethics will result in falsehoods. In fact I think that there is no disanalogy here, since I deny this latter claim: a point to which I return (see n. 15 below).

that are not entailed by some true moral principles. That is, whilst they reject

A [∃X: X is a finite set of true moral principles][∀y: y is a moral verdict] y is entailed by X and the non-moral truths

they can, consistently with this, accept

B [∀y: y is a moral verdict][∃X: X is a finite set of true moral principles] y is entailed by X and the non-moral truths.[7]

Let's call the position that involves rejecting **A** but embracing **B** *principled particularism*. The idea is that different moral verdicts will be entailed by different sets of principles; but there is no one set that will entail them all. This is the position that I shall explore in this paper. It might seem that it will involve denying outright the thesis that Cullity takes to be definitive of particularism, the thesis that there are no true moral principles. However, as we shall see shortly, there will turn out to be something right about his approach. Getting to that point will involve getting clear on just how principled particularism can be made to work.

II

Developing Principled Particularism. Whilst particularist writings are not clear on the matter, I rather doubt that anyone has so far embraced principled particularism.[8] Yet it seems to me to be an interesting and attractive position. To see why it is attractive

7. Again I am assuming that entailment should be read syntactically. Suppose it were read semantically: should particularists still reject **A**? They might contemplate accepting it, on the grounds that this would somehow fix the right interpretation. (Compare the discussion for arithmetic in Vann McGee, 'How We Learn Mathematical Language', *Philosophical Review* 106 (1997), pp. 35–68.) But I have no idea how this would go; in particular, I have no idea what would serve as the relevant axioms.

8. For some particularist discussions of the proper role of principles see Jonathan Dancy, *Moral Reasons* (Oxford: Blackwell, 1993), pp. 66–71; and David McNaughton, *Moral Vision* (Oxford: Blackwell, 1988), Ch. 13. Note that the idea that every moral truth is justifiable from some set of true moral principles is compatible with the idea that there can be regret when a principle is justifiably violated; and with the idea that no non-moral features have a constant 'moral valence' i.e. their presence will always either make an act better, or make it worse. On this last point see below, n. 12.

consider the two roles that principles have often been expected to play. In the first place they might be used in an *investigative* role, enabling us to discover the right thing to do. In the second they might be used in a *justificatory* role: to show that (and perhaps why) certain actions are right, to convince ourselves and others of their rightness.[9] It is a criticism that is often levelled at particularists that they cannot account for either of these roles.

The advocate of principled particularism will indeed think that principles have a very limited function in an investigative role. Principles will not provide us with anything like a decision procedure for telling whether an action is right. The reason is plain: it will be no good trying to discover whether a moral verdict is true by seeing whether it follows from a certain set of principles, since we can never be sure which set of principles to start with.[10] Nevertheless, the advocate of principled particularism will hold that principles play an important justificatory role. We can show that a given action is right by showing that it follows from some true principles and the non-moral facts. The principled particularist will thus be able to explain why principles play such an important role in our moral lives, whilst at the same time explaining the overblown claims that Kantians and utilitarians have made. Impressed by the fact that we use principles to justify moral verdicts, they have sought to codify the principles that we use; and that cannot be done.

That is why principled particularism is attractive. But there is a problem in developing it, one which comes from the very argument that particularists use to support their position. That argument, which we can call *the supersession argument* runs as follows: given any action whose features are described in non-moral terms, and a principle that says that a action having those features will be good, we can always think of some further feature which is such that, were the action to have that feature too,

<hr/>

9. I take this terminology from Russ Shafer-Ladau, 'Moral Rules' *Ethics* 107 (1997), pp. 584–611. I think that some of his conclusions need to be modified in the light of the distinction made here.

10. Given a strict understanding of what a decision procedure is, it is very unlikely anyway that we should have one for ethics: for it seems likely that to formulate ethical arguments we will need at least first order logic, and we know that we don't have a general decision procedure for validity there. But in a looser sense we might say that we have a decision procedure if we know that all of the sound moral arguments are those which invoke a certain finite set of moral principles. At least then we would know where to start looking for the proof.

it would become a bad action. So the principle is inadequate as it stands. It must be modified, or a further principle must be given outlining the exception. But once we have done that an exception to the amended principle(s) will be found, and we will be forced to amend again. And so on.[11]

The supersession argument is an argument for denying **A**, i.e. for thinking that there is no finite set of true finite principles that, together with the non-moral facts, entails, for all actions, whether or not they are right.[12] But the supersession argument seems to work equally well against **B**: it seems to follow that no deductively valid argument can be found that takes us from true principles and non-moral facts to the conclusion that any particular action is right. For deductive logic is monotonic: if an argument is deductively valid you cannot make it invalid by adding a further premise. So if the addition of a further premise can make an apparently valid argument invalid, it seems that the argument cannot really have been valid in the first place.

This is a formidable problem, but we should not despair. There is, I believe, a remedy. Lest it seem arbitrary or *ad hoc*, let me

---

11. Cullity refers to this process as 'undermining' rather than supersession ; I prefer the latter term, since it captures the idea that the superseding moral consideration involves a positive, as well as a negative, claim.

12. Let me reinforce a point made by Cullity. The argument for particularism is sometimes said to be holism, i.e. the view that non-moral features do not have a constant moral valence, but are good or bad depending upon the other non-moral features present. But that in itself doesn't entail particularism about principles. A homely example will make the point. Worm based compost heaps work best at a certain level of acidity. Make them too acid or too alkaline, and the worms that eat the rubbish will fail to flourish and ultimately will die. Suppose I have some material that I am thinking of adding to my heap. Will it be good for the heap, or bad for it? I won't know by knowing only the acidity of the material. Suppose that it is strongly alkaline. If the heap is too acidic, as they often are, then its addition will be good. But if the heap is already strongly alkaline, perhaps as the result of an over-zealous application of lime, then it will be bad. Similarly, the *amount* of material matters: the worms need to be fed, but they don't want to be swamped, or aerobic decomposition might set in and fry them. Compost heap management is thus a holistic business, in Dancy's sense: addition of the same stuff can be good or bad depending on the state of the heap. Nevertheless, it would be ridiculous to say (or at least, ridiculous to say on these grounds) that there is no finite set of principles governing it. We can perfectly well work out what the ideal conditions for the worms are, and derive our principles from that. It is just that the principles must make reference *both* to the nature of the material to be added *and* to the state of the heap: whether it is good to add some material will be a function *both* of the acidity and volume of the material *and* the acidity, volume and worm population of the heap. The argument for particularism is thus not just that moral considerations are holistic, but, in addition, that there are infinitely many of them.

first try to motivate it intuitively. In defending **B** we want to say that certain features of the world, together with certain principles, make a certain action right. The worry then is that there *could be* other features of the world which, together with other principles, which would undermine that verdict by making the action not right. But at that point we want to say something like this:

> So what? Why be worried by hypotheticals? If there *were* these other features they would make the action not right. But there aren't. We are concerned with the features that actually do obtain, and they, together with the principles, make the action right.

How do these considerations translate into the availability of a deductive argument? The basic idea is clear enough: we want our deductive argument to state that the facts we're talking about are all the relevant facts. Of course we might be wrong about that claim; there might be other facts that we should have considered. But with just about any argument we might be wrong about the premises. What we want is a deductively valid argument which, if we are right about the facts and about them being all the relevant facts, will take us to the conclusion of what we ought to do.

If the idea is clear enough, showing quite how to implement it is a bit more tricky. To keep things simple, we will consider only moral arguments that contain a single conditional principle with a single universal quantifier and that employ *modus ponens*.[13] Moreover, the examples I shall present are utterly uninteresting. It is the *form* of the argument that I want to explore.

Let us first introduce some terminology. Suppose we have a set of non-moral predicates $\{F_1, F_2 ... F_m\}$; and suppose that these occur in a moral principle of the form $\forall x ((F_1x \& F_2x \& ... \& F_mx) \to F_cx)$ and in a corresponding set of non-moral sentences $\{F_1a, F_2a, ... F_ma\}$. Then we say that that principle and those non-moral sentences are *superseded* by another moral principle $\forall x((G_1x \& G_2x \& ... \& G_nx \to G_cx))$ and corresponding set of non-moral sentences $\{G_1a, G_2a, ... G_na\}$ just in case:

(i) $(G_1x \& G_2x \& ... \& G_nx)$ entails $(F_1x \& F_2x \& ... \& F_mx)$, but not *vice versa*;

---

13. I don't think that this is too unrealistic an assumption; and it would, I think, be easy enough to generalize, but at the cost of making my presentation very hard to follow.

(ii) $F_c x$ is incompatible with $G_c x$.

For instance, the principle 'If something is a killing, you shouldn't do it' and the non-moral sentence 'This is a killing' is superseded by the principle 'If something is a killing and done in self-defence, you may do it' and the non-moral sentences 'This is a killing' and 'This is done in self-defence.'

The particularists' argument was that for every true principle and set of facts, there was some other true principle and set of *possible* facts that would supersede it. But that does not imply that each true principle and set of facts is *actually* superseded; that is, it does not imply that there is a true principle and a set of *true* non-moral sentences that supersede it. We now want to build into each moral argument the claim that it is not actually superseded. How do we do it? First, we need to add to each argument a new premise, which we might call '*That's it*':

That's it: There are no further relevant moral principles and non-moral facts; i.e. there is no true moral principle and set of *true* non-moral sentences which supersede those which appear in this argument.

And then we need to add a clause in each principle to the same effect. We can do this by adding it as a further conjunct of the antecedent. So we get moral arguments like this

I.   P1   This is a killing
     P2 $\forall x$ ((x is a killing & *That's it*) $\rightarrow$ you shouldn't do x)
     P3   *That's it*
     C   You shouldn't do this.

The particularist claims that this argument is bound to be superseded by other valid arguments, for instance

II. P1   This is a killing
     P2   This is done in self defence
     P3 $\forall x$ ((x is a killing & x is done in self defence & *That's it*) $\rightarrow$ you may do x)
     P4   *That's it*
     C   You may do this.

But the fact that II is a *valid* argument that supersedes I does not show that there is a *sound* argument that supersedes I. If there is a sound argument that supersedes I, then I cannot be sound, since the *That's it* premise in **I** will be false. Thus we can embrace **B**, or more accurately (and assuming that every argument can be phrased as one with a single principle), **B***

> **B*** [∀y: y is a moral verdict][∃x: x is a true, finite moral principle] y is entailed by x, the relevant non-moral truths (i.e. those that interact with the principle x) and *That's it.*

Let us stop for a moment and fix up one sloppiness that has been allowed to go unchecked. Earlier I gave a definition of what it is for one principle and set of non-moral sentences to supersede another. But this definition was restricted to sentences of a certain form, and that form made no space for the inclusion of *That's it* in the principle. So we need to add to that definition as follows:

> A moral principle of the form $\forall x\ ((F_1x\ \&\ F_2x\ \&\ ...\ \&\ F_mx\ \&\ \textit{That's it}) \rightarrow F_cx)$ and a corresponding set of non-moral sentences $\{F_1a, F_2a, ...\ F_ma\}$ are *superseded* by another moral principle $\forall x\ ((G_1x\ \&\ G_2x\ \&\ ...\ \&\ G_nx\ \&\ \textit{That's it}) \rightarrow G_cx)$ and corresponding set of non-moral sentences $\{G_1a, G_2a, ...\ G_na\}$ just in case:
>
> (i) $(G_1x\ \&\ G_2x\ \&\ ...\ \&\ G_nx)$ entails $(F_1x\ \&\ F_2x\ \&\ ...\ \&\ F_mx)$, but not *vice versa*;
> (ii) F_cx is incompatible with G_cx.

This reveals a certain circularity in our definitions: *That's it* is defined partly in terms of the idea of being superseded; and being superseded is defined partly in terms of *That's it.* This is a tricky area, but I don't think that the circularity is pernicious. It is simply that we need to understand the two notions together.[14] Nevertheless, the use of *That's it* might well raise a suspicion of triviality. In the next section I investigate whether this suspicion has any foundation. At this point let us just note that we can finally say what was right about Cullity's characterization of particularism about principles: whilst it need not deny that there are

---

14. On the general issue see Stephen Yablo, 'Definitions, Consistent and Inconsistent', *Philosophical Studies* 72, (1993), pp. 147–75.

any true moral principles, it does deny that there are any that do not contain *That's it.*[15]

III

Is 'That's It' Legitimate? *That's it* involves a degree of self reference; it contains the expression 'this argument' which refers to the very argument in which it occurs. This has the consequence that the *That's it* premise will have a different content in each argument in which it appears.[16] The same goes for the *That's it* clause in each principle. In turn this means that principles will only have a truth value in the context of an argument. But self-reference isn't bad by itself; and I can't see that what we have here will lead to paradox or contradiction. If there are worries they come either from the thought that *That's it* makes moral arguments trivial, or that it imports unacceptable moral considerations into the premises. Let us take these worries in turn.

Arguments can be trivial in many different ways. One way is to be question-begging. Thus an argument that contained among its premises the claim that a certain action was the right one wouldn't be very useful. But adding *That's it* isn't going to be tantamount to doing that. *That's it* makes the very different claim that no considerations beyond those mentioned in the argument are going to be relevant. And in saying this it is going to be highly contentious. Those disagreeing with a moral argument will frequently contend that the problem is exactly that there are further relevant non-moral facts that are being ignored. Indeed, the *That's it* premise does bring a degree of scepticism to any moral argument. If there are infinitely many principles, and

15. We are also now in a position to answer the worry raised in n. 6, namely that arithmetic and ethics are not analogous, since whilst Gödel showed that any attempt to axiomatize arithmetic would be *incomplete*, the particularist holds that any attempt to capture ethics in a set of principles will actually lead to *falsehood*. Certainly the particularist will hold that many attempts to capture ethics with principles will lead to error; utilitarianism is one example. But not all sets of principles will do so. A good set of moral principles, formulated with *That's it* clauses and employed in arguments containing *That's it* premises will lead to no falsehoods. They will, however, be incomplete, for there will be many circumstances in which *That's it* will not be true. There is thus no important disanalogy with arithmetic here.

16. Nonetheless, we can still think of entailment as defined syntactically. We just need to ensure that within any one argument each occurrence of the indexical expression 'this argument' gets the same interpretation.

infinitely many non-moral facts, then our confidence in the truth of *That's it* cannot amount to certainty. But scepticism of this kind seems quite right.

A second triviality worry concerns whether *That's it* guarantees that any argument that contains it will be valid. Certainly there are self-referential premises that have this character. Thus consider

Valid: This argument is valid.

Valid does seem to bring validity to any argument to which it is added as a premise, at least in an informal semantic sense of validity.[17] Does *That's it* have the same effect? I see no reason to think that it does. It certainly seems that we can give invalid arguments containing it, whether validity is understood syntactically or semantically. For instance

    P1   This is a killing
    P2 $\forall x$ ((x is a killing & *That's it*) $\rightarrow$ you shouldn't do x)
    P3   *That's it*
    C   You should do this.[18]

Nevertheless, there remains a worry about triviality.[19] The worry is that every moral principle will turn out to be true; or more precisely, true in every argument in which it occurs (recall that owing to the presence of *That's it*, moral principles only get

17. I.e. the sense in which an argument is valid iff every world in which its premises are true is a world in which its conclusion is true. Proof: suppose, for reductio, that there were an argument A that contained *Valid* as a premise and was invalid. An argument which is invalid is necessarily invalid. So, in every possible world, *Valid* would be false. So there would be no possible world in which the premises of A are all true; so there would be no world in which they are true and the conclusion is false. So A would be valid. Worse still: the argument

    P: This argument is valid
    C: God exists

seems to be both valid and sound. We have already seen that, since it contains *Valid* as a premise, it is valid; and since its only premise says that it is valid, it must be sound. But then the conclusion will follow, whatever it might be. Clearly there is something wrong with *Valid*. For discussion see Stephen Read, 'Self-Reference and Validity', *Synthese* 42 (1979), pp. 265–74.

18. Note: the problem of an argument with just *That's it* as premise doesn't arise, since the notion of supersession simply isn't defined for such arguments.

19. Thanks to Tim Williamson for raising it.

a truth value when they occur in arguments). Consider one of
the principles mentioned above:

$$\forall x \ ((x \text{ is a killing \& } \textit{That's it}) \rightarrow \text{you shouldn't do x}).$$

Let us suppose that that principle is true in whichever argument
it occurs. Then presumably the same principle with the contradictory conclusion

$$\forall x \ ((x \text{ is a killing \& } \textit{That's it}) \rightarrow \text{you should do x})$$

will be false in whichever argument it occurs. Let us take one
such (valid) argument:

(1)   P1   This is a killing
      P2 $\forall x \ ((x \text{ is a killing \& } \textit{That's it}) \rightarrow \text{you should do x})$
      P3   *That's it*
      C   You should do this.

The principle P2 is a universal generalization, so for it to be false
in this argument, it must have at least one instantiation of the
form

$$((A \text{ is a killing \& } \textit{That's it}) \rightarrow \text{you should do A})$$

which has a true antecedent and a false conclusion. For the antecedent to be true, both of its conjuncts must be true; and that
means that *That's it* must be true. *That's it* says, of course, that
the argument (1) is not superseded. Yet, and here is the triviality
worry, it looks as though every argument might be trivially
superseded. For consider the argument

(2)   P1   This is a killing
      P2 $\forall x \ ((x \text{ is a killing \& Grass is green \& } \textit{That's it}) \rightarrow \text{you}$
           shouldn't do x)
      P3   Grass is green
      P4   *That's it*
      C   You shouldn't do this.

Here we have simply taken a moral principle that, by hypothesis,
we are taking to be true, and a sound argument in which it features; we have inserted into the antecedent of the principle a true
non-moral sentence; and we have added that sentence to the
argument as a further premise. The resulting argument is sound.

By the definition of supersession that we gave earlier, this argument does seem to supersede the unsound argument, (1), with which we started. So the *That's it* premise that (1) contained is false; and so the moral principle which it contained, which we wanted to be false, has not been falsified after all. Moreover, it looks as though we could play the same trick with any instantiation of that principle; and indeed, with any instantiation of any apparently false principle. It seems that every moral principle will be true: either substantially true, in virtue of featuring in sound moral arguments; or trivially true, in virtue of this supersession trick.

Now perhaps this is not an utterly disastrous result. After all, we have already noted that the presence of *That's it* means that moral principles only get a truth value in the context of an argument. Once we have embraced this relativity to arguments, perhaps we should not worry about which moral principles are true, but about which feature in sound arguments; we might hope that those that are not trivially true are those that do (or could?) feature in sound arguments. (Argument (1) has not been shown to be sound. Indeed, the very argument we gave for thinking that the moral principle it contained was true traded on the fact that it was not, since it traded on the falsity of the *That's it* premise.) However, that is far from obviously right; and anyway it would be good if we had some way of denying truth to certain moral principles.

I see only one way of doing this, which works by being a bit less liberal about what we count as a moral principle in the first place. Recall that the problem arose because apparently false moral principles were superseded by arguments containing principles that were built from true moral principles with extra nonmoral clauses—such as the claim that grass is green—inserted into their antecedents. But must we count these gerrymandered constructions as moral principles? We need to be more restrictive: moral principles are minimally contentful. Weaken a moral principle by adding an unnecessary clause to its antecedent, and what you get is not a moral principle at all. It's not obvious quite how the details of this proposal would be worked out.[20] But something like it is quite in line with our intuitive conception of what

20. It has something in common with the objection to weakening found in relevance logic; and in working out the details one might expect to find similar difficulties to those encountered there.

a moral principle should be. Indeed, not only is it needed to block the current worry. Some such qualification seems to be needed if we are to say that moral principles must serve to *explain* moral verdicts.[21]

So much for the worry that *That's it* makes moral arguments trivial. What of the worry that it imports too much into the premises? We have already addressed this to some extent when we asked whether it was question begging. But there is further worry that, without actually being question begging, the presence of *That's it* might somehow undermine the whole point of the arguments in which it occurs. The thought is something like this: the interesting part of the principled particularist's claim was that, for any action that we ought to perform, we could give a deductive argument for performing it that used as premises just principles and non-moral facts. But once we add some further premise, we need to be careful that it isn't of a sort which serves to take away the interest of the claim.

Again, I don't think that there is any real concern here. In effect *That's it* consists of two related claims: a claim that there are no further relevant non-moral facts, and a claim that there are no further relevant principles. We thought it quite legitimate for the premises of a moral argument to consist of non-moral facts and moral principles: we were not, after all, trying to derive an 'ought' from an 'is'. So why should it not also include universal generalizations over non-moral facts and moral principles? Admittedly they make use of the idea of relevance; but this we have defined in terms of the notion of supersession; and there does not seem to be anything odd about that definition. Since the quantification ranges over an infinite domain, we cannot think that our understanding of the universal generalizations comes from surveying that domain. But no one other than a very hard-line verificationist would conclude that we therefore do not really understand them, or that they have no significance. They remain eminently falsifiable.

In fact something like *That's it* will be needed by very many moral theories and theories of practical action when put in

---

21. I haven't broached the difficult issue of moral explanation here. My aim is the limited one of showing how a particularist could embrace principles. I am not saying anything about the further features that such principles must have if they are to serve as explanations.

deductive form. Suppose you think that the thing to do at a party is to talk to the most influential person. You will not know what to do if all you have is a list of people who are at the party, together with details of how influential they are. In order to know who to talk to, you will also need to know that these are *all* the people at the party. Similarly, and more plausibly, suppose you were a utilitarian. Then you couldn't determine which action to perform on the basis of a list of pleasures and pains caused by possible actions of yours. You would need to know, in addition, that these was *all* the pleasures and pains that each action caused; and that these were *all* your possible actions. Indeed it wouldn't help even if, *per impossibile*, you listed absolutely every non-moral fact. You would still need to add the premise that these were all the facts: you would need something analogous to *That's it*. Of course it is easy to describe the non-moral facts in such a way that something like *That's it* is smuggled in; we talk about the *total* utility caused by an action. We should realize though that this is just shorthand for the claim that there is this much *and no more*.

It might seem then that the real difference between the role of *That's it* in principled particularism and the role of similar premises in utilitarian arguments is this: whilst both need a premise that says that there are not further relevant non-moral facts, it is only in principled particularism that we need a premise like *That's it* which also makes a claim about there being no further relevant *principles*. But even here the distinction is not so clear. Certainly a utilitarian argument that a certain action is right need only invoke the utilitarian principle that one should perform the action yielding the greatest utility, together with a list of the total utility resulting from each possible action, and a claim that these are all the actions. But if we are to conclude that this is the *unique* action that is right, we will need to know that the utilitarian principle is the *only* correct one; we need to say that this is the only relevant principle. We wouldn't normally put this in to a utilitarian argument, since it is presupposed; but strictly we need it.

IV

Conclusion, and a Brief Application to the Law. I hope that I have said enough to make principled particularism look plausible, and to quieten worries about the legitimacy of *That's it*. As I said at the outset, I find principled particularism an interesting doctrine. It acknowledges the particularist point that we can always find an exception to any moral principle; whilst at the same time making good sense of the role that principles play in justifying our moral conclusions. It also, I think, makes good sense of our use of principles in teaching people to be moral. We give principles that apply in most cases, but always with an implicit *That's it* condition attached. An insensitivity to this on the part of the learner is likely to be met, not with admiration for their logical acumen, but with impatience at their over-rigid approach. Perhaps too it will be met with the admonition that *the exception proves the rule*. This suggestive but much misunderstood expression comes from the law, an area to which I now turn. I shall say a little more about it at the end of a very brief discussion of how the principled particularism might apply in legal contexts.

In 'Model of Rules I'[22] Ronald Dworkin argues that legal positivism, understood as the thesis that all law derives from a set of socially accepted rules identified by a rule of recognition, cannot acknowledge the role of principles. The term 'principle' has a special sense in Dworkin's paper: roughly, unlike rules, principles do not apply in an all-or-nothing fashion, but rather apply with a certain weight, the weight being sensitive to the case.[23] At the end of his paper Dworkin considers the possibility that positivists might simply acknowledge all he says about the importance of principles, but insist that all law derives from a set of socially accepted rules and principles, together with an assignment of their appropriate weights in different cases. This set might be then regarded as the rule of recognition. To this Dworkin responds

> This solution has the attraction of paradox, but of course it is an unconditional surrender. If we simply designate our rule of recognition by the phrase 'the complete set of principles in force' we achieve only the tautology that law is law. If, instead, we tried

22. In *Taking Rights Seriously*, (London: Duckworth 1977).

23. Note too that this is likely to be a case where the particularist claim will need to be the stronger one mentioned in n. 2. Legal principles don't typically allow courts to arrive at legal conclusions from premises stated in non-moral vocabulary; rather, they enable the move from certain evaluative legal and moral notions (thick ethical concepts) to verdictive ones.

actually to list all the principles in force we would fail. They are controversial, their weight is all important, they are numberless, and they shift and change so fast that the start of our list would be obsolete before we reached the middle. Even if we succeeded, we would not have a key for law because there would be nothing left for our key to unlock.[24]

This is weak. If we did compile such a list it is not true that there would be nothing left for our key to unlock. We would have a formidable tool: a complete account of what the correct legal judgement would be in every case. So we need to turn to Dworkin's reasons for thinking that we could never compile it. Here the problem as Dworkin identifies it seems to be mainly technical: the principles shift so fast we could never pin them down. This invites the response that if only we had enough people on the job, with enough resources, then we could get it done. What we want is an argument for thinking that we could never compile the list, no matter what our resources. And it is here that particularist considerations come in. For isn't the thought that, no matter how long and detailed a list of principles and weights we had, we could always think of new cases which would require new principles, or at least, a change of the weights? Dworkin hints at this when he says that the principles are 'numberless' (I take it he means countably infinite, rather than non-denumerable). But why doesn't he say so explicitly? One reason might be that such a claim would seem to be in conflict with another feature of the law. In giving a judgment on a case a court does seem to give a set of rules and principles, together, perhaps, with some weighting on those principles, from which the verdict is said to follow. And in so far as the judgment counts as a precedent, subsequent courts will be required to distinguish the facts in cases in which they want to rule differently. So it might seem then that, once we acknowledge the role of rules and principles in justifying a given decision, we are forced to accept that the total set of such things could, in principle, be given.

I hope that I have shown in this paper that there is no such pressure. Principled particularism provides us with just the resources we need to bring the two theses together. We can think of legal decisions as always containing implicit *That's it* clauses.

24. Ibid. pp. 43–4.

When a distinction is made in a subsequent judgement, it is typically that clause that is denied. Indeed what better way of understanding the legal maxim, mentioned above in a non legal context, *Exceptio probat regulam in casibus non exceptis*: the exception proves the rule in the cases not excepted?[25] When we explicitly identify a case as an exception to a rule, we invoke *That's it*. But by treating it as an exception, rather than using it to show that the rule is wrong, we thereby implicitly reaffirm the rule for the cases in which *That's it* is not triggered.[26]

25. It is unfortunate that this maxim is commonly given the fallacious and far less interesting interpretation (endorsed by *Brewer's*) in which 'proves' is taken to mean 'tests'. This interpretation makes no sense of the use to which the expression is typically put. In discussing the maxim I make no claim about its standing in current Anglo-American law.

26. Thanks to audiences at the Universities of Edinburgh, Glasgow, Leeds, Stirling and Vermont where I tried out some of these ideas; and to Alexander Bird, David Christensen, Garrett Cullity, Jonathan Dancy, Anthony Duff, Frank Jackson, Rae Langton, Peter Milne, Philip Pettit, Michael Smith and Timothy Williamson.

FROM KANT TO POST-KANTIAN IDEALISM

by Sebastian Gardner and Paul Franks

I—Sebastian Gardner

GERMAN IDEALISM

ABSTRACT German idealism has been pictured as an unwarranted deviation from the central epistemological orientation of modern philosophy, and its close historical association with German romanticism is adduced in support of this verdict. This paper proposes an interpretation of German idealism which seeks to grant key importance to its connection with romanticism without thereby undermining its philosophical rationality. I suggest that the fundamental motivation of German idealism is axiological, and that its augmentation of Kant's idealism is intelligible in terms of its combined aim of consolidating the transcendental turn and legitimating the kind of (objectual) relation to value articulated in German romanticism.

I

The aim of this paper is to sketch an interpretation of German idealism. The interpretation, briefly stated, is that German idealism as a whole is to be regarded as driven at the most basic level by axiological considerations. What my defence of this idea—not itself novel—is intended to add is a specific suggestion as to what the relevant axiological considerations are and how they operate in the formation of German idealism, together with an account of what this entails regarding its philosophical significance.[1]

The mere thesis that German idealism is bound up in some important fashion with considerations of value would scarcely distinguish German idealism from any other major philosophical school or tradition. Equally uncontentious is the observation that the axiological dividends of German idealist metaphysics are remarkable. The stronger thesis to be defended here, however, is

---

1. The issues raised by speaking of German idealism 'as a whole', and the ambiguities of 'is to be regarded as', will be picked up on, though of course not laid to rest or resolved in this paper.

that German idealism is to be regarded as grounded ultimately on a conception of value which is articulated in German romanticism, and which in turn German idealism aims to show to be rationally accessible, and that this two-way relation can be acknowledged without ceasing to think of German idealism as continuous with Kant's idealism. This stronger thesis differs from some other views of German idealism.

There is a widespread presumption that the hyper-speculative character of the metaphysics of German idealism shows plainly that its fundamental orientation is at odds with the central epistemological orientation of modern philosophy, and in the minds of many this fact gives immediate grounds for a highly negative estimate of German idealism's strictly philosophical interest, whatever broader cultural importance or narrowly historical interest it may be allowed to have. In relation to this view, my claim that German idealism is value-driven will appear to be no news, and grist to the mill. Here the point of dispute is instead whether the philosophical rationality of German idealism is enhanced or undermined by its axiological dependence.

Among those who by contrast look sympathetically on German idealism, there is pressure to reconstruct its development as centring not on considerations of value but on problems of theoretical reason, in the first instance those epistemological and metaphysical problems formulated and addressed by Kant in the first *Critique*. Not only does this approach promise to elucidate the obscurities of German idealism by means of the relative clarity (or at any rate greater familiarity) of Kant, it also has firm historical grounds in the trajectory of philosophical development which is suggested by the sequence of texts that first appeared in response to Kant. Furthermore, it may seem that the best way of countering the charge of unwarranted deviation from the epistemological tradition is to show that, on the contrary, German idealism is wrestling with the same problems—the threat of scepticism, the shortcomings of empiricism, the arbitrariness of the great rationalist systems—that underpin Kant's theoretical philosophy, and that it is merely attempting, at least in the first instance, to overcome Kant's aporias.

There is also, among some of German idealism's defenders, a tendency to suppose that the best reconstruction of German idealism will be one that brings it into line with (and thereby shows it to be formative in the creation of) the post-metaphysical, broadly naturalistic climate which appears to be the legacy of both Anglophone and continental European philosophy of the last two centuries. This orientation is visible in some of the most striking recent work on Hegel.

The thesis that German idealism is value-driven, as I wish to understand it, comes into conflict with this post-metaphysical tendency, for reasons that will emerge. With regard to the more general view of German idealism as developing out of the same epistemological and metaphysical issues as preoccupy Kant, the disagreement concerns only its degree of completeness.

II

As these brief remarks indicate, there is in the interpretation of German idealism, as in other hard interpretative cases in the history of philosophy, including that of Kant, the problem that we have to deal with a number of interdependent variables—philosophical truth, relation to its historical predecessors, distance from or proximity to our contemporary philosophical outlook, and so on—none of which can be fixed without taking a stand that is open to dispute.

What is likely to be agreed, however, is that the development of German idealism presents, in relation to Kant, an obvious puzzle, concerning the transformation of a philosophical system that enshrines (arguably: that is constructed on the basis of an assumption of) human cognitive finitude, into a type of system that not only removes all limitations in principle from human cognition, but also embeds human cognition in a metaphysical context which accords human subjectivity, in different ways, an absolute status. The puzzle can be put in a variety of idioms: as a move from a weak, or contingent, conception of the subject-object relation to a strong conception, of subject-object identity; or as the transformation of a philosophical system which conceives its claims perspectivally, and philosophical truth as grounded in an appeal to necessities of representation, into an outlook that requires philosophical truth to be a-perspectival, or the revelation of a self-comprehending perspective. In this respect, if in no other, there seems to be a permissible sense in which, despite the profound differences between Fichte, Schelling and Hegel, one may speak of German idealism as a whole.

Now there are of course many different ways of attempting to account for the transition from Kant to post-Kantian idealism, and here we encounter another methodological difficulty, viz. that the kind of explanation we seek will be determined by how the explanandum is conceived, and that this is not a fixed given. If the development of German idealism is described in terms of, and regarded as simply consisting in, a series of sufficiently definite historical moves, then the task of explanation will be conceived as one of providing an analysis of specific transitions (from Kant to Reinhold and Maimon, from Reinhold to Fichte through Schulze, and so on), and it may then seem adequate to point to the various perceived internal difficulties in the Kantian system as initiating the development, each later stage being propelled by some perceived inadequacy in its predecessor.

One reason for doubting that such an explanation will be complete, is that it appears to show at most, not why German idealism developed in the wake of Kant, but why Kant's philosophy did not gain firm and enduring acceptance. From Kant's shortcomings it can be inferred only that the resulting post-Kantian philosophical situation should have been characterised by either controversy surrounding the value of Kant's system, or a consensus regarding its inadequacy, perhaps attended with the construction of new variants, such as Reinhold's Philosophy of the Elements and J. S. Beck's doctrine of the standpoint. It is in any case questionable that, had the prevailing disposition been protective rather than supersessive, Kant's philosophy could not well have survived, pretty much intact, the criticisms which were made of it immediately by Kant's contemporaries, and adduced later by the German idealists as reasons for pursuing the spirit of Kant's philosophy beyond its letter: that is to say, it is far from clear why Kant's philosophy, given its then unparalleled capacity to seemingly accommodate and meet, in a comprehensive and systematic fashion, the principal demands placed on philosophical thought by modernity, should have failed to establish itself as a new and robust philosophical orthodoxy.

Yet another, methodological reason is provided by the general line of argument which warrants the provision of 'high-level' hypotheses in the history of philosophy. Any attempt to provide a complete account of German idealism in terms of successive historical stages, step by step, faces the difficulty of what to say about the total development. If the total development is more than the sum of the stages, then there is again a risk of having to exaggerate Kant's deficiencies in order to be able to picture their overall trajectory as necessitated, thereby raising the question why, if Kant's philosophy was such a mess, it could intelligibly have been appealed to as a worthy basis for future developments; while if the development is no more than the sum of its parts, then German idealism, to the extent that there is any such thing 'as a whole', is made to appear a kind of accident.

For these reasons, I suggest, we should agree on the description of German idealism as involving a puzzling inversion of Kant's philosophy which intimates the need for a unitary, global explanation—one that prescinds, to some limited degree and with due caution, from the detail at the ground level of historical development.

III

As a first approach to the puzzle, it may be noted that Kant's system, in the form that it assumes in Kant's own writings and presentation, allows itself to be restructured, as several post-Kantians pointed out. This is the case in two respects in particular: first, the basic argument for transcendental idealism; second, the relation of the theoretical and the practical philosophy.

The argument for transcendental idealism in the *Critique of Pure Reason* is in fact twofold: an argument in the Transcendental Aesthetic from space and time, and an argument in the Antinomy of Pure Reason. The relation between the two arguments is not fully clear. Nor, more generally, is it entirely clear whether transcendental idealism is intended to be a premise (a bold hypothesis to be verified by the results of its experimental application) or a conclusion of the *Critique*, i.e. whether a linear argument for transcendental idealism is supposed to be found in the work. In addition, the argument in the Aesthetic, together with other parts of the *Critique*, in particular the Transcendental Deduction, also seem to intimate the possibility of what Karl Ameriks has called a 'short argument' for transcendental idealism, one that proceeds from reflection on the conditions of possibility of objects (of representation) in general to their transcendental ideality.[2] This is exactly what we find when the case

2. Karl Ameriks, 'Kantian Idealism Today', *History of Philosophy Quarterly* 9, 1992, 329–42, and *Kant and the Fate of Autonomy: Problems in the Appropriation of the Critical Philosophy* (Cambridge: Cambridge University Press, 2000), Ch. 3.

for transcendental idealism—or more precisely, the case against transcendental realism and for some idealist alternative; the case for the 'transcendental turn'—is rehearsed by the German idealists.

The relation of theoretical and practical reason in Kant's system similarly allows for restructuring. The historical order of Kant's presentation of the various parts of the Critical system appears not to determine straightforwardly or definitively the correct view of the system's logical organisation. While the texts which compose Kant's corpus proceed from the epistemological and metaphysical problems of theoretical reason to the sphere of freedom, the suggestion emerges, in discussion of the transcendental ideality of the self in the *Critique of Practical Reason*, of a relation of dependence, or at any rate a possible arrow of philosophical progression, running in the opposite direction—such that one may begin to envisage the possibility of embedding theoretical reason in practical reason or in some other, less narrowly specified sphere of reason's employment, a strategy that again is found in the German idealists.

However, the mere fact that these possibilities are left open by Kant's texts again does not of itself explain the emergence of German idealism. Specifically, the following points are unexplained. First, what it was in the outlook of the German idealists that made these possibilities of restructuring, readily discernible to us because we have seen them explored by Fichte and Schelling, salient to them. Second, that the route of a 'short argument' for transcendental idealism should have been explored at all, in view of the fact that the German idealists do not appear to have identified the same difficulties with the arguments of the Aesthetic and Antinomy that perhaps to us now seem so clear. Third, that its exploration, together with the reconfiguration of the relation of practical and theoretical reason, should have extended to new, absolute idealisms rather than back to Kant's transcendental idealism, i.e., why the alternative of transforming rather than simply reconfiguring—'repairing'—Kant was taken. Fourth, that there should have been in the development of German idealism such an intense preoccupation with staking an

3. *Critique of Practical Reason*, 5:6, in Kant, *Practical Philosophy*, trans. and ed. Mary Gregor (Cambridge: Cambridge University Press, 1996), p. 141.

'either/or' opposition of idealism and realism, or criticism and dogmatism (the terminology varies, as does the distinction itself). Fifth, what facilitated the clear appreciation on the part of the German idealists, unlike many other of Kant's contemporaries, that the core of Kant's so-called idealism lies in the institution of a new form of philosophical discourse, methodology and explanation, rather than in the adoption of an ontological, Berkeleyan position.[4]

IV

It is frequently said in accounts of German idealism that an interest in systematicity, or in forging unity, 'organic' unity, became philosophically forceful in the post-Kantian era. While it cannot be ruled out in advance of further enquiry that an interest in systematic unity for its own sake is simply the end of the matter, the implication of this way of putting things is as often as not to suggest an intrusion of extra-philosophical, quasi-pictorial concerns into philosophical thought.

This would not follow, of course, if the interest in systematicity could be reconstructed as a convincing philosophical motive: for example, if it could be shown that the authority of reason was genuinely at stake in the attempt to construct an all-comprehending and self-validating philosophical system, or that the concern for systematicity is crucial for the epistemological, countersceptical objectives of German idealism. But it is doubtful that any such reconstruction in terms of the authority or possibility of reason can avoid referring to a strong conception of reason which already bears the marks of German idealism, and most unlikely that epistemological motives take us all the way to German idealist metaphysics. In addition, the possibility of an explanation of German idealism that lays its seeming metaphysical exuberances at the door of German romanticism—a suggestion often made by critics of German idealism, and argued in some

4. It is true that Kant himself draws a historical line between previous, transcendental realist and the new, Copernican philosophy, but it hardly emerges from the body of the *Critique* as more fundamental than, say, Kant's new relation to empiricism and rationalism. Similarly, Kant's disavowal of Berkeleyanism is famously problematic.

detail by Edward Craig fairly recently[5]—should be acknowledged frankly as posing a serious challenge: in view of the thick web of historical interconnections between the relevant figures, and the multitude of conceptual, thematic and terminological affinities, it seems far from absurd to suppose that German idealism is at bottom simply Hölderlin's *Hyperion* transposed into a Kantian key.[6]

Thus, if a drive to systematicity and unity is the proximal source of German idealism, this factor requires some further explication, and if the romanticism connection is to be granted the importance that it appears historically to have had, without jeopardising the strictly philosophical interest of German idealism, then it too needs to be grasped in some way that reveals its philosophical rationality.

V

How might this be done? What else, beyond a concern for systematicity per se or an interest in re-expressing certain cultural and artistic developments in a philosophical idiom, might be adduced as a motive for German idealism?

The specific question to focus on is that of what *use* might be served by a stronger grade of idealism than that of Kant, given that (as I am assuming) there is no internal necessity for Kantian idealism to resolve itself into any of the post-Kantian idealisms—and that, it may be added, costs are attached to this move. The costs consist in a sacrifice of the careful balance achieved by Kant between the conflicting parties in the wars of reason, and in a heightened tension with the instinctive realism of pre-philosophical consciousness, supplemented by the difficulties that are created through assuming a much greater burden of explanation—through making philosophical explanation answerable once again to the principle of sufficient reason.

If we return to the two respects in which Kant's system is open to being restructured, it may be observed that one result of re-articulating idealism in the manner of German idealism is to construct a philosophical position with a greater capacity to resist

5. Edward Craig, *The Mind of God and the Works of Man* (Oxford: Clarendon, 1987), chs. 3–4.

6. Craig *op. cit.*, pp. 132, 162, 171–2; Craig talks of a 'craving for' and obsession with 'unity', pp. 136, 158. Cf. the view of Wilhelm Windelband, *A History of Philosophy*, vol. II, trans. James H. Tufts (New York: Harper, 1958), pp. 529–31.

transcendental-realist naturalism, i.e. to broaden the front on which transcendental idealism can be defended successfully. Though in the *Critique of Pure Reason* Kant appears to regard the argument with transcendental realism as resolved decisively in his own favour, it is plausible to think that there remains one species of metaphysical position against which Kant's arguments for the transcendental turn are at most only partially effective: namely a position of the same kind as that which we now describe as externalist naturalism, a naturalism that is not grounded methodologically on the resources of classical empiricism, but which instead premises philosophical explanation on the assumption of a standpoint outside human subjectivity, which is treated as an object fit to receive externally grounded explanation, rather than as that which provides the source and pattern of philosophical explanation. Awareness of the power of such a rival to transcendental philosophy—of its ability to evade the pressure that Kant puts on the empiricist to accept the transcendental turn, and perhaps its power to match in its own terms the explanatory achievements of transcendental idealism—is shown in the post-Kantian preoccupation with Spinoza.

The German idealist combination of the 'short argument' for transcendental idealism with a reattunement of theoretical and practical reason is intelligible in the light of the threat posed by Spinozist/naturalist transcendental realism. The situation of Kant in arguing against such a position may be put like this. Scrutiny of the arguments in the *Critique of Pure Reason* shows that its fundamental criticism of transcendental realist positions cannot be that they contain any strict, internal contradiction, but rather that they leave unexplained, and inexplicable, after a certain point, the relation of subject to object. In making this complaint Kant appeals, however, to a certain (familiarly 'Cartesian') conception of philosophical explanation, viz. that it should be cast in terms native to the perspective of subjectivity and serve the reflexive end of making this perspective lucid and adequate to itself. Kant's complaint presupposes, therefore, a prior weighting of the metaphysical significance of subjectivity which, to a certain sort of Spinozist/naturalist transcendental realism, must appear arbitrary and dogmatic. The transcendental realist may, in addition, retort that transcendental idealism in turn accumulates (measured in terms of the transcendental realist's own philosophical methodology) its own set of inexplicables.

The German idealist response—in so far as it may be stated with such massive simplification—is first to concede that as far as theoretical reason is concerned, the situation here is at an impasse, i.e. to allow that philosophical reason arrives in the theoretical context at a point of indifference in the choice between transcendental idealism and transcendental realism.[7] At this point German idealism then does two things. First, it promises to introduce amendments to Kantian idealism—the theme of subject/object identity, monism—that will to some partial extent incorporate the Spinozist outlook. Second, it appeals to non-theoretical considerations to sway philosophical reason from its point of indifference in favour of taking the transcendental turn, i.e. (expressed in Kant's terms) it grounds transcendental idealism on the primacy of practical reason. At the same time, it extends the list of data that are deemed unaccountable by Spinozist/naturalist transcendental realism, so that the range of its inexplicables includes, not just the relation of cognition, but also our self-attribution of theoretical and practical spontaneity, the possibility of autonomy, the fact of reason, the feeling of the sublime, our sense of a trans-natural vocation, and so forth. Of course, the appeal to the practical or axiological perspective—along with the German idealist account of the source of the authority of this perspective—can also be repudiated from the standpoint of Spinozist/naturalist transcendental realism without strict inconsistency. All the same, the result of German idealism's refinement of the grounds for the transcendental turn is a much more robust response than can be found in Kant to the threat posed by such positions: since it can be claimed plausibly that there is nothing left over—if it is not to be merely a nihilistic will—that could give reason for declining to take the transcendental path.

VI

Assuming this consolidation of the transcendental position to be essential to the design of German idealism, next it should be

---

7. In e.g. Schelling's *Letters on Dogmatism and Criticism* (in *The Unconditional in Human Knowledge: Four Early Essays* (1794–1796), trans. and ed. Fritz Marti (Cranbury, N.J.: Associated University Presses, 1980)) and in §5 of Fichte's First Introduction to the *Wissenschaftslehre* (*Introductions to the Wissenschaftslehre and Other Writings*, trans. and ed. Daniel Brezeale (Indianapolis: Hackett, 1994)).

asked why Spinozist/naturalist transcendental realism should have come to be perceived as sufficiently threatening to motivate the project of post-Kantian idealism, in spite of, once again, the additional costs that it bears.

It is here that German romanticism is profitably introduced into the story. To again put things in highly simplified terms: it will be agreed that a dominant theme in the literary and philosophical writings of the German romantics is the subject's relation to nature, and that German romanticism evinces a preoccupation with establishing in or through the subject's consciousness of the natural world a relation to value, furthermore, to value conceived as unconditioned or infinite, whence the infusion of religious qualities and ideas into the German romantic experience and theory of nature, all of this being undertaken, however, in full awareness of the antithetical modern scientific image of nature (with the result that German romantic consciousness characteristically reveals uncertainty as to whether value can be located in some literal sense within nature, or whether nature should rather be conceived as a vehicle for conveying symbolically the realm of value that is located supernaturally).

Now if this frame of mind is set alongside the Kantian conception of nature and value, and it is asked how the two interact, a set of reflections is generated in the light of which Kant's philosophy will come to seem axiologically deficient.

In the present context, what is philosophically significant about German romanticism is not that it has a philosophically original answer to the question of what value is, which it does not, but rather that it articulates and draws attention to the importance of a kind of *relation to value* that is either absent from or at least not present in a full and integrated manner in Kant. While agreeing with Kant that naturalism fails to supply the kind or grade of value which is required by human subjects, i.e. that it is a mistake to think that value can figure in or be extracted from the field of experience as circumscribed by the interests of modern science, German romanticism nevertheless insists on regarding value as in some sense an object of experience, and our relation to this object as teleological, i.e. such that the subject who enjoys consciousness of this object necessarily finds itself endowed with purposiveness by virtue of this relation.

This is admittedly a very hazy formulation of what distinguishes an objectual relation to value, but it resonates appropriately with relevant passages in German romantic writings and the *Glaubenphilosophen* who stand behind them, and it is sufficiently definite to make plain that it is a conception the model for which is provided clearly by aesthetic experience, and that stands in firm contrast with a conception of the being of value as consisting exhaustively in its function of determining action. Value conceived as manifested in this objectual mode allows itself to be conceived more readily in a straightforwardly realist manner than value conceived in a strictly practical mode, and this satisfaction of the natural realism of pre-philosophical consciousness, in conjunction with the teleological dimension, is plausibly a ground for regarding the romantic world-view as of enduring philosophical importance.

In the light of this conception, a number of questions concerning Kant's conception of value suggest themselves. If it could be established non-circularly that the romantic conception of value is necessarily nothing but philosophical fantasy, then German romanticism could have no rational impact on Kantian philosophy; and if the relation between romanticism and Kant's philosophy were wholly antithetical, then it would be necessary to repudiate the latter in its entirety, in the manner of Jacobi, in order to affirm the objectual relation. But the attempt to establish such a negative conclusion from Kant's perspective encounters difficulties, and there are elements in Kant's thought that make it in a complicated way and to a partial degree receptive to the romantic view.

Although the kind of relation that we have to value, as it emerges from Kant's analysis of moral consciousness, does not meet the conditions for an objectual relation, and the aspiration to relate to value objectually will be diagnosed by Kant as reflecting the misunderstandings of our cognitive powers characteristic of *Schwärmerei*, Kant's system allows the concept of such a relation to be formulated: Kant's own system is centred on the concept of a form of unconditioned value, the ground of which lies in the intelligible world and thus with objects that are transcendentally real; at least the shadow of an objectual relation to value is present in Kant's system in the form of the objects of hope which are supplied by the postulates of pure practical reason; and the *Critique of Judgement* can seem to intimate (I shall suggest in the next section) an ultimate unity of fact and value, albeit as again a merely problematic notion. Furthermore, it is hard to see on what grounds Kant might refuse to allow that the belief in such a relation belongs to natural consciousness, or deny that the idea of such a relation has the 'interest of our reason' on its side. The question thus arises whether the 'bargain' that Kant strikes between fact and value—the restriction of theoretical reason to sensible objects in exchange for the extension of pure practical reason to the supersensible—is not perhaps overly restrictive. Encouragement in this direction derives from uncertainty whether in Kant's theory value is not merely a function of (necessities of) representation, and so a reflection of our (albeit pure rational rather than empirical) subjective powers. This question arises in the context of Kant's discussion in the *Groundwork* of ends in themselves, and more sharply with respect to the postulates of practical reason. Kant's introduction of the postulates raises the expectation of stronger axiological and teleological relations. However, the objects of the postulates remain enclosed within the practical perspective, and the status of these objects and our relation to them—a recurrent topic of discussion in German idealism—is famously puzzling, in so far as Kant's theory can seem to be saying that practical necessities of representation entail the necessity of our representing certain states of affairs as obtaining non-practically. In this way Kant's overall philosophical position can come to seem partially compromised with naturalism: Kantian value can appear to reduce to certain necessities governing the relations of representations within the subject, thereby failing to satisfy the instinctive realism of common sense, while the Kantian restriction of theoretical reason's objective validity to empirical objects frustrates the demand for an objectual relation to value.

The German romantic context makes it plausible, I think, to regard the German idealist augmentation of Kantian idealism as the product of the interaction of Kant's philosophy with a different conception of our axiological needs from that of Kant. The result of this interaction is not a wholesale substitution of the romantic conception for the Kantian—the objectual relation need not be set down as a necessary condition for all and any relation to value—but rather a synthesis of the two: German idealism attempts to show that the transcendental turn, along with central elements in Kant's system, including central elements in his moral theory, need not frustrate the axiological demands articulated in German romanticism, and that it may on the contrary supply these demands with a metaphysical rationale and demonstrate the possibility of their fulfilment, while these demands themselves may be taken to motivate the transcendental turn.

If this is correct, then the ultimate advantage that accrues from a stronger grade of idealism than Kant's is axiological: with the transition to a conception of the subject-object relation as identity, a relation to value of a kind that is empirically unconditioned and yet not merely a function of practical representation, becomes conceivable. This interpretation provides also an explanation for the heightened post-Kantian perception of the need to deflect the threat posed by Spinozist/naturalist transcendental realism, in so far as this task is revealed to be interdependent with that of instituting philosophically a new conception of value: the greater the threat posed by Spinozist naturalism—the more it threatens to claim for itself the full range of objects possible for us, a claim for the defence of which Kant's theoretical philosophy may seem to have provided additional resources—the more difficult it becomes to envisage the possibility of any genuine relation to value, and the more demanding the conditions for value are perceived as being, the more urgent it becomes to neutralise Spinozist/naturalist transcendental realism.

VII

The specific ways in which German idealism realises the aim of establishing an objectual relation to value cannot be detailed here. To a considerable extent they are visible at the surface of German idealist writings. One that may be mentioned, however, because it sets a pattern for the axiological significance of German idealism as a whole, concerns Fichte's introduction of the concept of positing into transcendental philosophy. Positing is a primitive concept in Fichte's mode of philosophical explanation, and it obeys the rule that whatever is said to be posited cannot be determined to lie on one side or another of the is/ought distinction, prior to further philosophical analysis disclosing the further conditions of synthetic unity of what is posited, and determination of whether these conditions are fulfillable rather than merely problematic, and of how they are fulfilled. Thus, when it is claimed by Fichte that the self is posited as infinite, this is equivalent neither to the claim that there exists actually and as a matter of fact a self that is infinite, nor to the claim that the self ought to be or to render itself infinite. Since the distinction of what really is the case, from what merely ought to be the case, can come into play only at a later point, it cannot be carried back to elucidate what is meant by Fichte's speaking of something as posited.

What it means to posit in Fichte's sense cannot consist, however, merely in something negative. Nor can Fichte's talk of acts and products of positing be reduced to talk of mere possible objects and states of affairs, designated by concepts and unasserted thoughts lying in the mind of the philosophical subject, since this just raises the question of what is the status, warrant and philosophical function of those concepts and thoughts. One might expect to find that Fichtean positings have the same kind of status as the conditions of possibility detailed in the Analytic of the *Critique of Pure Reason*, or that of the propositions that Kant envisages as to be accepted non-problematically from the practical point of view. To understand Fichte in either of these ways, however, makes, as far as I can see, insufficient sense of the patterns of philosophical explanation advanced in the *Wissenschaftslehre*. Whereas Kant's discussion of conditions of possibility can be understood (up to a point, waiving the question whether this interpretation of Kant is correct) as pertaining to a merely epistemological order, or order of justification, the same cannot be done for Fichte: even if Fichte's own descriptions of his methodology, of positing as *Handlung*, a 'real act of mind', and so forth, are disregarded, the layering of grounds in the *Wissenschaftslehre* is explicitly designed to take us behind the back of cognition as a whole, and to show how cognition ('presentation') emerges necessarily from antecedent metaphysical structures. This transcendence of epistemological or justificatory relations appears to be integral to Fichte's conception of a philosophical system as a self-completing and self-grounding structure that possesses a single first principle. Similarly, it is not an option to suppose that thoughts of what is posited are merely practical ideas, notions that we entertain in the context of determining what to do, if the 'practical point of view' is intended to denote a perspective that presupposes an antecedently and independently determined sphere of action. While this would seem the natural way of understanding how the concept of the practical point of view operates in Kant, it would make no sense of Fichte's conception of the primacy of the practical, since this is intended to underlie, and so cannot presuppose, the construction by theoretical reason of a world of objects in which the self is positioned as agent. The practical point of view in Fichte, in so far as it is distinct at all from the point of view of positing in general, cannot postdate the institution of reality as determined by theoretical reason, and so to speak of certain thoughts and concepts as 'envisaged from the practical point of view' cannot mean that their significance is restricted to determining action in contrast to determining reality, i.e. that their status is *merely* practical, as opposed to metaphysical. There is consequently, I think, no alternative to a construal of Fichte's talk of positing as in intention descriptive of a metaphysical structure that is held to ground and generate the two domains of what is 'actually and as a matter of fact' the case and of what is (ought) to be realised practically. This metaphysical structure would accordingly reveal a single source for *is* and *ought*, allow a sense in which reality and value are one, and create an objectual relation to value at a global level, i.e. prior to the derivation of more specific forms of value in a system of duties, in so far as all instances of object directedness then allow themselves, prima facie, to be grasped as manifestations of unconditioned purposiveness, and as instances of that with which value is identical.

This line of thought, to the effect that German idealism witnesses an overstepping of the ordinarily understood distinction of belief and desire, has furthermore a Kantian ancestry of sorts. In the discussion of intellectual intuition in the *Critique of Judgement*,[8] Kant makes a number of points concerning the distinction of what cognition is or would be for an intuitive intellect, from what cognition is for finite subjects of sensible intuition, including the point that the distinction—presupposed by the concepts of the practical and the teleological—of the actual from

8. See *Critique of Judgement*, trans. Werner S. Pluhar (Indianapolis: Hackett, 1987), §§76–7.

the possible collapses in the case of intellectual intuition; from which it is a very short step to the notion, which would find natural room for development in the context of a programme of restructuring the theoretical/practical division in Kant's system, that the very distinction of practical from theoretical reason may be treated as a function of our cognitive structure, i.e. that the division of our faculties in terms of their different directions of fit to objects is itself to be regarded as a limiting feature of human subjectivity.

VIII

In conclusion, three points. First, there is an obvious qualification to be entered regarding the status that may be claimed for the view of German idealism sketched here. As said earlier, getting German idealism into focus 'as a whole' presupposes some distance from the historical detail; but until the interpretation has been worked out with reference to this detail, the most that can rightfully be claimed is either that it provides a simplifying rational reconstruction of the whole, or that it at least illuminates one strand of the hugely complex phenomenon of German idealism.

Second, the implication of the axiological interpretation is I think—though this is a separate matter, which requires further argument—to relocate the centre of gravity in German idealism before Hegel, in Schelling. It does not follow from the axiological interpretation that Hegel's is not the most interesting and important form of German idealism, but it does follow that, if this is so, then it is in virtue of Hegel's having executed a philosophical project that had been designed already, explicitly and comprehensively, by Schelling. This runs counter to the tendency found in a lot of work on Hegel, and even among those who repudiate Hegel's own teleological view of the history of post-Kantian philosophy, to regard Hegel's philosophy as instituting a new basic framework which subsumes that of the earlier post-Kantian idealists, rather than as distinguished by methodological innovations within an inherited framework. Alternatively, it implies that, if Hegel does overtake his predecessors with respect to his basic conception of the project of philosophy, then he to that degree departs from the central impetus of German idealism.

Third, it should be emphasised that the axiological reading entails a metaphysical, ontologically committed interpretation of German idealism: if German idealist metaphysics seeks to accommodate the axiological demand articulated in German romanticism, then a non-metaphysical, ontologically deflationary construal of German idealism, even if it were to make complete sense of the internal machinery of the German idealist systems, omits their prime mover and final end. (From a naturalistic, post-metaphysical standpoint, this counts as a reason for thinking that the axiological reading cannot be right, but not, if the axiological interpretation is correct, from the standpoint of German idealism.)

FROM KANT TO POST-KANTIAN IDEALISM

by Sebastian Gardner and Paul Franks

II—Paul Franks

GERMAN IDEALISM

ABSTRACT German idealists regard Spinozism as both the realism that out-flanks Kant's idealism and the source of the conception of systematicity with which to fortify idealism. But they offer little argument for this view. To fill the gap, I reconstruct arguments that could underlie Jacobi's and Pistorius's tenta-tive but influential suggestions that Kant is or should be a Spinozist. Kant is indeed a monist about phenomena, but, unlike Spinoza, a pluralist about nou-mena. Nevertheless, it is arguable that the Third Antinomy can be solved by a more thoroughgoing Spinozistic monism. The resulting Spinozism outflanks Kant by acknowledging Jacobi's charge that philosophy annihilates immediacy and individuality, whereas Kant's commitment to things in themselves can seem a half-hearted attempt to avoid the charge. However, the German idealist con-tention is that only a synthesis of such a Spinozism with Kantian idealism can retrieve immediacy and individuality, thus overcoming nihilism.

A striking feature of German idealism is that its proponents seem to regard the systematic derivability of every philo-sophical insight from a single absolute first principle as a neces-sary, indeed, as a sufficient condition for the solution of philo-sophical problems. This is puzzling in its own right, but doubly so since the German idealists see themselves as completing Kant's revolution. For Kant's conception of human finitude seems directly opposed to such a view.

As Gardner notes, the transition from Kantianism to German idealism might be illuminated 'if the interest in systematicity could be reconstructed as a convincing philosophical motive: for example, if it could be shown that the authority of reason was genuinely at stake in the attempt to construct an all-compre-hending and self-validating philosophical system. . .'[1] However, Gardner finds 'it . . .doubtful that any such reconstruction in

---

1. Gardner, 'German Idealism I', 6.

terms of the authority or possibility of reason can avoid referring to a strong conception of reason which already bears the marks of German idealism. . .'[2]

A thoroughgoing reconstruction of the German idealist interest in systematicity cannot be attempted here.[3] But one aspect of the problem suggested by Gardner will be considered. On his characterization, Spinozism plays two roles in the transition. It is the optimal version of transcendental realism, which outflanks Kant's arguments in the *Critique of Pure Reason*, hence the chief opponent that a perfected idealism must overcome.[4] Yet it also provides some of the resources with which idealism can be perfected.[5]

One such resource, I suggest, is the idea of a system in which an absolute first principle both necessitates its derivatives and is impossible without them. Such a system is *monistic* in the sense that there is no real distinction between principle and derivatives.[6]

To explore why the German idealists undertook to synthesize Kantianism and Spinozist monism, I will consider a brief moment, prior to the beginning of German idealism, in which—*mirabile dictu*—Kant himself was taken for a Spinozist. Study of this moment can help one to understand not only unsuspected affinities between Kant and Spinozism, but also reasons why a merger might be attractive.[7]

I

It would be hard to overestimate the influence of Jacobi's 1785 Spinoza book on the reception of Kant's *Critique* and on the

2. Gardner, 6–7.

3. See my forthcoming book, *All or Nothing: Skepticism, Transcendental Arguments, and Systematicity in German Idealism* (Cambridge, MA: Harvard University Press).

4. Gardner, 8.

5. Gardner, 9.

6. See Suarez, *On the Various Kinds of Distinctions* (*Disputationes Metaphysicae, Disputatio VII, de variis distictionum generibus*), trans. Cyril Vollert (Milwaukee: Marquette University Press, 1947). In the Cartesian tradition, two terms are really distinct iff each can exist independently of the other, while in the Leibnizian tradition, two terms are really distinct iff each is intelligible independently of the other. Here I will follow Kant in assuming the Leibnizian conception.

7. I cannot deal here with the relationship between Spinozism and the actual philosophy of Spinoza. Monism, as characterized here, seems to be a commitment both of Spinoza and of variants of Spinozism influential in Germany in the 1780s and 90s.

origins of German idealism.[8] Every German idealist first read the *Critique* in light of Jacobi's provocative contention that philosophy led inexorably to Spinozism and thence to nihilism.

Jacobi himself had read the *Critique* before writing his book. In a footnote to a letter to Mendelssohn in which he outlined what he took to be Spinoza's argument for monism, Jacobi cited, for the sake of elucidation, some 'passages from Kant, which are entirely in the spirit of Spinoza'.[9] In these passages, Kant argued that our representations of space and time must be intuitions, not concepts, because the relationships between space and its parts, and between time and its parts, are such that the parts do not precede the wholes, as do the parts of an object fit for wholly conceptual representation; rather the parts are possible only through limitations of the wholes. Instead of explaining the sense in which Kant's argument was 'in the spirit of Spinoza', however, Jacobi proceeded to cite passages from Spinoza 'as accompaniment to these words of Kant'.[10]

Jacobi's suggestion was protested in an anonymous review, probably written by C. G. Schütz:

> Either Mr Jacobi or his reviewer has totally misunderstood Mr Kant's sense and opinion in the cited passages. Mr Kant says: there is only *one space*; Spinoza: there is only *one substance*. Kant says: all that we call *many spaces* are only parts of the *unique, all-encompassing space*; Spinoza: everything finite is one and the same as the infinite. How both speak here in the very same spirit, how Kant can here serve as elucidation for Spinoza, we do not in the least comprehend. ... However, we concede that, in the passage from Spinoza, which Mr. Jacobi quotes on p. 125, where he speaks

8. Über die Lehre des Spinoza in Briefen an den Herrn Moses Mendelssohn (*Concerning the Doctrine of Spinoza in Letters to Herr Mendelssohn*), in Jacobi, *Werke*, eds. Klaus Hammacher and Walter Jaeschke (Frankfurt and Stuttgart: Meiner and frommann-holzboog, 1998), 1, 1, translated in *The Main Philosophical Writings and the Novel 'Allwill'*, trans. and ed., George di Giovanni (Montreal: McGill-Queens University Press, 1994).

9. Jacobi, *Werke*, 1, 1: 96 n. 1, translated in di Giovanni, 218 n. 30. Jacobi cites Kant, *Critique of Pure Reason*, A25, A32.

10. He cites properties 2–5 of the intellect from *Treatise on the Emendation of the Intellect*, *Spinoza Opera*, ed. Carl Gebhardt (Heidelberg: Carl Winter), 2: 39, translated in *The Collected Works of Spinoza*, ed. and trans. E. Curley (Princeton: Princeton University Press, 1985), 43–4; also the paragraph on the modes of thinking by which we imagine things, and the paragraph on beings of reason, both from the Appendix Containing Metaphysical Thoughts to *Descartes' 'Principles of Philosophy'*, Gebhardt, 1: 234, translated in Curley, 300–1.

of the concept of *quantity*, the thought that representations of line, surface and body do not comprehend quantity but rather only serve to delimit [it], has an affinity with Kant's thoughts about space.[11]

To be sure, both Kant and Spinoza employed the notion of a whole prior to its parts. But it was highly misleading to suggest that Kant was therefore moved by the spirit of Spinoza. After all, what connection could there be between Kant's commitment to a single space and the Spinozist commitment to a single substance?[12]

In fact, neither Jacobi nor Schütz is entirely correct. There *is* a connection between Kant's commitment to a single space and Spinoza's commitment to a single substance. Yet Kant's view is not *wholly* in Spinoza's spirit.

The connection may be brought out through consideration of the following line of Kantian argument.[13] Concepts of things are composed of real determinations—that is, predicates signifying properties capable of composing essences. If concepts of things are to be possible—one might say, if conceptualizable things are to be possible—then real determinations must be available. There must therefore be a stock of available real determinations, the sum-total of whose possible combinations would be the sum-total of possible concepts of things. Indeed, this stock must be available *prior* to the *actual* existence of anything, for it constitutes the *possibility* of anything, and things are possible before they become actual, if indeed they ever do. However, this *omnitudo realitatis*, as Kant calls it, is itself merely a stock of *possible thoughts of possible properties*, and cannot subsist without some

11. *Allgemeine Literatur-Zeitung* 36, 11 February 1786, reprinted in *Rezensionen zur kantischen Philosophie* 1781–87, ed., Albert Landau (Bebra: Albert Landau Verlag, 1991), 272 (my translation). See also Schütz to Kant, February 1785, *Werke* (Berlin: de Gruyter, 1900-), 10: 430.

12. Jacobi's response, in his second edition, is not very illuminating. He prefaces his quotations from the *Critique* with the words: 'Kant may serve to render this concept more graspable. That the Kantian philosophy is not accused of Spinozism, one need not say to any sensible person.' See Jacobi, *Werke*, 1, 1: 96.

13. This argument for God's existence is central to Kant's pre-critical work. See *Werke*, 1: 395–6, 2: 83–7. In the *Critique*, A571/B599-A583/B661, Kant characterizes the argument as illusory. Later, however, he views it as articulating a necessary demand of reason, which, however, concerns only how we must think, not what must exist. See *Werke*, 8: 138n., 8: 154.

actual basis. That basis, Kant argues, must be God, considered as *ens realissimum*, the unique being from whose real determinations all other real determinations may be derived. What is important here is that Kant himself comes to see a connection between the way in which the sum-total of all realities— grounded in a single, divine substance—precedes its parts, and the way in which space precedes its parts: 'All manifoldness of things is only so many different ways of limiting the concept of the highest reality, which is their common substratum, just as all figures are possible only as different ways of limiting space.'[14]

Indeed, the disanalogy between the *omnitudo realitatis* and space is as important as the analogy. Within the *omnitudo realitatis*, as Kant understands it, every possible thing is uniquely individuated by a combination of positive real properties that pertain to it intrinsically. This is not, however, how we, with our finite minds, individuate objects. As Kant argues in the *Critique* and the *Metaphysical Foundations*, we have cognitive access only to objects that affect us sensibly, hence objects that are spatio-temporal and that exist within a dynamic community in which each object exerts law-governed force on every object that simultaneously occupies some part of space. Thus we can individuate a given object only through sensible properties that implicitly or explicitly involve dynamic relations and, if two or more objects have exactly the same sensible properties—a possibility that cannot, Kant thinks, be excluded *a priori*—we can distinguish them through the fact that they are 'intuited in different places at the same time'.[15] Indeed, no intrinsic property—no property of the sort that helps individuate things within the *omnitudo realitatis*— can be known by us to be instantiated. Moreover, Kant sometimes employs this result in the following argument: if the objects knowable by us were things in themselves, as transcendental realism contends they must be, then those objects would be individuated via intrinsic properties; since, however, the objects knowable by us are in fact 'nothing but relations', they must be transcendentally ideal.[16]

---

14. A578/B606. Translations are from *Critique of Pure Reason*, trans. and ed., Paul Guyer and Allen W. Wood (Cambridge: Cambridge University Press, 1998).

15. A263/B319.

16. See, e.g., B67, A265/B321, A277/B333, *Werke*, 8: 153–4.

There is, then, a far more thoroughgoing affinity between Kant and Spinoza than Schütz suspects. For Kant agrees with the Spinozist thesis that empirical objects are not substances in the traditional metaphysical sense. Indeed, it follows from the First Analogy that empirical objects may be aptly characterized as modes of the *one* substance we can know: the invariant matter that underlies all empirical alteration. Kant's empirical world is monistic.

Still, this does not entitle Jacobi to characterize Kant's view of space and time as 'wholly in the spirit of Spinoza'. For Kant is not a monist about the *intelligible* world. To the chagrin of many readers, he seems to maintain that a world of things in themselves underlies the world of empirical objects. As we have seen, he sometimes assumes that, insofar as they meet reason's demands, these things in themselves are individuated by intrinsic properties within the *omnitudo realitatis*. But he also assumes that there are *many* things in themselves, not one, notably in his solution to the Third Antinomy and in the moral philosophy enabled by that solution, where *we* are said to be things in themselves, insofar as we are free agents, capable of autonomy.

II

At least one early reader of Kant's *Critique*, however, thought that Kant's affinity with Spinozism was even greater than I have so far suggested. For he thought that Kant was also committed to monism about the intelligible world.

The reader in question is H. A. Pistorius, author of several important reviews of Kant's works. In 1786, a year after Jacobi's Spinoza book, he thought that he had discovered a 'deduction of Spinozism' from Kant's philosophy. For transcendental idealism requires that:

> There is, provided overall that something exists, only one sole substance, and this is the sole *thing in itself*, the sole noumenon, namely the intelligible or objective world. This limits itself, this is the sphere which has neither beginning nor end. This is the sole ideal of pure reason. Thus, according to this [Kantian] theory of the apparent and the real, the ideas of reason are and must be specified in exactly the same way as Spinoza specified them. For

him, as is known, the world is the sole substance, the self-completing series, or the unlimited sphere, which for him plays the role of the Godhead.[17]

Pistorius hesitated to say that Kant actually was a Spinozist, which would be truly 'malicious'. Nevertheless, he argued, transcendental idealism led to Spinozism, whether or not Kant was aware of it.

Pistorius's attempt to *deduce* Spinozism—to show that Kant *must* be a monist—fails.[18] But a passage in his review suggests a more promising line of thought which he does not develop:

> According to this [Kantian] system, reason demands the completion of the series of natural events and causes, it seeks a limit outside the same, ascends from conditioneds to unconditioneds, and must assume a limit, an unknown something as the unconditioned, because otherwise it can never find the sought after completion and satisfaction.—If I am not mistaken, then reason, educated and guided by this theory of appearance and truth [i.e., transcendental idealism] can and must find this completion nowhere else but in the series itself.[19]

This suggests that Spinozism provides a solution to the Third Antinomy, where Kant is concerned with reason's demand for 'the completion of the series of natural events and causes'. Indeed, one might well reach this conclusion if one reads Kant's Third Antinomy through the lens of Jacobi's Spinoza interpretation. To show why, I will now juxtapose Jacobi's Spinozist argument for monism to the argument for the antithesis in the Third Antinomy. What results is not a Kantian deduction but rather a Kantian *motivation* for monism.

In his letter to Mendelssohn, Jacobi attributes to Spinoza a six step argument for monism.[20] The first step expresses commitment to the principle of sufficient reason, understood as requiring, for every possible why-question, not only a justificatory response sufficient to answer that question, but also a justificatory

---

17. Pistorius, review of *Erläuterungen über des Herrn Professor Kant 'Critik der reinen Vernunft' von Joh. Schultze*, *Allgemeine deutsche Bibliothek*, 60, No.1 (May 1786), reprinted in Landau, 326–352.

18. See my forthcoming book.

19. Pistorius, 329.

20. I am not concerned here to evaluate Jacobi as an interpreter of Spinoza.

response that does not raise any further unanswered why-question:

> I. At the ground of every becoming there must lie a being that has not itself become; at the ground of every coming-to-be, something that has not come-to-be; at the ground of everything alterable, an unalterable and eternal thing.[21]

This corresponds to a principle ascribed by Kant to reason:

> If the conditioned is given, then the whole sum of conditions, and hence the absolutely unconditioned, is also given, through which alone the conditioned was possible.[22]

Jacobi's second and third steps give an argument parallel to the argument for the antithesis in Kant's Third Antinomy:

> II. *Becoming* can as little have come-to-be or begun as *Being*; or, if that which subsists in itself (the eternally unalterable, that which persists in the impermanent) had ever been by itself, without the impermanent, it would never have produced a becoming, either within itself or outside, for these would both presuppose a coming-to-be from nothingness.
>
> III. From all eternity, therefore, the impermanent has been with the permanent, the temporal with the eternal, the finite with the infinite, and whosoever assumes a beginning of the finite, also assumes a coming-to-be from nothingness.[23]

The parallel argument in the *Critique* is as follows:

> Suppose there were a *freedom* in the transcendental sense, as a special kind of causality in accordance with which the occurrences of the world could follow, namely a faculty of absolutely beginning a state, and hence also a series of its consequences; then not only will a series begin absolutely through this spontaneity, but the determination of this spontaneity itself to produce the series, i.e., its causality, will begin absolutely, so that nothing precedes it through which this occurring action is determined in accordance with constant laws. Every beginning of action, however, presup-poses a state of the not yet acting cause, and a dynamically first beginning of action presupposes a state that has no causal connec-tion at all with the cause of the previous one, i.e., in no way follows

---

21. Jacobi, *Werke* 1, 1: 93, translated in di Giovanni, 217.
22. A409/B436.
23. Jacobi, *Werke* 1, 1: 93–4, translated in di Giovanni, 217.

from it. Thus transcendental freedom is contrary to the causal law
. . . and hence is an empty thought-entity.[24]

What Jacobi calls the beginning of becoming corresponds to
what Kant calls an absolute beginning. And the argument for
rejecting the former parallels the argument for rejecting the latter. Suppose there was an absolute beginning, at which point the
absolutely unconditioned started to generate series of conditioned conditions. Then there must have been a time prior to
the absolute beginning, when the absolutely unconditioned was
not engaged in such generation. But now there are only two possibilities. Either there is a sufficient reason why the absolutely
unconditioned passes from inactivity to generation at the relevant time, a reason that was lacking before that time. Or there
is no sufficient reason for the change. In either case, the result is
inconsistent with the commitment expressed by Kant's principle
of the unconditioned and by Jacobi's step one. The second case
is obvious. In the first case, the sufficient reason cannot arise
from the absolutely unconditioned itself, or else it could not have
been lacking earlier. Therefore the sufficient reason must arise
from elsewhere. But then what we have been calling the absolutely unconditioned turns out to be conditioned.
It is at this point that Jacobi's and Kant's arguments diverge.

> IV. If the finite was with the eternal from all eternity, it cannot be
> outside it, for if it were outside it, it would either be another being
> that subsists on its own, or be produced by the subsisting thing
> from nothing.
> V. If it were produced by the subsisting thing from nothing, so too
> would the force or determination, in virtue of which it was pro-
> duced by the infinite thing from nothingness, *have come* from
> nothingness; for in the infinite, eternal, permanent thing, every-
> thing is infinitely, permanently, and eternally actual. An action first
> initiated by the infinite being could not have begun otherwise than
> from all eternity, and its determination could not have derived
> from anywhere except from nothingness.[25]

As I understand it, this argument has the same basic structure
as the previous one, but is concerned, not with temporality, but

24. A445/B473-A447/B475.
25. Jacobi, *Werke*, 1, 1: 94, translated in di Giovanni, 217.

with modality. The previous argument, we might say, showed that the absolutely unconditioned cannot *temporally transcend* a generated series of conditioned conditions. That is, the former could not have pre-existed the latter. The current argument claims that the absolutely unconditioned cannot *modally tran-scend* a generated series of conditioned conditions. That is, it cannot even be *possible* for the former to exist when the latter does not. For, if it is possible, then there must be some sufficient reason why the latter actually exists. Again, there are only two cases. Either there is no sufficient reason, or there is a sufficient reason which cannot arise from the absolutely unconditioned itself. In either case, reason's demand has not been met: the possibility of the series of conditions has not been grounded in an absolutely unconditioned.

Let us look more closely at Jacobi's text. Step four distinguishes two ways in which the finite could be 'outside' the eternal or the infinite. The first way is mentioned only to be set aside. For it is obvious that the finite cannot be a 'being subsisting on its own'. Although the finitude of the finite has not been explicated, it must involve some way of lacking self-sufficiency and needing a ground. The second way is for the finite to be produced *eternally* from nothing by the infinite. Since the production is eternal and does not have an absolute beginning in time, the problem discussed in step two—the problem of temporal trans-cendence—is avoided. But a similar problem—the problem of modal transcendence—remains. For if talk of eternal production is to mean anything, it must mean at least that it is possible for the producer to exist without the produced. And now there is no way to avoid the argument given a paragraph ago.

Consequently, Jacobi concludes on Spinoza's behalf, the finite cannot be outside the infinite. Now, it may well seem, at this point, that there simply cannot be any way to fulfil the initial commitment to the principle of sufficient reason. If, to use Jacobi's terminology, the finite is eternally in the infinite, then is the infinite not conditioned by the finite just as much as the finite is conditioned by the infinite? After the failure of both temporal and modal transcendence, how *can* the infinite be absolutely unconditioned?

Although Kant considers only the failure of temporal trans-cendence, his remarks are pertinent to Jacobi's situation too. The root of the difficulty may be put as follows. One thinks of the absolutely unconditioned as the first member of the series of conditions it grounds. But then, although one has sought to safeguard the distinctiveness of the absolutely unconditioned, say by assuming its temporal (or modal) transcendence, nevertheless the absolutely unconditioned inevitably becomes *homogeneous* with the other members of the series. And then it becomes subject to the law of the series—to the demand for an antecedent condition—and so it is no longer the absolutely unconditioned with which one hoped to satisfy reason's demand once and for all. Consequently, if this difficulty is to be overcome, it can only be by ensuring the *heterogeneity* of the absolutely unconditioned to every member of the series of conditions.[26]

I will call this the heterogeneity requirement. Now, Kant does not consider the possibility that there might be more than one way to meet the requirement, hence more than one way to keep faith with reason's demand. Instead he goes on to develop *one* solution which, he claims, does the job. Namely, heterogeneity is at least logically possible if the series of conditions is not mathematical but *dynamic*—that is to say, if the pure category under which the conditions are connected and which one hopes to extend to the unconditioned is, for example, the category of causality. Furthermore, the transcendental idealism that Kant has already motivated on other grounds can flesh out the notion of heterogeneity, since he has already had to assume a distinction between appearances and things in themselves, to both of which the categories pertain. So there is no contradiction in the idea of a uncaused cause among things in themselves that is responsible for a series of conditions among appearances.

I suggest that Kant's solution is at best only one possible way of meeting the heterogeneity requirement, while Jacobi's Spinozistic solution promises to be another:

> VI. Hence the finite is in the infinite, so that the sum of all finite things, equally containing within itself the whole of eternity at every moment, past and future, is one and the same as the infinite being itself.[27]

26. A528/B556-A532/B560.
27. Jacobi, *Werke*, 1, 1: 95, translated in di Giovanni, 217.

In effect, while Kant proposes that the absolutely unconditioned be *transcendent to the series as a whole*, indeed to the
empirical world within which the series unfolds, Jacobi proposes,
on Spinoza's behalf, that the absolutely unconditioned be *immanent within the series as a whole*, indeed immanent to the empirical world within which the series unfolds. *Both* proposals avoid
the problematic situation in which the absolutely unconditioned
is supposed to be transcendent to the first member of the series,
which has the effect of pulling the absolute into the series and
compromising its unconditionedness. *Both* proposals render the
absolutely unconditioned heterogeneous with respect to every
member of the series.

We have now derived Pistorius's suggestive formulation: 'Reason . . . can and must find this completion nowhere else but in
the series itself.' But what exactly does it mean for the absolutely
unconditioned to be immanent within the series as a whole, or
to be 'one and the same' as 'the sum of all finite things'? In his
next paragraph, Jacobi offers some clarification:

> VII. This sum is not an absurd combination of finite things,
> together constituting an infinite, but a whole in the strictest sense,
> whose parts can only be thought within it and according to it.[28]

The proposal is not, then, that the infinite is identical with the
extension of the class of all finite things. Rather, I suggest, the
proposal is that the sum of all finite things constitutes what Kant
calls the *omnitudo realitatis*, a whole that completely determines
its parts in virtue of its absolute first principle: the *ens realissimum*. Indeed, it is just here that, as we saw earlier, Jacobi cites
Kant's views on part/whole relations to shed light on Spinozistic
monism. According to my suggestion, the claim that the infinite
is 'one and the same' as 'the sum of all finite things' needs to be
handled with care. What it means is not that there is *no* distinction to be drawn between the *ens realissimum* and the *omnitudo
realitatis*. It means, rather, that the distinction is not *real* but
modal, and that the *ens realissimum* is the ground of the *omnitudo
realitatis*.[29] So no finite thing is really distinct from its infinite

---

28. Jacobi, *Werke*, 1, 1: 95–6, translated in di Giovanni, 218.

29. Two terms are modally distinct, according to the Leibnizian tradition, iff one is
intelligible independently of the other but not vice-versa.

ground. And, although the infinite ground cannot be without the finite, nevertheless the infinite conditions—that is, grounds—the finite, while the finite does not condition the infinite, which is therefore absolutely unconditioned.

Indeed, we have now derived, in effect, another formulation of Pistorius: 'There is, provided overall that something exists, only one sole substance, and this is the sole *thing in itself*, the sole noumenon, namely the intelligible or objective world.'[30] This does not mean that the sole substance is the intelligible world *as a manifold*. It means rather that the sole substance is the intelligible world *as a unity*. One might say that the absolutely unconditioned constitutes *the worldhood of the intelligible world*. It is the principle that renders it a whole prior to its parts, which are completely determined through their delimitation of the whole.

Here, then, is an argument for the thesis, essential to German idealism, that the demands of reason can be satisfied by a monistic system in which an absolute first principle both necessitates its derivatives and is impossible without them. It is an argument for 'a strong conception of reason which . . . bears the marks of German idealism', not merely an invocation of that conception, presupposed as valid.[31] Moreover, it is an argument with demonstrable Kantian affinities, available to readers of Jacobi.

III

Supposing that transcendental idealism and Spinozistic monism both offer the hope of solving the Third Antinomy, and setting aside unquestionably important questions about the coherence and detail of each proposal, what considerations might favour one over the other?

Given Jacobi's influence, it is helpful to ask, more specifically, how proponents of the two programmes might respond to his contention that philosophy as such leads inexorably to nihilism, a consequence that he thinks is brought out more clearly by each stage in the succession from Spinoza to Kant, from Kant to Fichte, and from Fichte to Schelling.

30. Pistorius, 330.
31. Gardner, 6–7.

In his Spinoza book, Jacobi raises the issue of nihilism only implicitly, notably when he cites Spinoza's thesis that 'determination is negation'.[32] That is to say, there are no intrinsic determinations; rather, things have their properties and are individuated in virtue of their relations to the other things they are not. As we saw in Section I, Kant affirms this thesis with respect to appearances, but not things in themselves. Jacobi offers the following gloss: 'Individual things, therefore, so far as they only exist in a certain determinate mode, are *non-entia*, the indeterminate infinite being is the one single true *ens real, hoc est, est omne esse, et praeter quod nullum datur esse.*'[33] That is, only the *omnitudo realitatis*—the totality of determinate things, which is not itself a determinate thing and is thus 'indeterminate'—is genuinely real, while determinate things are not. Presumably, Jacobi says this because he thinks it obvious that genuinely real entities cannot be determined solely negatively. In a Spinozist system, the *omnitudo realitatis* alone is not determined solely negatively. But, for that reason, it is not determined at all. So Spinozism leaves no room for—or, as Jacobi puts it later, Spinozism annihilates—determinate things.

'Nihilism' does not signify a single issue for Jacobi, and his various formulations are far from clear, but there are sufficient family resemblances to permit the following account.[34] Reason in the proper sense is a perceptual faculty whose objects are given to it immediately, as unconditional and unproblematic grounds. But, in the name of what they improperly call reason, philosophers demand justification of what ordinarily requires no justification. Thus, the everyday relationship between perception and inference, between immediacy and mediation, is inverted, and primacy is accorded to inference. As soon as the demand for

32. Gebhardt, 5: 240 , translated in Spinoza, *The Letters*, trans. Samuel Shirley (Indianapolis: Hackett, 1995), 260.

33. Jacobi, *Werke*, 1, 1: 100, translated in di Giovanni, 220. Jacobi quotes the last eleven from *Treatise on the Emendation of the Intellect*, Gebhardt, 2: 29: '[. . . the origin of Nature . . . is indeed this being, unique, infinite,] that is, it is all being, and beyond which there is nothing.' The translation is my own. Compare Curley, 34.

34. For detailed discussion, see Franks, 'All or Nothing: Systematicity and Nihilism in Jacobi, Reinhold, and Maimon' in *The Cambridge Companion to German Idealism*, ed., Karl Ameriks (Cambridge: Cambridge University Press, 2000), 95–116, 'Does Post-Kantian Scepticism Exist?' in *The Yearbook of German Idealism* (forthcoming, 2002) and 'Skepticism after Kant' in *Skepticism and Interpretation*, eds. James Conant and Andrea Kern (forthcoming).

justification is accepted, natural faith in perception has been lost and the everyday immediacy of grounds has been annihilated. Philosophers like Spinoza then seek to perfect the form of their inferences. But no perfection of form can restore that lost immediacy without which there can be no genuine grounds whatsoever.

This schema may be variously applied. Sometimes Jacobi is concerned with the annihilation of epistemological immediacy, as when he criticises representationalism. Sometimes, as in Spinoza's case, the annihilated immediacy is ontological: it is the immediacy with which things and persons have their properties and thus have the individual characters that make them the things and persons they are. On still other occasions, Jacobi is combating ethical nihilism, for example in his novel about the character, Edward Allwill, who lacks the immediate individuality required for virtue: he is all will, investing himself entirely and hence seductively in transient passions, so that all his opinions and attachments are mediated.

Confronted with this family of complaints, then, how do transcendental idealism and Spinozism fare?

For Kant, as we have seen, the determination of appearances is negation. Having no intrinsic properties whatsoever, they are determined and individuated in virtue of their dynamic and spatio-temporal relations to one another. So Kant's conception of the empirical world is open to Jacobi's nihilism charge. However, Kant may be said to *accept* the charge. Hence his argument that appearances have no intrinsic properties and so cannot be transcendentally real. Hence, too, his thesis that the matter of appearances must somehow be grounded in things in themselves, which, in accordance with reason's demand, we must think as subjects of intrinsic properties. Here, Jacobi thinks, Kant expresses his residual faith in what is properly called reason.

Kant finds room in the intelligible world for a plurality of really distinct things, because of two views held by him and rejected by Spinoza. First, Kant regards the *ens realissimum* as possessing every absolutely infinite intrinsic property, whereas Spinoza ascribes to his first principle infinite attributes, which are not intrinsic properties, whatever exactly they are. Second, Kant regards finite things in themselves as possessing finite versions of God's intrinsic properties, and is committed to an analogical relationship between the predicates ascribed to finite things and the predicates ascribed to God, whereas Spinoza rejects any such relationship.[35] Given these views, Kant can reconcile the dependence of all things on God with real distinctions, not only between finite things but also between each finite thing and God. On the one hand, finite things in themselves are dependent on God, not only for their actualization, but also for their transcendentally real possibility, which cannot be rendered intelligible without reference to God as the *ens realissimum* who grounds reality. On the other hand, however, finite things are substances apart from God and from each other. For, just because their properties are derivative versions of God's properties, which are intrinsic to Him, finite things are what they are in virtue of properties intrinsic to them.

At first glance, then, it seems that transcendental idealism fares better with respect to nihilism than Spinozism. For, although Kant may be said to annihilate the everyday immediacy of things in the empirical world, he is committed to genuine things in themselves underlying appearances, and indeed he argues in his moral philosophy that we may justifiably regard ourselves not merely as appearances but as genuine individuals. In contrast, unless it departs dramatically from some central views of Spinoza, Spinozism is bound to be thoroughgoingly nihilistic.

At second glance, however, it is less clear that, if one takes Jacobi's worries seriously, one will consider Kant's doctrine of things in themselves a satisfying response. Even if we were to succeed in making sense of the thesis that unknowable things in themselves underlie the appearances we know, this could hardly restore the lost immediacy of the things that we ordinarily take ourselves to perceive and that we ordinarily take to immediately possess individual characters. If Spinozistic modes are *non-entia*, then so are Kant's empirical objects. Moreover, in the one case where Kant can, at least for practical purposes, determine a thing in itself—namely, himself as a free agent—it is contestable whether that which is so determined may be said to be an individual. For its character can be determined only as the rationality and capacity for autonomy shared by all rational

---

35. See Kant, *Werke*, 8: 154; Spinoza, 1p17s, Gebhardt, 2: 62–3, translated in Curley, 426–7.

beings. Thus one can come to think of Kant's transcendental idealism, not as a satisfying response to Jacobi's nihilism worry, but as at best a half-hearted acknowledgement of the worry's depth. In contrast, Spinozism can seem to confront nihilism with full seriousness, embracing without reservation the conception of reasoning as inferential mediation that Jacobi takes to be constitutive of the philosophical tradition, and exploring its consequences.

One can now appreciate the sense in which Spinozism may be thought both to outflank Kant's *Critique* and to provide the resources with which to perfect idealism. Spinozism outflanks the *Critique* because it provides a solution to the Third Antinomy that competes with Kant's transcendental idealism, a solution unsuspected by Kant, which involves no superficial response to the charge that philosophy is nihilistic. Moreover, the Spinozist solution avoids the obscurities of Kant's two worlds, for which it substitutes two aspects: the thing viewed partially, in relation to other modes of the same attribute, and the thing viewed in relation to the whole and its first principle.

Suppose, now, that one undertakes to reconstruct, within a monistic system that is Spinozistic in form, certain impressive Kantian themes arguably neglected or under-theorized by Spinoza—say, the spontaneity of the mind, the constitutive function of principles of judgment, and the dialectical interplay of the faculties, among others. Assume further that, under the joint influence of Jacobi and Kant, one regards such a system as the ultimate achievement of the philosophical tradition and the maximal expression of (that tradition's conception of) reason. One will then find that nothing less than the authority of reason itself is at stake in the system's ability, not merely to acknowledge, but to respond to the charge of nihilism. Such a response would require the system to accommodate immediacy, in all the varieties required by everyday relations to grounds—not only the ontological variety on which I have focused here—while eschewing altogether any appeal to the intrinsic properties residually retained by Kant. Some of the keynotes of German idealism may be understood in this light, such as Fichte's thesis that individual subjects, capable of immediate self-reference and acknowledgment of norms as immediately practical—are constituted through reciprocal recognition.

IV

What may be said, from this perspective, about Gardner's axiological interpretation of German idealism? The consonance between our views is indeed striking. However, the problem of articulating philosophically what Gardner calls an objectual relation to unconditioned value,[36] expressed in romanticism, seems to me to be one instance of the more general problem of accommodating within a monistic system the varieties of immediacy involved in everyday relations to grounds. I see no reason to focus on values, rather than grounds of other kinds, unless it can be shown that the way in which the problematic of nihilism plays itself out in axiology deserves to be privileged—either because it was privileged within German idealism's historical origins, or because it should be privileged within contemporary reflection on German idealism's continued pertinence.[37]

36. Gardner, 10–13.

37. Thanks to Karl Ameriks, Joseph Blenkinsopp and Hindy Najman for their comments and assistance.

EMOTIONAL TRUTH

by Ronald de Sousa and Adam Morton

I—Ronald de Sousa

ABSTRACT Taking literally the concept of emotional truth requires breaking the monopoly on truth of belief-like states. To this end, I look to perceptions for a model of non-propositional states that might be true or false, and to desires for a model of propositional attitudes the norm of which is other than the semantic satisfaction of their propositional object. Those models inspire a conception of generic truth, which can admit of degrees for analogue representations such as emotions; belief-like states, by contrast, are digital representations. I argue that the gravest problem—objectivity—is not insurmountable.

I

Generic Truth. A 'true likeness' is not one that is not false. When we say that Tolstoy's novels are true to life, we don't mean to claim that they are, after all, non-fiction. In these and some other domains we speak of truth, but assume we are not speaking strictly. Must this be the case for *emotional truth*? The phrase sometimes refers to kindred properties such as *authenticity*, a difficult notion worth elucidating, but about which I have little to say. I propose instead to take literally the idea of truth-valued emotions.

The concept of emotion is Janus-faced. In one direction emotions face inward, either as 'perceptions referred to the soul' (in Descartes), or as perceptions of bodily states aroused by some exciting cause (in William James). In the other direction emotions face outward, suggesting that (at least some) emotions provide us with correct or incorrect representations of something in the world outside us. It is in this facing-out stance that emotions might claim to be literally true or false. In pursuit of this hypothesis, I shall offer some reasons for assigning a broader scope to the concept of truth as correspondence, and survey some of the difficulties that such an extension to emotions of the idea of literal truth may bring.

A mental state M can be said to be true or false, only if

(1) it is subject to a norm N;

(2) N is determined by M itself, yet
(3) N looks for its satisfaction to some reality existing inde-
    pendently of M.

These are necessary but not sufficient conditions for standard
ascriptions of truth-value. I shall postulate that they are sufficient
to capture the core of a generic notion of truth, which might be
summed up in this slogan: *A story defines its truth, but whether
it is true can never be part of the story.* My question, then, is how
this might apply to the relation between an emotion and that
which, if anything, the emotion represents.

In philosophy the entities to which truth value is attributed
directly are commonly held to be not mental states, but propositions. Mental states that incorporate propositions in a suitable
way (I shall speak generally of 'attitudes') inherit truth-value
from their propositional objects. But it is unclear what propositions are. It seems safe to regard them as posits tailored to
play just two roles: as objects of propositional attitudes, and as
bearers of truth-value. Among the attitudes, beliefs then remain
typical of those that admit of truth or falsity. They obviously
satisfy the conditions just stated: a belief (1) specifies or 'expresses' a proposition; (2) it thereby determines a norm, according to
which it is true or false; and (3) the satisfaction of that norm is
independent of the belief's existence.

A tight connection therefore seems to hold between truth and
belief. For as is often noted—and as witnessed by Moore's paradox—the *aim* of belief is truth. Nevertheless, it would be misleading to say that truth-value belongs essentially to belief. For, as
Frege made clear, we need to allow that propositions may remain
unasserted. Otherwise the antecedent and consequent of any conditional would be asserted merely in virtue of figuring in the conditional, trivially short-circuiting Modus Ponens. More
generally, belief's monopoly on truth might be infringed in two
ways. First, some attitudes may lack propositional objects and
yet also be true or false. *Perceptions* may provide examples.
Second, one might attribute a truth-like property to other propositional attitudes, differing from beliefs in their aim. An
example would be *desires*. In this second class of cases, one might
ascribe truth-value derivatively to the attitude on the basis of the
truth-value of its object. Thus one might say that my desire for

oyster ice-cream is true iff I get some. But a more interesting analogy with the truth of beliefs would focus not on the semantic satisfaction of propositional objects, but on the attitude's attainment of its aim, its *success*. For belief, success is truth; but it lies elsewhere for other attitudes.

Emotions may stake a claim under both headings. Like perceptions, they sometimes lack a propositional object. And as in the case of desires, the truth of their propositional object does not define their success even when they can be said to have one. To see this clearly, recall Robert Gordon's observation that some emotion ascriptions are 'factive', while others are 'epistemic'.[1] The former, such as *S is embarrassed that p*, presuppose that the subject knows that *p*, while the latter, such as *S fears that p*, presuppose that the subject does not know whether *p*.[2] Obviously in the latter case, the truth-value of *p* does not determine the appropriateness of the emotion. Even in the factive case, however, the truth of *p* is not sufficient to *vindicate* the emotion. By contrast, the truth of *p* always vindicates the belief or the assertion that *p*.

But if semantic satisfaction does not determine the aim of an emotion, what does? To answer this we need to proceed on two fronts. We must explore the way in which a state without a propositional object might be true; and we must ask what might define the success of an emotion, in a way precisely analogous to the sense in which truth defines the success of a belief. The former quest will look for inspiration to the model of perception. The second will explore what it is for an emotion to be, in the relevant sense, successful.

Proceeding somewhat indirectly, I begin by acknowledging some of the difficulties that might threaten to scuttle the project before it gets off the ground. The most insistent difficulty, concerning the prospects for emotional objectivity, will bring me back both to the analogy of perception and to the reconstruction of a relevant notion of emotional truth as success. I shall conclude by sketching some reasons to adopt the suggestion that the

---

1. Gordon 1987, 26 ff.

2. What Gordon actually says is that *emotions* are factive or epistemic. But that cannot be quite right, for several reasons that don't bear on the present point. (See de Sousa 1991).

specific domain of propositional truth, for which we are accustomed to reserve the literal meaning of truth, is distinguished by its digital as opposed to analogue mode of representation.

II

Some Logical Problems. A basic feature of the paradigm truth-valued states—propositions, assertions, or beliefs—is that they can be negated. Furthermore, where the embedded proposition exhibits a subject-predicate structure, it can be negated in two ways, yielding contraries distinct from contradictories. Thus p is false if and only if $\sim p$ is true, while Fa is false if $not\text{-}F(a)$ is true. Is any such pair of standards for negation applicable to emotions?

Some named emotions are commonly felt to be polar opposites (love and hate, hope and despair, admiration and contempt, gratitude and resentment). Such pairs may plausibly be regarded as contraries, while equanimity—rather than indifference— might relate to both as their contradictory. But how are the norms of contrariety to be grounded?

Compare the case of desire. Beliefs demand consistency: if p and q are inconsistent, that inconsistency is automatically an indication that belief that p and belief that q cannot both be right. By contrast, someone might suggest that no such demand exists for consistency of desire. For two desires may aim at incon-sistent states of affairs without entailing that at least one must be mistaken.

This is partly right, but harbours an important confusion. It presupposes that a single criterion of consistency is appropriate to both beliefs and desires. But that presupposition begs the ques-tion against the distinction alluded to above, by confusing the *satisfaction* conditions of desire with conditions of *success*. For any two beliefs, compatibility coincides with consistency. But for two desires to be consistent, it is not necessary that their contents be jointly satisfiable, but only that their contents be jointly *desirable*.[3] So while a desire for p and a desire for q (where q implies $\sim p$) are clearly incompatible, it does not follow that they should be regarded as inconsistent. And while this raises difficult questions about how to cash in the claim that two desires are

3. de Sousa 1974.

inconsistent, it makes room for inconsistent desires without requiring that consistent desires also be for compatible objects.

Emotions are similar, but messier. The reason is that there is no single proper object of all emotions. Each emotion is linked to its own specific evaluative continuum, and so defines its own proper object, and thereby the dimension along which contrariety might be defined for that emotion.

To illustrate how the distinction between truth and satisfaction might work out for a standard emotion, consider the example of fear. This can readily be construed as having been honed by natural selection to favour the avoidance of danger. The formal object of fear—the norm defined by fear for its own appropriateness—is the Dangerous. *Fear that p* is satisfied iff *p* is true, but it is *successful* iff *p is actually dangerous*. In general, for any emotion sufficiently complex to afford the identification of a propositional object:

E(p) is *satisfied* iff p is true
E(p) is *successful* iff p actually fits E's formal object.

Where the emotion admits of a target (t) but lacks a propositional object (as in certain kinds of fear), semantic satisfaction consists in successful reference, while success still depends on whether the target fits the formal object:[4]

E(t) is *satisfied* iff t exists
E(t) is *successful* iff t actually fits E's formal object.

In all cases, the emotion's success is independent of semantic satisfaction. Fear of monsters is not semantically satisfied, but may be successful. The converse may be the case in fear of spiders.

Emotional truth, then, refers not to semantic satisfaction, but to success. I follow widespread practice in saying that fear's assessment of p or t as dangerous consist in some sort of *evaluation* of p or t. Success is tied to the correctness of that evaluation, and I will need to say more below about how the

---

4. This skirts around a current debate about whether there can be non-conceptual contents of perception. Some hold, while others deny, that perceptual content may be non-conceptual. Even in Pittsburgh, however, where all content is conceptual and every concept owes its identity to the inferences it licenses, it doesn't follow that every perception must boast a propositional object.

evaluation relates to the rest of the emotional experience. But this suffices to suggest how the notion of opposition, if any, appropriate to a given emotion is internal to that emotion. And while this provides no handy criterion of emotional contrariety, it at least suggests a way in which such a concept might have application, as well as explaining why it is difficult to cash out in practice.

Another disanalogy is sometimes adduced between belief and desire and might apply *a fortiori* to emotions. When deliberating about what to do, there comes a moment when it is appropriate to say: *now is the time to decide*. And then one does so, definitively and rationally. But deliberating about what to *believe* is different. For that amounts to making up one's mind about what is *true*, and there is always a gap between the rationality of making up one's mind about p and the truth of p. At best there can come a moment when I am justified in making up my mind. But that cannot give me a rationally sufficient ground for the *truth* of the proposition. At best, it can be the right moment to decide only on the rationality of *behaving as if it were true*.[5]

Yet this contrast too is misleading. Admittedly, the pressure of time can furnish a reason to decide (that it is rational) to believe that p, but can never be *evidence* for p. What is rational to believe is only my best bet under current constraints. Nor is deciding to believe p equivalent to deciding to act as if p were true. But the following parallel still holds: while the pressure of time and other constraints can be a perfectly good reason for *deciding* (*that it's rational*) *to do p*, it can't be grounds for the proposition that *p is objectively best*, or even that p is what will seem best in the light of infinite consideration.

The crucial disanalogy between beliefs and other attitudes lies elsewhere. Only one of two incompatible beliefs can be true, and therefore only one can be successful. Among incompatible desires or emotions, on the other hand, no single desire or emotion need be uniquely successful.

The very idea of an *objective best*, however, may seem to beg the question against a prevalent view that neither emotions nor

5. This point was made by David Owens in comments on a paper by Gary Watson, at a Montreal conference on Akrasia, May 2001. Since I draw on Owens' oral presentation and conversation, I can't be sure that he would endorse my formulation.

desires can be assessed in terms of anything objective at all. To this I now turn.

III

The Claim of Objectivity. On the problem of emotional objectivity, Plato made an early start on two fronts. The *Philebus* argued that pleasure can be false, not merely in the derivative sense of being associated with or caused by a false belief, but in itself. That claim, extended to (other) emotions, presupposes that there can be an objective correlative to pleasure or emotion that is not a mere projection. That demand is made explicit in the *Euthyphro*, where Plato posed the problem of whether the gods love piety because it is pious, or whether calling it pious is merely to claim the gods love it.

The meaning of 'objectivity' is subordinate to the contrast with 'subjectivity', and that term has at least a dozen different senses.[6] But a clear paradigm of objectivity can arguably be found in mathematical intuition. Imagine someone saying: *I understand your statement that all triangles have three sides, but I disagree.* One would be confident in objecting: *Your 'disagreement' suffices to show you have not understood.* But unexpectedly, at the other, most subjective end of the spectrum, it seems plausible to admonish someone who doesn't share my individual tastes with a curiously similar demand for *taste universalization*:

   (*TU*) *If oyster ice-cream tasted to you as it does to me, you could not fail to find it delicious.*

The cases seem very different, for in the case of taste we lack any independent way of supporting the counterfactual. Nevertheless, it is instructive to explore this further. Since taste exemplifies extreme subjectivity, it would not be surprising if it failed to meet the conditions for generic truth. If despite that it succeeds, on the other hand, we may assume that more complex emotions will also pass the test. If not, then to diagnose exactly how it fails might help us to discern how emotions must differ from taste if their claim to be truth-valued is to be vindicated.

6. de Sousa 2002.

If my taste for oyster ice cream (TOI) could be said to be truth-valued, the following must hold: (1) TOI must be subject to a norm of appropriate liking or aversion (the '*valence*'), (2) that norm of appropriate liking or aversion must somehow be defined by the character of the taste (the '*quale*'), but (3) the quale cannot suffice to determine the satisfaction of the norm in question.

One problem is to make sense of the quale's defining its own norm of success—the appropriateness of liking or aversion. A second problem is how to make the relation between the quale and the valence *contingent*: it must be possible for an inappropriate valence to be present or an appropriate one to be absent. In other words, if taste is really objective then taste universalization (*TU*) must fail.

Suppose we think of all actual experience, on the model of a mathematical domain, as located in a multi-dimensional space encompassing all possible experiences, had by any possible conscious beings. Only some very limited ranges of experience are available to any specific kind of conscious being. (Human experience of colour, for example, can provide only partial insight into the experiences available to tetrachromatic animals.) At any point in that space, the valence of a specific experience is one of the qualitative dimensions of experience. It would then follow trivially that two experiences could not be qualitatively identical while being opposed in valence. On this picture, is there any prospect of prying apart the valence of an experience and its quale?

There are two possibilities. Either valence is a component of complex qualitative experience, or it is supervenient on other qualia. Understood in the first way, valence could always in principle be dissociated from the concomitant qualia. If my experience of oyster ice-cream consists in qualia [*A*,*B*,*C*, *liking*], and yours in [*A*,*B C*, *aversion*], then we are not having the same experience. This would not preclude the required contingency. But what could be the measure of appropriateness between [*A*, *B*, *C*] and one or another valence?

It is tempting to appeal to Human Nature to set a standard of correctness. Given any quale, an evaluative response that falls foul of the norm will lack appropriateness, and on that basis we can call it perverted, abnormal, or *false*. The problem with human nature, however, is that if it refers to a set of interesting properties true of all and only humans, and robust enough to support normative standards, then there probably is no such thing.[7] Still, the suggestion is worth setting on ice for partial recuperation and reconstruction, as I shall suggest in a moment.

Now consider the second possibility, that valence supervenes on other qualia. If supervenience is understood deterministically, it will preclude the required contingency of the relation between quale and valence. But the laws governing that relation of supervenience might be stochastic, allowing two or more alternative outcomes. That would restore contingency, and providing one valence can be made out to be more appropriate than the other it would then satisfy the conditions for generic truth after all.

This last requirement remains very far-fetched in the case of taste. But it is much more likely to be met in the case of those emotions that are plausibly characterized as perceptions of value. Take, for example, the classic thought experiment in Mencius: you see a child about to fall into a well, and your apprehension of the situation immediately moves you, and you want to save the child. In this instance, what is apprehended is the *need to intervene*. Or better it is the nature of the total situation, in which *the need to intervene* roughly sums up the supervenient valence. Yet it is not impossible to witness the scene without being moved thus. Anyone whose experience lacks the appropriate valence, however, may be said to have an objectively false emotion.

This way of describing the situation avoids simple projectionism, insofar as what I perceive is not merely the shadow of my own response, but something about the character of a situation as a whole in the context not only of my own singular responses but of the feelings and interests of others. The choices to which I am led are products of a multi-dimensional landscape of values constituting a larger axiological whole. I call this view 'axiological holism.' It stipulates that we do not apprehend value in discrete units. but only in the light of a complex of factors that transcend individual experience. No single range of facts suffices for the success of an emotional response. Biological facts will speak to its origins and may thereby assign it a proper function in the sense of Millikan (1989), but they will not determine its relation to currently relevant norms. Social norms, in turn, are every bit as likely to be irredeemably nasty as biological ones.

7. de Sousa 2000.

(To endorse social norms as the touchstone of normativity would be to condemn all social reformers.) Individual biography sets up paradigm scenarios in terms of which each individual understands the world, but this defines only a narrow sense of fit between a current response and a present situation. That fit cannot be identified with value in any comprehensive sense, still less determine what is morally right.[8]

All of these factors—biological, social, or personal, and more—may properly be confronted with one another in the hope of arriving at something like reflective equilibrium. That holistic equilibrium is as close as we can come to reconstructing a notion of normative human nature. And perhaps it is close enough. In this way, we may find some emotional responses mistaken, just as Macbeth found ('Art thou not, fatal vision, sensible to feeling as to sight?') that a perception can fail the test of corroboration by different sensory channels. Vision provides distal information about our surroundings; yet visual illusions occur. Similarly emotions in general constitute apprehensions of axiological reality; yet not every emotion is equally to be trusted. We tell which is right and which is wrong much as we test the veracity of perceptual information: by appealing to corroborating evidence. Something like the method of reflective equilibrium is commonplace in science as well as in ethics; what is not often noticed is that the items that need to come to equilibrium are typically emotional responses. The search for reflective equilibrium plays an important role not just in moral deliberation but also where the issue is purely epistemic, where, as Christopher Hookway (1998) has argued, emotions such as the *feeling of plausibility* or *doubt* play a crucial role. Without such emotions, even the most comprehensively rational argument may remain powerless to move us.

Equilibrium, it may be objected, establishes only *coherence*. And it is an excessively weak theory of truth that is satisfied with coherence. Compare perception again. Each sensory channel provides a specific mode of information. But primary qualities are apprehended through different sensory channels. Multi-modal access is the warrant of objective reality. What then is the analogue of multi-modal access for emotions?

8. D'Arms and Jacobson 2000.

IV

The Scope of our Emotional Access to Value: A Musical Analogy.
A helpful analogy is suggested by a fascinating paper by Dmitri
Tymoczko on Milton Babbitt and John Cage.[9] Tymoczko
describes both composers as philosophers who, in their different
ways, questioned the relevance of beauty or pleasure to aesthetic
appreciation. Babbitt, in particular, aims to break the link
between value and the ordinary listener's emotional response to
music:

> Advanced music, to the extent that it reflects the knowledge and
> originality of the informed composer, scarcely can be expected to
> appear more intelligible than [higher mathematics] to the person
> whose musical education usually has been even less extensive than
> his background in other fields.[10]

But are the compositions based on these principles *musically*
intelligible, even to experts? 'Do they lead to perceptible features
of the music that can be understood through listening?' asks
Tymoczko. Babbitt's defence of his esoteric compositions seems
to presuppose that the relationships he elaborates are indeed perceptible as acoustic patterns, albeit only after special training.
But Tymoczko gives some reasons for doubt, and points out that
if, in fact, no amount of training can make the patterns perceptible even to the most sophisticated specialist, then the analogy
with mathematics fails. For Babbitt's compositions do not have
their being in the acoustic domain to which music usually
belongs.

Does that amount to an expansion of the scope of music, or to
a *reductio ad absurdum* of Babbitt's methods? There is, perhaps, a
faintly discernible third possibility: namely that the domain of
music is not actually circumscribed by our capacity to hear patterns, nor by the emotional responses typically evoked by the
acoustic domain. Whatever the merits of this view of music, it
provides a model for an alternative perspective on the objective
correlates—the potential truth-makers—of emotions in general.
Recall Tymoczko's objection to regarding as music what cannot

9. Tymoczko 2000.
10. Babbitt, quoted in Tymoczko 2000.

be appreciated by the ear, however well trained: If 'the relationships are out there, in the objective world, but we cannot apprehend them', they must then cease to count as music. *But
precisely*, Babbitt might respond, *what matters is that the relationships are objectively there. And if they are continuous with patterns
that can be heard as well as apprehended in other ways, that boosts
their claim to be regarded as objective. So much follows from the
principle of multi-modality as a touchstone of objectivity.*

The retort would have some force; and the thought generalizes
to non-musical emotions. If the values apprehended by emotions
are objective, we might expect that *they are not exhausted by
actual emotional responses.* This needn't commit one to the existence of a Platonic world of values which our emotions apprehend
only dimly; but it does evoke the possibility that, just as Babbitt's
music might be appreciated on paper, in the spirit in which a
mathematician apprehends a proof, even by those whose audi-
tory capacities are not up to hearing them, so one might, by a
non-emotional process of ratiocination, apprehend values inac-
cessible to the emotional capacities of people at some given stage
of personal, social or biological development.

On this view, something like *emotional experimentation* may,
by analogy to musical experimentation, enlarge the domain of
values to which we have access. But while the domain of values
is not independent of the facts about conscious beings, it is
neither simply projected from, nor ever exhausted by, the actual
repertoire of human emotions—any more than all possible
thoughts can be exhausted by the repertoire of actual humans
thoughts past, present, or to come.

V

A Test Case: Huckleberry Finn. Several philosophers have discussed Huck Finn's decision to give up on morality and take up
wickedness by stealing Jim out of slavery. Everyone agrees that
it is Huck's emotions, as opposed to his explicit moral principles,
which produce the true answer. In Huck, the two faces of emotion merge: his authentic emotion is also the *true* one. It corresponds to objective values which he apprehends, despite his
conviction that he is doing wrong.

But there is some dispute about how to best describe the case. McIntyre (1990) argues that the main lesson of the story is that if akrasia is defined as a conflict between what one *believes to be one's best reasons, all things considered* and the *real reason on the basis of which one acts*, an akratic action may be entirely rational, because one may be mistaken about one's own best reasons. She contends that Jonathan Bennett (1974) wrongly sees Huck as irrational because he characterizes 'Huck's dilemma as one in which general moral principles and reasons conflict with 'unreasoned emotional pulls'.'[11] Rather, she suggests, Huck need not be viewed as irrational even while he is akratic. For what he does is inconsistent not with his actual values but only with what he falsely believes to be his values.[12] Her point is not merely that some objective reasons might exist to justify the akratic action, but that the so-called akratic might, after all, be doing the right thing from her own point of view. Rationality in action is 'evaluative consistency,' and that could be attained even if the action were akratic in the sense just defined:

> Evaluative consistency may exist, for example, in view of the fact that if the agent had had more time to reflect, she would have changed her mind about what the best thing to do would be. Thus she would have been saved from akrasia not by changing her behaviour but by changing her evaluation of it.[13]

These considerations bring us back to the problem of determining what constitutes emotional 'reflective equilibrium'. Three tentative morals may be drawn:

First, it appears to be neither necessary nor sufficient that the various emotions participating in the weighing in search of equilibrium be conscious.

Second, despite the fact that standards of contrariety for emotions are, as we have seen, obscure, it is principally emotions themselves, and not propositions, which are weighed against one another in the quest for reflective equilibrium.

Third, in the case of Huck Finn, the veracity of an emotion is hard to disentangle from its *authenticity*. We touch here on what

11. p. 381, quoting Bennett p. 127.
12. McIntyre, p. 386.
13. Ibid.

I called at the outset the inward-looking face of emotion. The sense of emotional truth I have sought to articulate is one which posits a correspondence between the emotion, characterized by a specific formal object, and some property of the human-inhabited world. But the values apprehended by emotions depend in part on who we are. They are no less objective for that; but what reflects my own individual nature—what makes for my emotional authenticity—therefore comes to seem, after all, potentially relevant to the objective world of value.

VI

Species of Truth: Emotional and Propositional. I began by advocating an extension of our notion of truth as correspondence, based on a core intuition that can be summed up in the slogan: *a story defines its truth, but whether it is true can never be part of the story.* (A corollary notoriously dooms the ontological argument: *whether a thing exists cannot be part of its nature.*) This required, in effect, the satisfaction of three conditions, which I conclude that at least some emotions are able to meet.

(1) Emotions are subject to a norm defined by their formal objects: what I fear must be dangerous; she of whom I am jealous must figure in a certain sort of triangle; what angers me must be a wrong.

(2) The norm in question is determined by the emotion itself. This is often manifest in the fact that there is an air of tautology about the characterization of the formal object: he whom I love must be lovable; what I regret must be regrettable.

(3) But the appearance of tautology is misleading, because the attainment of success for emotions—the actual fit between the object or target of the emotion and its formal object—depends on a vast holistic network of factors which transcends my actual response.

If emotions are properly said to be truth-valued in a generic sense, then the narrower class of truth-bearers traditionally targeted by philosophy—propositions or belief-like attitudes—no longer need to be regarded as the paradigm truth-valued attitudes. They form only a subclass of truth-valued states, a.special case. What then is the difference that sets them apart?

My hunch about the answer is this: belief is digital; the representations involved in Truth's broader domain are analogue.[14] A digital representation is necessarily part of a system of representation, and can function only once all possible signals are assigned to a finite set of discrete symbols. An analogue representation, by contrast, admits of varying degrees of precision and an indefinitely large set of possible symbols.

This hypothesis suggests another way in which emotion resembles perception. For while we can sometimes perceive *that* some proposition holds, in other cases the content of direct perception seems typically to be analogue.[15] Furthermore it allays three worries raised by the notion of literal truth for emotions.

1. Generic truth legitimizes talk of more or less, by incorporating analogue correspondence, which can be more or less exact. But as traditionally conceived, truth admits of no gradations. A proposition is either true or false: *tertium non datur*. While this is rejected by advocates of ontological vagueness or fuzzy logic, it can be seen to apply at most only to a species of truth-bearer. Within a narrower domain of digitized representation, there are no degrees. So we get the kind of on/off truth we associate with well-defined propositions.

2. Digitality is not necessarily conventional, as shown by the example of the digital system embodied in DNA. But insofar as digital representation exists only in the context of a system of discrete values suited to indefinite copying, most digital systems are likely to be conventional. This should lead us to expect that the typical examples of truth in the sense precluding degrees will be bound to the conventional medium of language.

3. Digital representation is essential to secure fidelity in multiple reproductions of a stable 'message'. Insofar as they constitute a medium of social interaction, emotions tend to cluster into a limited repertoire of distinct entities, functioning as justifications and motivation for behaviour, regimented and 'digitized' as a system of limited significant types.[16] But in the rich variety of their experienced reality, the significance of emotions is not

14. Robert Nozick made a very similar suggestion in Nozick 1989, p. 93: 'Emotions provide a kind of picture of value ... an analog representation of it.'

15. Peacocke 1986.

16. de Sousa 1997.

limited to their role in influencing behaviour and social interaction. Regarded as experiences representing something outside themselves, their variety instantiates a limitless continuum, and they have no need to take on the digital character of propositions.

4. That standard truth-bearers are digital representations helps to explain the grain of truth in the often expressed anxiety about the distortion of reality introduced by abstractions. Abstraction is, by definition, a process of pruning details, of ignoring certain distinctions and aspects of reality. Since all thought requires abstraction, all thought is risky. None escapes the danger that the most important aspect of reality for present purposes is precisely that which our abstractions have left out. A vague aspiration to the 'whole truth', which no utterance can contain, lies behind Nietzsche's charge that (propositional) 'truths are illusions which we have forgotten are illusions'.[17]   The whole truth is an impossible ideal: but it usefully evokes an analogue conception of representation. It has exactly the absurdity of a map on a scale of one inch to the inch, in which every nanometer is faithfully represented to scale. If emotions are conceived as analogue representations of an axiological landscape, it may come to seem natural that they should admit of variable degrees of definition, instantiating a concept of *accuracy* that merges with generic truth.

References

Bennett, J. 1974. 'The Conscience of Huckleberry Finn', *Philosophy* 49, 123–34.
D'Arms, J., and Jacobson, D. 2000. 'The Moralistic Fallacy: on the "Appropriateness" of Emotion', *Philosophy and Phenomenological Research* 61, 65–90.
de Sousa, R. 1974. 'The Good and the True', *Mind* 83, 534–51.
de Sousa, R. 1991. Review of Gordon 1987, *Noûs* 25, 373–376.
de Sousa, R. 1997. 'Love Undigitized', in R. Lamb (ed.) *Love Analysed*, 189–207. (Boulder: Westview).
de Sousa, R. 2000. 'Learning to Be Natural', in N. Roughley (ed.), *Being Humans*, 287–307, 313–316. (Berlin, New York: de Gruyter).
de Sousa, R. 2002. 'Twelve Varieties of Subjectivity', in Jesus L. Larrazabal and Luis A. Pérez Miranda (eds), *Knowledge, Language and Representation* (Dordrecht: Kluwer), 135–151.
Gordon, R. M. 1987. *The Structure of Emotions: Investigations in Cognitive Philosophy* (Cambridge: Cambridge University Press).
Hookway, C. 1998. 'Doubt: Affective States and the Regulation of Inquiry', *Canadian Journal of Philosophy*, Suppl. vol. 24, 203–26.

17. Nietzsche 1993, 43.

McIntyre, A. 1990. 'Is Akratic Action Always Irrational?', in Rorty and O. Flanagan (eds) *Identity, Character, and Morality* (Cambridge, MA: MIT Press), 379–400.

Millikan, R. 1989. 'In Defence of Proper Functions', *Philosophy of Science* 56, 288–302.

Nietzsche, F. 1993. 'On Truth and Lies in a Nonmoral Sense', in R. Schacht (ed.) *Nietzsche: Selections* (New York: Macmillan).

Nozick, R. 1989. *The Examined Life* (New York: Simon and Schuster).

Peacocke, C. 1986. 'Analogue Content', *Proceedings of the Aristotelian Society Supplementary Volume* 6, 1–18.

Tymoczko, D. 2000. 'The sound of philosophy', *Boston Review* Oct/Nov 2000. Citations are to the unpaginated on-line version at http://bostonreview.mit.edu/BR25.5/tymoczko.html.

EMOTIONAL TRUTH

by Ronald de Sousa and Adam Morton

II—Adam Morton

EMOTIONAL ACCURACY

ABSTRACT It is accuracy rather than truth itself that is valuable. Emotional truth is a dubious though attractive notion, but emotional accuracy is much easier to make sense of. My approach to accuracy goes via an account of what makes a story accurate. Stories can be accurate but not true, and emotions can be accurate whether or not they are true. The capacity for emotional accuracy, for emotions that fit a person's situation, is an aspect of emotional intelligence, which is as important an aspect of rational human agency as the intelligent formation of beliefs and desires.

I

Cheap Truth. Truth comes in many forms, some cheap and some valuable. Distinguish two dimensions of cheapness. One dimension extends in the direction of vagueness, indefiniteness and generality. If I claim that some flowers are coloured, or that music is sometimes nice, what I say is true, but cheaply so. Another dimension extends in the direction of the range of attitudes that can be counted as true. Truth can be extended from assertive sentences to beliefs to questions and requests at very little price. When a person attitudes that p, and p, we can count her attitude as true. So a Yes-No question is true if the answer is yes; a desire is true when it is satisfied. And we can say that all Jane's desires on Tuesday were satisfied, which would be equivalent to 'if on Tuesday Jane wanted cats to fly, then cats flew, and if she wanted $34 + 76$ to be 994, then $34 + 76 = 994$, and ...'. Similarly, we can say that 'Hamlet killed Polonius is true' iff Hamlet killed Polonius, and that '$e^{\pi i} = -1$' is true iff $e^{\pi i} = -1$, without worrying about where in the world to find Hamlet, Polonius, and imaginary numbers. None of this is very demanding; the conceptual price is low, as the minimalist literature shows.[1]

---

1. See Williams 1976, Horwich 1998.

Emotional truth is easily achieved if one wanders far enough out along these dimensions. My fear that the dog will bite me is true if and only if the dog will bite me. My elation that life has many joys and my depression that life is a grim business are both true since life is a grim business with many joys. But there's no philosophical pride to be had from bringing home these trophies; any child with a butterfly net could have gone out and got them.

Now to the more valuable kinds. The opposite of vagueness is precision, and precision combined with truth gives accuracy. Accuracy certainly adds value to truth. For one thing it allows non-perverse speculation: the difference between scientific cosmology and metaphysical rambling is that cosmology distinguishes between finely differentiated hypotheses—whether fundamental constants have this value or this slightly different one—and tries to distinguish the different consequences they would have. And on the other dimension, the opposite of minimalist content-matching is to insist on a world-to-mind direction of fit in which determinate aspects of the state have to match determinate aspects of the world. (A substantive theory of truth—correspondence, as I'm slanting it—thus aims not at telling us what propositions are to count as true, but what kinds of truth to count as valuable, a point ignored by Lewis 2001.)

Emotional truth that had these value-adding features would be something to aim for. There would be a point to directing the evolution of our emotional states towards it, just as there is a point to directing the evolution of our beliefs towards the more valuable, but only the more valuable, forms of truth. Analogous to the way precision in theory allows responsible speculation, precision in emotion allows responsible intensity. If you have the *exact* emotion for the situation, then you can feel it whole-heartedly, without the danger of inappropriate blundering. A bull that dances through the china shop. And analogous to the world-to-mind fit of beliefs would be some notion of an emotion that is demanded by the situation. Elation where elation is right, depression or anger where that is right, whether or not the person has grounds to motivate their feeling this right thing.

These remarks are meant to elicit sympathy for de Sousa's project. To the extent that we have a grasp of the right emotion for a situation, the objectively right emotion, we can see analogues in emotion of the valuable features of true belief. But they are also meant to insinuate a doubt. The intuitions are linked not to the core idea of truth itself but to the value-adding aspects that make it worth having. In this paper I shall argue that some of these aspects are independent of the core. We can make sense of emotional accuracy without having to make sense of emotional truth, at least not in more than the cheap and easy way just described. Some of the consequences of accuracy-without-truth, though, are in many ways like those that de Sousa wants from emotional truth.

II

Accuracy Without Truth. Consider two stories:

> *Story* 1: A carriage rolled north down Baker Street through a thick London fog on a cold December day in 1887. As it came to Marylebone Road the passenger rapped on the driver's window and asked to be let out. Only the most acute of observers would have recognized the crippled Crimean war veteran who emerged as the famous detective Sherlock Holmes.

> *Story* 2: A boat drew slowly along the Baker Street canal in the balmy weather of London in the winter of 1887. As it joined the Thames a passenger leapt to the bank. That person continued his journey on foot.

Neither story is true. Possibly neither is false. But the first is in two respects more *accurate* than the second. Baker Street does not have a canal, and even if it did it would not reach the Thames. The winter of 1887 was not balmy. That is the first accuracy, fit: the first story fits the world as it is, even though it does not say anything true about it. The first story is also detailed in a way that the second is not: it gives a specific name to its protagonist, and describes his appearance. Though both stories can be matched with many non-actual worlds, the first applies to fewer than the second does: it is more restrictive. (We are probably speaking of infinitely many worlds in both cases, so 'fewer' is problematic. It would be best to consider cases where one story's worlds are a subset of those of another. But that would require four stories rather than the two I used.)

The two aspects interact. Detail allows fit. If a story has enough details that can be taken as true of an actual situation then it will fit it. Fit selects detail. If a story is taken as fitting a particular situation then we can assess the detailedness of its description of that situation. This suggests a tentative definition of accuracy. One story is a more accurate depiction than another of an actual situation when there are more elements of the one that are true descriptions of aspects of the actual situation than there are of the other. (One story might be taken to be intrinsically more accurate than another when there is an actual situation such that there are more elements of the one that are true descriptions of aspects of that situation than there are elements of the other that are true descriptions of any actual situation.) That will do for now; the definition is not meant to be taken very carefully. (It surely will not survive rough handling: taking stories as closed under logical consequence and then literally counting true sentences, etc.)

Some think that stories are true of worlds, and thus simply true when they are true of the actual world. I do not want to get into this question. The important point is that one not-true story can be more accurate than another. Science fiction is not very accurate, at any rate not accurate about the technological possibilities (or even usually the laws of nature) of the present actual world. Cowboy fiction is said to give a very inaccurate impression of life in the Wild West. Zola or Hardy probably do give relatively accurate reports of life in the times and places they discuss. But none of these stories are true. In fact, a story can have a good measure of accuracy while lacking not only truth but also possibility. Kurt Vonnegut's *Cat's Cradle* is full of historical, sociological, and emotional accuracy while describing something that just can't happen.

Accuracy as just described seems to presuppose truth. An accurate story has many elements that are true descriptions of an actual situation. But a more careful formulation takes care of this. A story can be taken as describing a situation no elements of which does it actually name. For example a story might begin 'The general had accumulated many powers, so many that concerned citizens plotted to assassinate him.' It might be taken as describing events in Rome in the first century BCE, or in many other times and places. But no element of it is simply true. Conversely a Jonathan Miller type production of 'Julius Caesar' might add enough detail that—incorporating all elements of the production into the story—it was an accurate portrayal of Tony

Blair and his entourage. The assassination itself would then be a non-descriptive detail that gained significance from its links to the descriptively accurate elements. Neither accuracy nor truth simply presupposes the other.

III

Emotional Accuracy. What does this have to do with emotions? The essential link is that a person's emotions involve representations, and these representations can be more or less accurate depictions of her situation. Contrast two classes of cases.

(1a) An engineer is laid off by her company. She realizes that the economic climate is not good for getting another job of the same kind, feels relieved that she does not have to face more boring programming disguised as design, and goes back to university to do a MBA.

(1b) An engineer is laid off by her company. She takes this as showing that she has neither the technical nor the personal skills for success in a demanding profession, becomes very unhappy, and does not look for another job.

(1c) An engineer is laid off by her company. She reflects on the less competent and less hard working colleagues who have kept their jobs and of the lack of respect her boss has always shown to her. She gets very angry, goes into his office and pours a cup of coffee over his head.

(2a) An engineer is laid off by her company. She thinks of all the desired things that will now never happen and is overcome with sorrow. She becomes very unhappy at the fate of abandoned animals, and cries whenever she sees a dog walking without a leash, or a non-fat cat.

(2b) An engineer is laid off by her company. The next day she finds her mind is full of confusing thoughts moving in all directions. There is something exciting about the confusion and she develops an enthusiasm for the company. She starts a web site on which satisfied customers and grateful employees can register their good feelings.

(2c) An engineer is laid off by her company. Feelings of anger rise up in her and she directs them at American policy in the middle east. She becomes a fervent campaigner for the internationalization of Jerusalem.

The cases under 1 resemble story 1 in a way that the cases under 2 resemble story 2. That will only be true of some ways of imagining the cases, filling in the details. But they are the natural ones, the ones that would first occur to one. Suppose that we have a detailed filling in of one of these cases, including on the one hand the engineer's beliefs, intentions, fears, and desires, and on the other hand her whole physical state and the state of her environment, the sensations she experiences, and the basic acts she performs. Call the first of these 'the emotion-story', and the second 'the situation'. Then the emotion-stories of the (1) cases are more accurate depictions of the situation than the emotion-stories of the (2) cases. More of the facts are accurately represented in these stories.

Consider (1a). The engineer's emotion is one of relief and redirected interest. These emotions are directed at specific aspects of her situation and do not make sense without them. They involve (or require, or even consist in) beliefs about the character of her work before she was laid off, beliefs about the character it would have assumed had she been one of those not laid off, desires to do one kind of work rather than another, intentions to act in one way rather than another, and so on. Contrast this with (2a). The engineer's emotion is one of sorrow directed at the plight of animals. But, at least on one natural way of filling in the details, there are no specific episodes of animal suffering that give detail and specificity to the emotion: many associated beliefs are not true of the engineer's life, and many associated desires do not lead to successful acts. (They're not true desires, in the cheap way of speaking I suggested above.) This is generally true of natural ways of imagining the (2) cases: they do not latch onto actual features of the situation as it is. In fact, in order to imagine oneself into the situation of the engineer in the (2) cases one has to imagine her misconstruing and misrepresenting what is going on and what the connections between events are. This is much less so in the case of the (1) cases. The emotions there not only are sustainable in the face of an accurate grasp of the facts and possibilities, they build on a network of representations of the details of the person's situation.

I am trying not to put this in an overly cognitive way. On a 1970s-type account the emotion just is a complex of states essential members of which are propositional attitudes, which in accurate cases have true propositions as their objects. I take it that a number of writers, notably de Sousa and Greenspan,[2] have shown us more plausible ways of recognizing that thinking is essential to emotion without turning emotions into thoughts. Without taking on the details of any of these accounts I shall assume that when one is in an emotional state there are patterns of belief and belief change, desire and desire change, and characteristic intentions, that are essential to ones being in that state rather than another. If a person is afraid then there is a pressure towards thinking that some things are dangerous, and a tendency towards wanting to avoid or escape some things, whether or not she succumbs to the pressure or goes along with the tendency. This is enough to make what I have called the emotion-story essential to the emotion, and thus to give the emotion an intrinsic degree of accuracy as a depiction of a person's situation.

I said that accurate emotions are sustainable in the face of an accurate grasp of the facts and possibilities. Why possibilities? Consider someone who takes as fearful something that cannot hurt him, or who greets with joy something that cannot do him any good. The emotions don't fit the situation not because the object will not harm or will not help; after all, it is appropriate to be afraid of a rattlesnake that in fact does not bite one. The lack of fit comes because something is thought to be capable of what it is not. More generally, an emotion can be inaccurate because it misrepresents the possibilities of the whole situation. Most emotions are action-guiding, taking action in a very general way to include strategies of thought. (This is a central idea in most of the papers in Goldie 2001.) They will not serve this role if they are unhinged from the actual situation of the agent; and they will not serve it if they do not respect what is actually possible and impossible, in fact what possibilities are more or less remote. So an accurate emotion must not only contain detailed representations that fit the actual situation; it must represent that

2. See de Sousa 1987, Greenspan 1988, also Goldie 2000.

actual situation as rightly situated in the galaxy of could-have-beens and would-have-ifs around it.

This might seem to distinguish accuracy of emotion from accuracy of belief. I think it does not, though. A belief can be inaccurate though true in a detailed way of the actual world. Consider for example a rich and complete system of unnatural Goodmanian concepts, cutting across natural kind boundaries in weird and peculiar ways, and consider beliefs expressed in terms of them. The belief that all emerats are granimals is true (emerats are emeralds that come to human notice before 1 Jan 3000 or otherwise rats, and granimals are green things noticed before that date or otherwise animals). But it misrepresents what emeralds and rats are like and taken together with other similar beliefs would misrepresent what is possible for them. So respect for how a situation is situated among its possible variants is something we should write into a better definition of the accuracy of belief, too, taking accuracy even further from truth.

Accurate emotions are not well described as true. After all, the analogy is with an accurate story, and many very accurate stories are not true. The difference shows up in the non-uniqueness of accuracy. All of (1a)-(1c) are accurate, accurate to the same facts about the engineer's life. I see no reason to think that any one *has* to be more accurate than the others; each could invoke as rich a body of beliefs and desires, fitting the person's situation and its possibilities as well as each other one. (That is why (1b) is included: emotions that we think of as less wise or less admirable may still be accurate. But see Section IV below.)

Another way of putting it. An accurate emotion is like a rich myth, deeply engaged with the details of some aspect of the world. A less accurate emotion is like a shallow or artificial myth, a Walt Disney substitute, which tries to depict mythical events that bear no detailed relation to what actually happens in people's lives. Or, the accuracy of an emotion is like the *observational* accuracy of a scientific theory, which can capture actual and potential observations more or less well. Theoretical and observational assertions and concepts can be intimately connected; neither may be intelligible without the other, and yet it is clearly true that observational accuracy does not guarantee truth. There can be rival equally observationally accurate theories, relative to any way of drawing the somewhat arbitrary line between observation and theory. And among non-true theories some will be more accurate observationally than others. For some purposes, e.g. navigation or bridge construction, observational accuracy will be more important than truth. We want a rich and reliable body of connections with the ways the world impinges on us. So too with emotions: among the variety of attitudes we could take to the situations we find ourselves in, we want those that give a rich and reliable set of connections to guide our further acting and feeling.

IV

Emotional Intelligence. My main point has been that among the emotions a person can direct at a situation some fit it better than others. The point can be extended: among the varieties of anger, or of sadness or exhilaration, that a person can direct at a situation some fit it better than others. So accuracy cuts across our usual classifications for the emotions. You can be miserable, elated, or curious, and be so in a way that does or does not accurately represent your situation. No emotion is intrinsically accurate. But some *distinctions* between emotions are necessary for a creature that is to have accurate emotions. Sadness must be distinct from depression; remorse, guilt, shame, and embarrassment must be kept apart. Falling into one of these when another fits the situation is a sure route to emotional mess. And finding one's way around a rich range of emotions is as demanding as finding one's way around a complex set of beliefs. It requires a special and admirable quality that it makes sense to call emotional intelligence.

Emotional intelligence will not always result in emotional accuracy, any more than theoretical intelligence will always result in true belief. And just as truth bears a complex relation to the coherence of belief, emotional accuracy bears an equally complex relation to the coherence of emotions, with one another and with a person's complex of beliefs and desires. Sometimes the more accurate emotions a person can have will not cohere well with one another or with the person's other states. This will typically be when the other states are defective, or when the situation is so complex that the person is not capable of coherent attitudes that represent it well. (But then, the universe *is* like that, compared to our little brains.) And, to pile on the warnings, there is no more guarantee that emotional accuracy will give us better lives than there is that we will be happier if we have true beliefs. To the perspicacious tyrant who kills you if you don't believe he is charming there corresponds the situation that is so unbearable that your sanity will not permit you to react to the way it really is. But, we all trust, these are aberrant outlying cases. In general, the route to truth leads through evidence and results in satisfied desire, and the route to emotional accuracy leads through the acquisition of a range of possible feelings and attitudes and the capacity to discriminate between them, and results in the harmony of thinking and feeling. More specifically, it tends to link the evolution of our beliefs, our desires, and our feelings, and allows the present state of each of these to put pressure on the others. It allows us to be whole people, by having patterns of thought that make two-way connections between what we believe and what we feel. (*Some* of the connections in one way are clear: when you discover the insect is harmless your fear should change. The connections the other way must consist in part of your emotions helping select relevance of evidence and direction of thought. If you feel instinctively afraid of the insect you look for reasons, both in what you can see around you and in what you know, which might settle the question of its dangerousness.)

Imagine then a progression. It starts with our hard-wired emotional responses, with their fixed affects and their simple paradigm scenarios. Emotional intelligence then intervenes, and we acquire the capacity to modulate our emotions to what we learn and what we come to want. (At the beginning we feel dismay at a situation; at a later stage we anticipate regret for the action we are choosing; at a yet later stage we anticipate regret if we take one choice and remorse if we take the other.) Suppose that the capacity were perfectly acquired. Then our emotions would match our situations to the extent that our information about then was accurate. Could they then be counted as emotional truths? The main factor to consider is the way they exclude one another. At the original primitive stage fear, say, and delight are mutually exclusive. And the exclusion is not just the effect of quirks and limitations: it is intrinsic to a simple fear that it leads one to intend avoidance and to a simple delight that it leads one to intend contact. They are emotions that cannot both be held, though we can oscillate between them. But each might be equally accurate. As de Sousa, following Tappolet (2000), would put it, the values of danger and of attractiveness are both present. So we shouldn't count them as truths. (It would be a strange kind of truth, such that having it committed one also to falsity. To fear is to take as not attractive.) But at later stages the exclusion lessens. We acquire more subtle emotions, such as a delighted horror. (You see the notorious association between sophistication and perversity.) Then it is possible to acknowledge that the situation is both dangerous and attractive. So as our emotions become more and more refined they come to be capable of representing more and more of the values present in our situations, in such a way that to acknowledge one is not to reject another.

Might there be an ideal end to this progression, where in any situation an agent could have emotions which accurately represent it, and which do not exclude any others that accurately represent it? I have no idea. I do fear that these kinds of heroically accurate emotions would have become so much like beliefs that they could not easily serve the functions of emotions. After all, as Greenspan and earlier work by de Sousa taught us, emotions are essential for defining patterns of salience that create pressures on the evolution of our beliefs and desires. These patterns are essentially selective; they make things possible for us by limiting the possibilities. But perhaps creatures with sufficient emotional intelligence would be able to assume these deliberately limiting perspectives while also remaining open to alternatives. Perhaps. We don't have to take a position on this, in order to conclude that there is such a thing as emotional accuracy, that it is valuable, and that intelligent thinking and feeling aims at it.

REFERENCES

de Sousa, R. 1987. *The Rationality of the Emotions*, Cambridge, MA: MIT Press.

Goldie, P. 2000. *The Emotions: a Philosophical Exploration*, Oxford: Oxford University Press.

Goldie, P. (ed.). 2001. *Understanding Emotions*, London: Ashgate.

Greenspan, P. 1988. *Emotions and Reasons*, London: Routledge.

Horwich, P. 1998. *Truth*, second edition, Oxford: Oxford University Press.

Lewis, D. 2001. 'Forget about the "Correspondence Theory of Truth"', *Analysis* 61: 275–280.

Tappolet, C. 2000. *Emotions et Valeurs*, Paris: Presses Universitaires de France.

Williams, C.J.F. 1976. *What is Truth?* Cambridge: Cambridge University Press.